Pamela Mordecai was born in Kingston, Jamaica, and educated there and in Newton, Mass., USA. A trained language arts teacher, she has worked extensively in media – she was a freelance television presenter for 17 years.

With Mervyn Morris she edited *Jamaica Woman* (Heinemann, 1980), the first anthology of poetry by Jamaican women. In 1987 she edited *From Our Yard: Jamaican Poetry Since Independence*. Her *Storypoems* for children appeared in the same year. *Journey Poem* (Kingston, Sandberry Press, 1989), Pamela Mordecai's first collection of poetry, was published in 1989. She has also written on Caribbean literature and language teaching and authored/co-authored some 13 textbooks for the region.

A former Publications Officer in the Faculty of Education, University of the West Indies, and Editor of the *Caribbean Journal of Education*, Pamela Mordecai now runs her own company in Kingston.

Betty (Elizabeth) Wilson, Pamela Mordecai's sister, has a Diploma in Education from London University and a doctorate from Michigan State University. In 1988 she gained a senior Fulbright Award.

A member of staff of the French Department of the University of the West Indies in Jamaica, she is also Assistant Chief Examiner for French for the Caribbean Examinations Council. Betty Wilson authored *Language Arts for Primary Schools* (Heinemann, 1983) with Don Wilson and Hyacinth Campbell and has translated Myriam Warner-Vieyra's French novel, *Juletane* for Heinemann's Caribbean Writers Series (1987). She is currently working on a comparative study of Caribbean and Afro-American women's prose writing, as well as a translation of another French Caribbean novel.

HER
TRUE-TRUE
NAME

Edited by
Pamela Mordecai
and Betty Wilson

9631

HEINEMANN

Heinemann Educational Publishers
A division of Heinemann Publishers (Oxford) Ltd
Halley Court, Jordan Hill, Oxford OX2 8EJ

Heinemann: A division of Reed Publishing (USA) Inc.
361 Hanover Street, Portsmouth, NH 03801-3912, USA

Heinemann Educational Books (Nigeria) Ltd
PMB 5205, Ibadan
Heinemann Educational Boleswa
PO Box 10103, Village Post Office, Gaborone, Botswana

FLORENCE   PRAGUE   PARIS   MADRID
ATHENS   MELBOURNE   JOHANNESBURG
AUCKLAND   SINGAPORE   TOKYO
CHICAGO   SAO PAULO

Series Editor: Adewale Maja-Pearce

Her true-true name. – (Caribbean writers series)
1. Fiction in French. Caribbean Writers, 1945 – Critical Studies.
I. Mordecai, Pamela II. Wilson, Elizabeth
III. Series
843

ISBN 0–435–98906–5

Photoset by Wilmaset, Birkenhead, Wirral
Printed in Great Britain by
Cox & Wyman Ltd, Reading, Berkshire

94 95 96 97 10 9 8 7 6

CONTENTS

ACKNOWLEDGEMENTS

We would like to thank the authors for their generous co-operation and help with biographical data; our translators: Fernanda Steele, Claudette Williams and Karin Wilson; Carmen C. Esteves, Rosario Ferré, Mark McCaffrey, Lisa Paravisini and Diana Vélez who allowed us to use their translations of hispanophone works; Nick Caistor for revisions; our colleagues, Annette Insanally, Mervyn Morris and Joseph Pereira at the University of the West Indies, Mona, and Susan Homar and Emily Krasinski of the University of Puerto Rico for their help in identifying and locating the Cuban and Puerto Rican extracts; the librarians in The West Indies Collection, UWI, Mona for their willing assistance.

The editors and publishers would like to thank the following for their permission to use copyright material. Omega Agüero for the extract from *El Muro de Medio Metro* by Omega Aguero, Unión de Escritores y Artistas de Cuba, Havana 1977, translated by Karin Wilson, 1989; Andre Deutsch Ltd for the extract from *Crick Crack, Monkey* by Merle Hodge, London 1970, the extracts by Jean Rhys: from *Sleep it off Lady*, London 1974, and the extract from *Tigers are Better Looking*, London 1968; Christine Craig for 'In the Hills' © Christine Craig, 1989; Editorial Alfa & Omega C por A for the extract from *La Narrativa Yugulada* by Hilma Contreras, Pedro Peix ed, Santo Domingo, translated by Fernanda Steele 1989; Editorial Antillana for the extract by Carmen Lugo Filippi from *Vírgenes y Mártires* by Carmen Lugo Filippi and Ana Lydia Vega, Puerto Rico 1983, translated by Lizabeth Paravisini 1989; Editorial Arte y Literatura for the extract from *Todos Los Negros Tomamos Café*, by Mirta Yáñez, Havana 1976, translated by Claudette Williams 1989; Editions du Seuil and Victor Gollancz Ltd for the extract from *A Bridge of Beyond* by Simone Scharz-Bart, Paris, France and London 1972; Editions Gallimard for the extract from *Amour, Colere et Folie* by Marie Chauvet © Editions Gallimard, Paris 1968, translated by Betty Wilson 1989; Farrar, Straus and Giroux, Inc, New York and Pan Books Ltd, London for the excerpt 'Marbles' from *Annie John* by Jamaica Kincaid, Picador, London. Copyright © 1983, 1984, 1985 by Jamaica Kincaid. Reprinted by permission of Farrar, Straus and Giroux, Inc, and the excerpt 'At the Bottom of the River' from *At the Bottom of the River* by Jamaica Kincaid, Picador, London. Copyright © 1982, 1983 by Jamaica Kincaid. Reprinted by permission of Farrar, Straus and Giroux, Inc; The Feminist Press for the extract from *Reena and Other Stories* by Paule Marshall, New York 1983; Rosario Ferré for the extract from *Papeles de Pandora*, Editorial Joaquín Mortiz, Mexico 1976, translated by the author and Diana Vélez 1989; Heinemann Educational Books Ltd for the extracts from *A Season in Rihata* by Maryse Condé, translated by Richard Philcox (Caribbean Writers Series 1987), *Juletane* by Mariam Warner-Vieyra, translated by Betty Wilson 1989 (Caribbean Writers Series 1987), *Beka Lamb* by Zee Edgell (Caribbean Writers Series 1982) and *Frangipani House* by Beryl Gilroy (Caribbean Writers Series 1986); Jonathan Cape Ltd for the extracts from *The Hills of Hebron* by Sylvia Wynter-Carew, London 1962; Longman Group Ltd for the extract from *Summer Lightning* by Olive Senior (Longman Caribbean Writers Series) Harlow 1986; Methuen, London and the Charlotte Sheedy Literary Agency Inc, New York, for the extract from *No Telephone to Heaven* by Michelle Cliff, London 1988; New Beacon Books for the extract from *Jane and Louisa Will Soon Come Home* by Erna Brodber, London 1980; Marion Patrick-Jones and Columbus Publishers, Trinidad, for the extract from *J'Ouvert Morning*, Port of Spain 1976; Peepal Tree Press (53 Grove Farm Crescent, Leeds LS16 6BZ) for the extract from *Timepiece* by Janice Shinebourne, 1986; Velma Pollard and the Caribbean Authors Publishing Co Ltd for the extract from *Focus 1983, An Anthology of Contemporary Jamaican Writing*, Kingston 1983; Magali García Ramis for the extract from *La Familia de Todos Nosotros*, Editorial Cultural, Rio Piedras, translated by Carmen C Esteves, 1989; Ana Lydia Vega for the extract from *Encancaranublado y Otros Cuentos de Naufragio*, Editiones Casa de las Américas, Havana, 1982, translated by Mark McCaffrey 1989; Virago Press for the extracts from *Whole of a Morning Sky* by Grace Nichols, London 1986; Virago Press and A P Watt for the extract from *My Love, My Love* or *Peasant Girl*, Virago, London 1987; Virago Press, London for the extract from *The Orchid House* by Phyllis Shand Allfrey, © Phyllis Shand Allfrey 1954, reproduced by permission of Curtis Brown Ltd, London; Williams Wallace Publishers Inc, for the extract by Dionne Brand from *Sans Souci and Other Stories*, Stratford 1988; The Women's Press for the extract from *Waiting in the Twilight* by Joan Riley, London 1987, and the extract from *Angel* by Merle Collins, London 1987.

The publishers have made every effort to trace copyright holders, but in some cases without success. We shall be very glad to hear from anyone who has been inadvertently overlooked or incorrectly cited and make the necessary changes at the first opportunity.

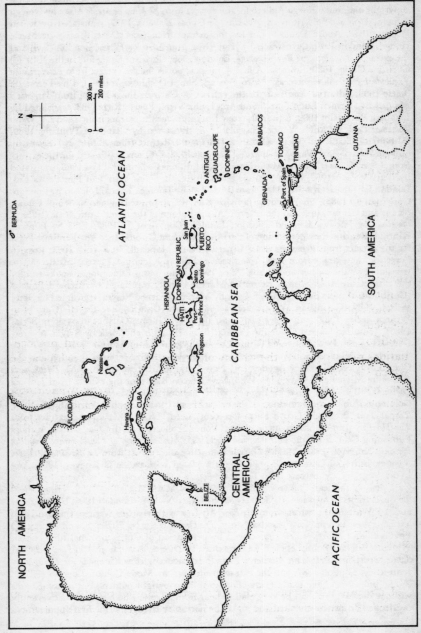

INTRODUCTION

We had immense difficulty with this anthology. The very volume of important 'quality' writing which we were trying to sift and sift again, reluctantly, in order to arrive at this final, tiny, sample was daunting. Our task was further complicated because we felt it was vital that our sisters from the non–English–speaking Caribbean should be represented. We have included works from the French– and Spanish–speaking Caribbean.[1] However, that meant an even smaller proportion of writers, and fewer pages from the English–speaking Caribbean in exchange.[2] Regrettably, for many reasons, we were unable to include writers from the Dutch–speaking Caribbean.

Finding texts and being in touch with authors across the vast spaces that separate anglophone, hispanophone and francophone countries represented a challenge more than a difficulty. There was a continuing problem in which we rejoiced: when it seemed we had just about managed to lay our hands on everything, there was always a new book, something just come to light or just off the press, that we had to scramble to get hold of.

Many people helped and we are grateful. We hope they will agree that the book, as it has emerged, reflects in some way the development of the tradition of women's writing in the region, the issues and preoccupations of that oeuvre, the variety of forms and the special exhilaration which Caribbean women writers bring to the use of language. It in no way adequately represents the achievement of the many women now writing in the region and barely represents the achievement of those whose work appears here.[3] What it hopes to be is a contribution to the long overdue task of making the writing of Caribbean women easily available to a wider audience. If it achieves that goal, our efforts will be more than rewarded. The extracts are arranged as the countries would appear on a map of the Caribbean, starting on the mainland and ending in Trinidad. For this suggestion we are indebted to Liz Gerschel.

Despite the fact that it is an important and not insubstantial body of literature, until quite recently Caribbean women's writing has received little attention from readers, critics and scholars alike. In her introduction to *Fifty Caribbean Writers*, Daryl Dance observes:

> Unfortunately serious and intensive critical attention has tended to focus on only a handful of the Caribbean writers. Many authors whose contributions to Caribbean literature are widely recognised

have received little or no extended treatment . . . many of the newer writers have received no attention at all, save for newspaper reviews.[4]

Of the ten 'notables' she mentions, two are women. Of the three 'new talents', two are also women. We note and welcome the shift in proportion as we applaud the choice of Olive Senior as the winner of the first Commonwealth Writers' Prize (a major literary award instituted in 1987). If Caribbean writers have been generally neglected it is no exaggeration to say that Caribbean women writers have been virtually abandoned. Writing in Dance's volume (published in 1986), Leota Lawrence remarks that, 'among West Indian writers, very few women are represented'.[5] Whereas the comment may have been true in 1978, it certainly was no longer true in 1986. The problem may well have to do with inadequate storage and retrieval systems, but the fact is that most of the 30 women in this anthology were already published at that time. The Savacou anthology entitled *New Poets From Jamaica* (1979) presented 13 poets, seven of whom were women.[6] *Jamaica Woman* appearing in the following year presented the work of fifteen women poets, none of whom had had a collection of her own published at the time.[7] Seven of them are also prose writers, Olive Senior being one. Eleven of the 28 poets in the more recent Jamaican anthology *From Our Yard* (1987) are women; six of these also write prose.[8] We emphasise that we have omitted from *Her True-True Name* at least as many women writers as we have included.

Prose works by women in the Caribbean date from the mid–nineteenth century[9] – some may be even earlier – but in the face of poor documentation and archival work that seems at its best biased, it would be unwise to make more than general comments on the historical/developmental aspects of the contribution of women prose writers in the region.

Most of the earliest women writers seem to have been creole (in this use of the word, white Europeans born in the West Indies): Mary Seacole's father was Scottish and her mother a Jamaican woman of mixed blood[10], but Jean Rhys and Phyllis Shand Allfrey were both Dominican-born whites. Jack Corzani in his comprehensive work *La Littérature des Antilles–Guyane Françaises* (1978) lists several early French Caribbean women writers who were white. The majority of women represented in this anthology are, like Mrs Seacole, *femmes de couleur*: they would be regarded as 'black' in a European or North-American context, but what Betty says of those writing in the francophone Caribbean probably holds true for their sisters elsewhere:

. . . in the fine distinctions of their own societies they range, like the heroines of their novels, over a wide and complexly designated colour spectrum: négresses, mulâtresses, capresses, chabines, femme à peau de sapotille, à peau d'acajou, and so on.[11]

Colour, as it is linked to class and life possibilities, is a persistent theme in the novels. We will return to it in a while. These women in many cases share a personal history involving movement from home country to European or North American metropolis. Some made the return trip; some went on to Africa or other Third World places. Perhaps half of those represented here came home to remain in the region. Even those like Rosa Guy and Paule Marshall who have lived the greater part of their lives outside the Caribbean, manage in almost every case to retain and articulate in their work a powerful sense of the island place and are able to affirm island culture and living, fraught though it may be with contradiction and weighed down by its history.

It is necessary to call attention, especially in the case of the anglophone Caribbean, to the remarkable volume of work produced by women since roughly 1980. (In the francophone and hispanophone Caribbean, too, a growing number of works by women are currently being published or republished.) The interesting question is, of course, whether these women had been writing much before that time and therefore whether what appears to be a sudden literary blossoming may not, at least in part, be a flowering of publishing interest consequent on the Women's Movement and the improved economic status of women, making them a market to be reckoned with.

If the sheer volume of recent writing by Caribbean women is impressive, what Pam calls 'the freedom and authority' of the woman's voice is no less so.[12] Extracts by Erna Brodber, Jamaica Kincaid, Simone Schwarz–Bart, Hilma Contreras, Olive Senior, Velma Pollard and Ana Lydia Vega are random examples from this collection of how Caribbean women respond to the world and harness language to create varieties of effects.

Nor is the shape of the novel, as explored by Caribbean women, restricted and 'traditional'. True, some of the earlier works are fairly solidly in the conventional mould. But a ground–breaker like Rhys was well ahead of her time, as is demonstrated here in the short (ghost) story, 'I Used to Live Here Once' and the longer, lustier creole piece 'Let Them Call it Jazz'. And though the autobiographical, *intimiste* viewpoint is often evident, there are excerpts in this collection which come from novels (some first novels) with strong political/socio–political preoccu-pations: Condé's *A Season in Rihata*, Collins's *Angel*, Cliff's *No Telephone to Heaven*, Edgell's *Beka Lamb*, Wynter Carew's *Hills of Hebron*, Shinebourne's *Timepiece* for example. They are none of them propagandist nor shrill. Rather, the political/socio–political context becomes a significant part of a dynamic of internal/external action. Politics, which is a composite and 'source', certainly, of 'external actions', seems in some cases almost to become a character, an agent in and of itself. If one considers that politics can constitute an uneasy presence in the works of writers as experienced as Lamming and Naipaul (*Water with Berries*, *Guerrillas*), the accomplishment of women at a stage when they are relative newcomers to the genre becomes more evident.

Political interest is not the only departure: a surrealist quality characterises the writing of the sole Santo Domingan contributor, Hilma Contreras; the story by the Puerto Rican, Rosario Ferré; as well as the robust neo–narrative of Antigua's Jamaica Kincaid; and, in yet another way, the writing of Guadeloupean Simone Schwarz–Bart. It is tempting to wonder whether this formal quality emerges from an early and persistent preoccupation with madness – 'la folie antillaise' – on the part of Caribbean women writers, beginning with Rhys's *Wide Sargasso Sea*, continuing in works like Wynter Carew's *Hills of Hebron* and Marion Patrick–Jones's *J'Ouvert Morning*, and more recently expressed in novels such as Myriam Vieyra's *As the Sorcerer Said* and *Juletane*.[13] One of the questions which critical discussion could profitably address is the presence – and absence – of madness as a subject, and the meanings to be secured from the nature and extent of its exploration in the writing of men and women of the region.

Schwarz-Bart's *The Bridge of Beyond* is also a kind of extended folk narrative, a chronicle of the survival of mothers, and daughters of mothers, through three generations. Its reach is epic, as is that of Merle Collins's *Angel*, though Collins's work is more of a political history. Humour is a dominant factor in Olive Senior's 'Do Angels Wear Brassieres?' and an important element in other works such as Merle Hodge's *Crick Crack, Monkey* and, in a gently ironic way, in Velma Pollard's *Karl*. Erna Brodber's *Jane and Louisa Will Soon Come Home* marries ordinary narrative to folk tale, stream of consciousness and dramatic monologue to create a form difficult to classify . . .

Evelyn O'Callaghan, discussing the writing of four Jamaican women, argues their case in terms of the acceptability and legitimacy of the autobiographical novel in West Indian literature.[14] While the women's work as represented in this collection is in many cases not 'autobiographical', it is always true, as O'Callaghan indicates, that 'the women are concerned with bringing the personal (private, emotional issues) into the public arena (literature)'.[15] Regardless of the preferred shape of the prose – folk tale, politico–historical epic, surrealist, plain traditional narrative – these works explore events as they affect the 'private' lives of those who make or suffer them. In this respect they would seem to be distinctly 'feminist', at any rate as we would wish to define the term.

Betty, commenting on francophone Caribbean writers says:

> Among the contemporary women writers, a greater number are originally from Guadeloupe than from Martinique, which is not true of male writers . . . a detail perhaps not without significance. Guadeloupe is generally seen as more militantly nationalistic and as leaning more towards independence, while Martinican society with a larger European, white, population, is still largely directed towards the metropole. Many of the writers were at one time or another actively involved with women's organizations and groups concerned with reform in the role and status of women.[16]

Where the anglophone Caribbean is concerned, if that literature has up till recently been a literature of middle-class values and bourgeois preoccupations, we need regretfully to assign the responsibility to male writers. The focus of most of the women's writing – especially recent writing – has been on grass roots concerns and ordinary people. Regardless of the settings of the works and whether these concerns are overtly addressed (as in *Hills of Hebron*, *Angel*, *Timepiece*, *Whole of a Morning Sky*) or covertly, within the novels' careful scrutiny of the individual consciousnesses sorting their way through personal joys and pains, there is an agenda which refers directly to issues of value: the worth of male to female persons and vice versa; the worth of black persons (or other persons of colour) to other black persons and to white persons and vice versa; the worth of persons who have–not to other persons who have–not, and to persons who have, and vice versa; and finally, the complex of these criss–crossing valuings, for no–one is sexed without race, or 'raced' without class, etc, etc. So that, even in those books without identifiably political content, a judgement is being made and invariably it is a judgement against the valuing of *things* and for the valuing of *people*. There is a sense in which the major concerns of women's writing can be reduced (or expanded) to these most simple, essential considerations. Issues of race and class, of gender, of slavery, of history, of persons and personhood and of oppression, certainly turn on this valuing.

Given the constraints of space, we address ourselves finally to three themes which seem to merit further discussion since they represent important foci in the extracts presented in this book: the relationship of men and women, the relationship of mothers and daughters and the quest for a sense of identity and wholeness, intimately bound up with the issue of names and naming. There are of course many others, some of which have been referred to before: childhood and adolescence; history; spirituality; gender, race, class and culture; politics; city and country.

The relationship of men and women, as it appears here, from the earliest work to the most recent, augurs ill. Almost invariably the man regards the woman as an object, neglects, abuses, ill–treats and diminishes her: the extract from Joan Riley's *Waiting in the Twilight* is a jolting case in point, as is the Cuban Omega Agüero's 'A Man, A Woman', gently understated, yet unequivocal in its message. As Pam has pointed out more than once, 'the problem of the restoration of community in the West Indies, the possibility for the West Indian to re–enter communal relationships, is intimately bound up with the resolution of the dilemma of man's relationship to woman'.[17] The insights offered in the work of these writers seem to support this position. A work like Beryl Gilroy's *Frangipani House*, while exploring at length the consequences of an unsatisfactory relationship between the heroine and her man, also points to the possibility of more fulfilling male–female relationships and the positive social effects which can redound. If the book is somewhat disappointing because it fails to show us the 'how' of this achievement, preferring merely to present the 'that', it nevertheless underlines the fact that a positive relationship between the sexes is a pre–condition for any community of caring.

The prospect for the relationship between mothers and daughters is somewhat brighter. One of the contrasts between male and female writing in the region is its depiction of the mother figure: in male writing the portrayal is almost always positive, whereas in female writing there are ambivalent and on occasion – as often in the francophone contribution – negative portraits. (An important exception is the work of Schwarz–Bart in which women with a powerful sense of themselves as the descendants of slaves who revolted, communicate to their daughters and their daughters' daughters the power to survive, to resist adversities, and to save not only themselves but those around them. It is a special vision.) In more recent writing from the anglophone Caribbean, however, the strength and endurance of women as mothers – often unsatisfactorily supported by their men – is celebrated. Joan Riley's *Waiting in the Twilight* is the saga of one woman's tenacity and endurance; both Jamaica Kincaid's books explore and affirm the mother–daughter relationship, in this case unusually supported by a good father. Brodber's womenfolk are good, if struggling mothers, as are many of the female characters in Nichols's and Shinebourne's novels. There is also a diachronicity in this impulse: so that Collins's *Angel* stretches through generations; Edgell's *Beka Lamb* as much concerns her grandmother as her mother; and Hodge's *Crick Crack, Monkey* (in the chapter extracted in this anthology and from which the collection takes its title) presents Tee's grandmother as providing her with roots, a source of goodness, wholeness and reality which contrasts with life in Port of Spain, trammelled up with middle-class aspirations and false values.

Beryl Gilroy's *Frangipani House* deserves mention again here, for its central figure is a mother/grandmother 'abandoned' to an old people's home. The interaction in the novel is largely between women: nurses and fellow inmates who are present, children and children's children who are, for the greater part of the book, abroad and therefore remembered. It is an important contribution to the whole literature and, with Schwarz–Bart's first novel, *Un Plat de Porc aux Bananes Vertes* (untranslated), unique of its kind and immune to the accusation sometimes levelled at Schwarz–Bart's *Bridge of Beyond*, of romanticising the woman's dilemma. What is important is that Gilroy's judgement is a positive one: she discovers characters with the strength and capacity to care in the midst of decrepitude, poverty and isolation.

We come finally to the issue of identity and the quest for wholeness, central to Caribbean literature and a continuing preoccupation of both male and female writers. The contribution of the women rests on two crucial foundation stones, both already mentioned: first, their commitment to introducing personal, private matters into the domain of fiction and setting them at the heart of things; second, their exploiting the possibilities of language, as the men simply have not done.

Dance, introducing *Fifty Caribbean Writers*, comments:

> Language and identity are inseparable . . . In this quest the West Indian author and his *dramatis personae* generally make three journeys, starting with the journey to England (or more recently, to the United States or Canada), the journey in other words into the White Western world . . . generally this journey reinforces the fact that the cold and alien land is not home and that the traveller must divest himself of his Europeanisation or his Westernisation.[18]

The second journey is the journey to Africa (or India) to discover roots, and finally there is the return journey, one which many find impossible, according to Dance, because their European education has taken them too far from 'their people, their roots, and thus themselves'.[19] We think it is fair to say that for many, economic possibilities, including access to publishing, dictate this exile.

Along with Césaire, both Brathwaite and Walcott in their poetry and critical writing have emphasised the importance of what Walcott calls 'the Adamic task of giving things their names'. Brathwaite's concept of 'nation language'[20] and Walcott's caution that, 'To change your language you must change your life', underline the fact that there has been a continuing awareness of the need to liberate the Word, to make it into a vehicle adequate for our own Caribbean being and perceiving.[21]

So that this journeying and sometimes coming home – a pattern in the lives of many of these women writers as well as of their characters – is a spiritual/psychic search in which one of the things which the writer may put at hazard is the owning of his/her language. Significantly, different responses to this journey emerge for francophone, anglophone and hispanophone women. The reasons for this are complex: having to do *inter alia* with the extent to which the imperialistic way of life was entrenched in the different colonies, differing patterns of slave life and culture, and a relatively lengthy period of gestation – or at least non–access to publication – for the anglophone and hispanophone women writers.

Writing on a francophone novel, Betty points out that the protagonist's story is Guadeloupe's story ('histoire' in French is both 'story' and 'history') and that the process of the heroine's liberation becomes 'the sketch of a possible blueprint for the political evolution of the French West Indies'.[22] Thus the country's political and cultural situation is 'mediated symbolically through the healing of the woman, with which it coincides and is synonymous'.

The writing in the francophone Caribbean goes the same route: within the works of individual writers as well as historically through time, and following in Césaire's path, the perception progresses in a pattern much like this heroine's emerging consciousness.[23] The writers represented in this anthology have arrived at a point of affirmation and self-consciousness and an engagement with politics that reflects both of these: Vieyra's vision is cautionary and pessimistic; Chauvet's is apocryphal; the totality of Condé's work defies barriers of time and space and explores the black experience in history in all its dimensions – in Africa and throughout the diaspora. And Simone Schwarz–Bart in particular, as Marie–Denise Shelton points out, 'articulates a poetry of presence and plenitude against absence and fragmentation' through her network of 'liberating myths'.[24] Tituba, Nanny, Solitude and Télumée are all figures of resistance and survival.

In the anglophone writers an early sickened vision in the largely pessimistic work of Jean Rhys gives way to a portrayal of three women in Phyllis Shand Allfrey's *Orchid House* involved in uneasy quests for liberation. (Of Rhys it must be said that the work is complex, valuing island culture, black people and the creole language, as is evident in 'Let Them Call It Jazz'. At the same time the white creole person as presented in her Caribbean stories does not live happily in the island place.) Marion Patrick–Jones's two novels, focusing on the middle classes, though not exclusively, pillory Trinidadian society for its narrow, negative, materialistic vision. It is Hodge's *Crick Crack, Monkey* that begins the work of rescue. Tee at the end of that book seems about to capitulate to middle-class folly, but the ordinary, inter–personal business (caring, full of humour and vitality) in Tantie's household and Ma's country place, represent a solid grounding for her, so that we feel that she at least goes to battle equipped.

In the post 1980s writing, as we have said, the mood is optimistic. Perhaps as a result of a forced silence on the part of the anglophone women who, for whatever reasons, did not find themselves in print up to that time, it was possible for them to complete the 'development process', so that when they finally began to write, like Topsy, they arrived full-grown. The only one of the recently published Caribbean writers who does not affirm at least aspects of being in the Caribbean place is Michelle Cliff, who along with Rhys could be regarded as being more in the alienated tradition of a 'francophone' than an anglophone consciousness. Personal history perhaps provides important clues: like Rhys, who also felt isolated, Cliff is 'white' – or as light–skinned as makes, to the larger world, little difference. Also like Rhys, she went to the kind of school – quite comprehensively described in *No Telephone to Heaven* – which promoted the values of the metropole. Like Rhys, she left her island early and never really came home. One of the prices she has paid is a compromised authenticity in some aspects of her rendering of the creole. (Interestingly enough, the name of her heroine of both *Abeng* and *No Telephone to Heaven*, Clare Savage – 'White Chocolate' – suggests in reverse the meaning of *La Négresse blanche*, title of an early francophone Caribbean novel by Mayotte Capécia, harshly condemned by Fanon for its heroine's alienation.)

It is important to underline the fact that recent writing by anglophone Caribbean women is rigorously honest in its rendering of the societies. There is no ritual pursuing of pseudo–feminist agendas; rather there is sufficient detachment to allow for women to make the protagonists in their novels male (Velma Pollard, for example), not through any mimetic impulse but deliberately, as part of the creative statement. There is also a sense in which the women have lined up solidly behind the poet and folklorist, Louise Bennett's point of view, for historically Bennett's work, while it is painfully (sometimes gleefully) aware of her society's pretensions, foibles, failings and fragmentations, has always affirmed the island place, its language, its culture, and its right to work out its salvation in fear and trembling. Evelyn O'Callaghan's comment on four Jamaican writers could serve for almost all the Caribbean sisters:

> In accurately rendering ... women's lives, the writers make a contribution to West Indian literature by furthering the claim that the region has a dynamic and complex cultural life of its own.[25]

She mentions that Lorna Goodison 'in praising West Indian writers like Earl Lovelace for stressing the positives of Caribbean cultural achievement, repudiates the literary stance of bewailing our lack'.[26] She quotes Goodison as saying, 'It seems to me pointless to spend so much time washing down the corpse and dressing it, when officially you don't dead yet'.[27] Readers unfamiliar with creole language may miss the irony, the playfully promised vitalities behind that final phrase . . . Maybe is true some name Clare Savage, but not plenty; not everybody stay like the woman in 'Let Them Call It Jazz' what manage to find a room near Victoria; but some like Mama King (*Frangipani House*), and Clara ('bright', 'true', 'clean') and Gem (*Whole of a Morning Sky*), and Angel (*Angel*), and Télumée Miracle (*The Bridge of Beyond*) done find them true–true name.

PAM MORDECAI
BETTY WILSON
Kingston, 1988

NOTES

1 Hereafter 'francophone' and 'hispanophone'.

2 Hereafter 'anglophone'.

3 Professor Brenda Berrian in a recently compiled bibliography lists over six hundred women writing in the Caribbean.

4 Daryl Cumber Dance, *Fifty Caribbean Writers: A bio-bibliographical critical source book*, Greenwood Press, Conn., USA, 1986, p. 7.

5 Dance, ibid, p. 225.

6 Edward Kamau Brathwaite (ed.), *New Poets From Jamaica: An anthology, Savacou 14/15*, Kingston, Jamaica, 1979.

7 Pamela Mordecai and Mervyn Morris (eds.), *Jamaica Woman*, Heinemann Educational Books (Caribbean) Ltd, Kingston, Port of Spain, 1980.

8 Pamela Mordecai (ed.), *From Our Yard: Jamaican Poetry Since Independence*, Jamaica Anthology Series, No. 2, Institute of Jamaica Publications Ltd, 1987.

9 *The Wonderful Adventures of Mary Seacole in Many Lands* (by Mrs Seacole), an important early work, was published in London in 1857.

10 See Christine Craig, 'Wonderful Adventures of Mrs Seacole in Many Lands: Autobiography as literary genre and a window to character', in *Caribbean Quarterly*, Vol. 30, No. 2, June 1984, p. 34.

11 Elizabeth Wilson, 'Women's Writing in the French West Indies: an Overview', unpublished paper in Caribbean Seminar Series, University of the West Indies, Mona 1985.

12 Pamela Mordecai, 'Wooing with Words – Some Comments on the Poetry of Lorna Goodison', in *Jamaica Journal*, No. 45, 1981, p. 34.

13 A term used by Simone Schwarz-Bart in *Pluie et vent sur Télumée Miracle*, Paris, Editions du Seuil, 1973, (Translation: *The Bridge of Beyond*, translated by Barbara Bray, Heinemann Caribbean Writers Series, London, 1982).

14 Evelyn O'Callaghan, 'Feminist Consciousness: European/American Theory, Jamaican Stories' in *West Indian Literature and its Political Context: Proceedings of the Seventh Annual Conference on West Indian Literature*, Rio Piedras, Puerto Rico, 1987, p. 31.

15 O'Callaghan, ibid, p. 32.

16 Elizabeth Wilson, Introduction to *Juletane*, Heinemann Caribbean Writers Series, London, 1987, pp. vi–vii.

17 First in Pamela Mordecai, 'The West Indian Male Sensibility in Search of Itself: Some Comments on *Nor any Country, Mimic Men and the Secret Ladder*' in *World Literature Written in English*, Vol. 21, No. 3, Autumn 1982. Also in 'Into this Beautiful Garden – Some Comments on Erna Brodber's *Jane and Louisa Will Soon Come Home*, in *Caribbean Quarterly*, Vol. 29, No. 2, June 1983.

18 Dance, op. cit., p. 5. See also Wilson, 'Le Voyage et l'espace clos: island and journey as metaphor', in *Out of the Kumbla: Womanist Perspectives on Caribbean Prose*, Boyce Davies and Savory Fido (eds.), Africa World Press, 1988.

19   Dance, op. cit., p. 5. As the woman in Jean Rhys' story (p. 157) says: 'I came so far that I lose myself on that journey.'

20   Edward Kamau Brathwaite, *History of the Voice: The Development of Nation Language in Anglophone Caribbean Poetry*, New Beacon Books, London, Port of Spain, 1984.

21   Derek Walcott, 'Codicil' in *The Castaway*, Cape, London, 1965.

22   Elizabeth Wilson, 'Sexual, Racial and National Politics: Jacqueline Manicom's *Mon Examen de Blanc*', in *Journal of West Indian Literature*, Vol. 1, No. 2, June 1987, p. 50.

23   Aimé Césaire, *Return to my Native Land*, Penguin.

24   Marie-Denise Shelton, 'Caribbean Women Writers in French', paper presented at Caribbean Women Writers Conference, Wellesley, Mass., USA, April 1988.

25   O'Callaghan, op. cit., p. 43.

26   O'Callaghan, op. cit., p. 43.

27   Lorna Goodison, quoted in O'Callaghan, op. cit., p. 43.

Note   The diamond symbol ◆ is used in the extracts to indicate where cuts have been made to texts. Spaces are left where the breaks correspond directly with the originals.

GUYANA

Beryl Gilroy

Beryl Gilroy, originally from Guyana, has lived in England for many years. A counselling psychologist, she directs her own private clinic in London, where she works mainly with black women. She has also been a teacher, researcher and writer and was the first black headmistress of a North London primary school. Beryl Gilroy has written many language arts textbooks. In 1976 she published Black Teacher *(Cassells), an account of her experiences as a teacher.* Frangipani House *(Heinemann, 1986) was her first novel; her second,* Boy-Sandwich *(Heinemann) was published in 1989.*

Frangipani House tells the story of Mama King, a defiant old lady who resists the efforts of her well–meaning children to confine her to an old people's home and to deprive her of work, an old and faithful friend. Gilroy's creole voice and her poetic evocation of the landscape and atmosphere of her native Guyana, as well as her depiction of the indignities associated with aging, make this an important work.

Frangipani House

The frangipani trees were laden with sweet-scented orange-coloured flowers, but the most wanton of their petals took short rides astride the wind and slowly swirled to the ground. They had the appearance of snippets of ribbon strewn across a green baize carpet by wilful hands.

The more keenly Mama King watched the petals dancing and gliding on the wind the more memories escaped from her, causing her mind to scurry and scamper after them. Were those memories about her girls or about Miss Tilley's house that smelt of rotting oranges? She shook her head as if trying to jerk memory from some secluded corner of her brain – out of the crevice in which time had buried it but the memory stayed in its grave. Nurse Tibbs watched her and wondered what was going on. She continued her circular walk around an area heaped with petals, and picked some up and then, like a child caught doing some forbidden thing, she shyly dropped them again. She walked towards the low shed and scraped off those petals that adorned its bald, corrugated pate. Once more she thought of Danny. The house in which they first lived had such a roof, and when the sun heated it to boiling point, large, black spiders came out, seeking shade. But she walked with Danny when work was done and sat on the clean sand, and listened to the river chortling as it flowed, and watched the mangrove trees motionless in the dull, leaden darkness.

She hardly noticed when the memory she had been seeking came out of hiding. But she greeted it with a welcome smile. Of course, the colour reminded her of her daughters, both dressed in orange coloured costumes for the school play. She stared out into the distance, allowing spools of recollections to unwind.

'They did want Token for Snow White. But she too tall. She make a good dwarf, though. She say everything she had to say. Everybody clap. I feel so proud. I take in plenty washing to rig them out for the play and when it happen I forget the rheumatism in me hand from the hot an' cold water. The teacher so please wid Token. I notice how she grown – fullin' out and then all of a sudden, Token sick. She wouldn't eat a thing – only drink, an even that. She get fine – fine – fine! I say "God if you wan' she, take she", and I watch she turnin' to skeleton before me eyes. Then somebody tell me 'bout Maraj – a old, coolie man who know 'bout sickness.

'Where he live no bus does go. So Token an' me, we go by Donkey Cart for five hours and we reach there. He look at Token – she got nara. She guts twist. It easy for children guts to twist. He 'noint Token belly – she holler for mercy, but he 'noint her two more time. She eat dat same night. I kneel down in front of Maraj. I say "I ain' got money – only dis brooch. It solid gold. Take it."

' "Keep your brooch. We all is poor people," he tell me. "Feed ten beggar one for every year you chile livin'. I don' wan' money. Tonight I go to sleep. Tomorrow I can wake up somewhere else. Thank God for everything."

'People always good to me. The teacher never charge me a cent. She teach Token for nothing. Then she teach Cyclette. When I ask her about money – how much I got to pay she say, "Who talkin' 'bout payin'! They will remember me when I get old. Cast your bread on the water. Dat's what the Bible say". It look like yesterday when Token pass for nurse and Cyclette for secretary. Because they had a little complexion, they get work easy. Token was a good nurse. The patient dem like her and Cyclette could make a typewriter sing, laugh – run and jump. Only yesterday they was little. Danny would proud of them. Poor Danny – I wonder where he stay now. Dead and gone. I believe so. Nobody see him or meet him. Even people who been to Aruba. I wonder where Danny gone?'

'Mama King,' Matron shouted from the door. 'You staring like you mad! People who stare like that have empty, idle mind. Why don't you think positive, instead of standing around and staring at nothing?'

'Since I come here I look, but all I see is what past and gone. You have now. All I have is long ago. Go and count you money. It got old people blood on it?'

In a mocking, over-deferential manner she curtsied to the Matron, then twisting her body through the small space that the Matron's bulk had left unoccupied, she went back into her room to rock her feelings to rest. She walked round and round the bed and then once again, unable to resist its beckoning, lay down and closed her eyes.

'Matron think I doing nothing,' she said quietly to herself 'but thinking is hard work.'

'I sit down and my whole life pass before me – like a film at a picture show. I get so tired but yet I can't stop. And everybody think my mind empty, my head empty and my heart empty. I see people, dead and gone, walking and talking and young. And out of my old worn out body, a young woman walk out and life is like roll of new cloth waiting to roll out.'

She fell asleep.

She woke around dusk but she did not get up, and when Nurse Douglas entered her room she faked sleep.

'Come on, Mama King. I know you wake up. You want cocoa-tea or coffee?'

'I want cocoa-tea.'

While she sipped the cocoa, a flight of blue Sakis hurrying home in the dying light caught her eyes. The sun, plump and comfortable behind wisps of gossamer-mauve clouds, sank slowly out of sight. It was the end of another day.

'I wonder how long I been here. How long they keeping me here! How long I going to live Lord? I wonder how long?'

'Nurse,' she called, 'I want to go home. I miss everything.'

'Mama King, you lucky. Life is a treadmill. You been on it for years and years. You daughters push you off. Don't grumble. Don't complain. Count your blessings.'

Mama King sucked her teeth. 'You don' teach you grandmother to suck egg. I wan' go home, I wan' pen and paper to write me daughters. They must come and take me out of this terble place.'

'Well, tell you what, when you mind clear you can write. Wait till tomorrow. I will get you pen and paper and I will post the letter for you.'

'I wan' the paper now,' Mama King insisted. 'And the pen, and the ink.' Lucid, aggressive and determined, she kept on demanding writing materials until the nurse complied. She wrote a message to Token like a child given lines for punishment.

'Token, I want go home. I better. I hate this place.

Token, I want go home. I better. I hate this place.'

She wrote until all the lines on the paper were covered. She had written it thirty times. Then she addressed the envelope and sealed in the letter allowing the nurse to take it from her and put it in her pocket.

'I will post it for you,' Nurse Douglas promised. 'I going home just now.'

Mama King had doubts about the letters she asked the nurses to post. She never received any replies and every complaint she made was either swept aside like rotten wood in a rough wind, or ignored as if she complained in a foreign language. The women were expected to think themselves privileged and lucky to be under Matron's care.

◆

Mama King resumed her seat by the window, and on the grass outside, a patchwork of events from her life lay sprawled before her in a kind of half–light.

'Since Danny gone my feelings for men shrivel like grass in dry weather. Ben Le Cage did come roun' once or twice but he is like mucka-mucka.* He make you scratch yourself morning, noon and night with worry. He live wid woman after woman – get chile after chile and as fas' as he get them, he forget 'bout them. I can' believe he get them normal. He mus' get fed up doin' the same thing so much time with so much women. He never think 'bout God dat man! I didn't take notice of him. I say I is a married woman – I aint one of you hole an' corner. He didn't like that. "You got two girl children", he say. "Who will take you wid two girl? Boy more useful. Girl is trouble. Before they twenty they go and get belly." I chase him out when he say that. He want to bring bad luck on my two girl.'

The cadences of her own voice seemed to lull her into a deep sleep. Only the muffled sounds of moans and sighs that seemed to be fragments of anguish rising from the graveyard inside her, synchronised with her breathing. 'She never dreamt,' she said. She had never been able to recall a single dream but that evening one stuck in her mind and frightened her.

She was a child again walking demurely beside her mother along a road stretching far into the distance. There was no one else in sight but she could hear voices singing familiar tunes. The road suddenly became liquid and there she was swimming in the cool, chattering water. But her mother had disappeared and there was Matron scowling and scolding and shouting at her. Everything happened in an instant. She had grown old and Danny, as young as when she last saw him, had appeared on the

*A plant, the juice causes itching when in contact with skin.

4

scene. She rushed up to him but he eyed her with suspicion and cutting resentment.

'*I don' want you,*' he said. '*You old! You ugly! I want this nice clean skin woman.*'

He embraced Matron and then pushed his wife out of their way. She felt a searing pain on her shoulder where he had touched her and she screamed. The nurses rushed in. Her face, covered with sweat emphasised the astonishment and pain in her eyes. 'I dream,' she whispered, 'I dream . . .'

'It's only a nightmare, Mama King,' comforted Nurse Carey. 'It's gone now. Only me and you here now.'

Mama King still sobbed. Her heart was so full of hatred, although she did not know for whom, that at the slightest touch she would split open like a ripe calabash dropped on stone.

'Ginchi,' she called, 'Ginchi!' But her friend had long since gone home. She rushed to the window. There was nothing to see – just a slither of moon and whipped egg–white clouds scurrying away to the other side of the globe.

More than anything else she wanted work. She always had a special relationship with work. Her body needed it as it needed food and clothes. And now, time and life, her daughters and the matron had all conspired to deprive her of her faithful friends, work and hardship. She felt as though they had punched and kicked her and given her many terrible blows.

She began once more to prowl round and round the room like a caged animal. Even the window had clouded over. She ran her fingers along the sill and so found comfort and peace. Why had work deserted her for no reason to speak of? True, she had been sick, and even getting older but since when work turn its back on poor, old people?

'*If work come now and stan' up before me, I give her a big-big cuffing. Lord, how wonderful are thy works! All works belong to God.*'

◆

For the first time in a long life, Mama King was aware that things were being done to her, or given to her, or taken from her. Nurses administered potions and pills, fed her and washed her. Doctors examined her, and investigated the working of her life-worn body. Although she watched with the curiosity of a child, worry sneaked out of the corners of her mind to torment her. Regret for the cursory care she had given her children made her restless. Work had been the culprit that wrecked her life, robbed her of her perspicacity and deprived her children of her love. Things were different when her life was given over to the care of her grandchildren. Somehow she had less energy but they had more care. Grandchildren brought time, and ease and a quiet flow of happiness. She told them stories and played with them. She did not need to conquer and control them. She laughed and they laughed when she said:

'Over the copper forest, over the iron mountain, over the stormy sea, there was a rich King monkey who had soft teeth.' Out of a radiant corner of her mind voices suddenly called out, 'Go on grandmother tell us more.'

She could see a crowd of faces behind the voices. It was as if they were under chalky water looking up at her. She sat up in bed but the faces had vanished. Miss Ginchi's grandson Carlton walked in and sat down. He took her hand and said, with little emotion, 'Grandma Ginchi dead and bury yesterday.'

She did not speak. Her eyes moved slightly.

'I miss her, I miss her talking and her rowing. I miss the food she used to cook,' Carlton continued. 'I miss her putting on her good dress on a Sunday. I have nobody in the world for family.'

'Don't cry. You got me when I get better. You can live with me. I got a house. I still have a house? I will give you it when I dead. You take it.'

'Yes, Mama Ginchi and me clean it few weeks back. Poor Mama Ginchi, you know I never think she would ever go away. When they put her in the grave my heart get cramp. The grave was full of water. They bale out the water with a bucket from church. It had plenty tadpole and dead grass. The water colour like ginger beer.' Mama King listened. Only her eyes showed emotion, by the way she closed them or opened them as he spoke.

'She had a nice service. They sing Onward Christian Soldier.'

'Hm.'

'She had plenty wreath. Nice flower. She did like flower, yaller.'

'Hm.'

'I wish you did come. Plenty people come.'

'Hm.'

'I think I going away from here. Where she get me from? She never tell me. I wish I had mother. I would be able to go there now.'

'When the big drought come and rice burn up, she catch some people thiefing food from she farm. When they see her, they swim cross the trench, run away. They lef' you under some bush. They never come back for you. She never see they face or know they name. That's how you come. They wasn't much to tief but these two young people find

6

something. They was good people because they run away and didn't turn roun' and cuff her down.'

Carlton raised his eyebrows at the news of his history and said, 'She was good to me. She give me everything. She was good to me. I got plenty to thank her for. She could leave me in the sun to dry out. But she take me! She save me! She was father and mother for me. I goin' way. I can' live in tha' house no more.'

'Hm.'

'I going Mama King. I never going to see you again. Goodbye!'

'You can cope wid de worl'?'

He nodded. 'I think I can. I don't wan' too much. Just food and work.'

He walked out of the hospital, confident that he would see the world through his own eyes and through those of an indomitable woman. He would walk cautiously on his own feet, testing every rock and stone before putting his weight to it as she had done. He would grasp life with padded hands – hands padded with caution and experience of a life well-lived. A new kind of strength surged through him and he knew then he had grasped his manhood. 'Be a good man,' she once said. But what was a good man? He had heard talk of Danny and Ben Le Cage. He had met other men. But were they good? He did not know. Maybe a good man gives his seed to many women. Maybe he works hard as the women do. Maybe he does not work at all. Manhood is strength? He had always been a donkey-boy. Yes, manhood is strength. He had never thought of himself as a man before. Just Miss Ginchi's grandson. A donkey-boy who was happy to help and oblige.

He went back to the house and started putting his few things together. The house was quiet. There were no relatives to hang around and celebrate the death for days on end. The kitchen smelt of Miss Ginchi's last meal, the bedroom of her medicaments and the lavender water she liberally used, and the sitting-room of all those people who had laughed there, as they listened to her talk and her stories. He lit a candle and placed it by the bedroom window. Was it a symbol of the searing sadness he felt when he thought of her? Was it the star of her loyalty and kindness – a star that always burnt so brightly?

'Ow, Mama Ginchi, whey you gone? Whey you gone?' He cried until the surge of anguish receded.

Then he remembered the chickens. They had not been fed. Half-heartedly he fetched rice and corn and threw it for them. Sadness was in his voice as he called them. They came hurrying and pecked ravenously. It did not matter who fed them corn. Only the dog seemed to sense the final nature of the parting from his mistress. He howled and ran off into the night. 'Buller,' shouted Carlton. 'Buller come back!' But it sat alone upon the shadow-stricken grass, raised its head to the stars and continued its plaintive howling.

Carlton noticed lights in Mama King's house. 'Surely,' he thought, 'she was still in the hospital?' He went over to investigate.

'Who's that?' he called. 'Mama King!' The door opened almost at once.

'Hi, Carlton,' Markey shouted. 'Hi, it's good to see you. Come in! Our family are all here. Come in.'

'Hi Carlton. Remember me, Solo?'

'Hi Carlt', greeted Cindy.

The two older women continued their discussion as if nothing else existed in the whole wide world. In spite of the luggage that stood all around the little room, Carlton found a place to sit. He overlooked the changes brought by time and money. He overlooked the differences caused by living in a more demanding society. He smiled and his thoughts were of a time that for him alone had stood still.

◆

Mama King's reprieve now allowed her time for easy free-ranging reflection. Each afternoon she sat pondering the number of times that life had reconstituted her – first as child, then as woman, wife, mother, grandmother, mad-head old woman, beggar and finally old woman at peace at last.

On some evenings a parade of her contemporaries, all now dead and gone, passed before her mind's eye. She nodded with approval and frowned with disapproval at the quirks of fate and time. One gap in the record of knowing particularly troubled her. And once again she asked herself: 'Wha' happen to Julia McAbe' daughter, Tina? Tina the determined. Tina, who could conquer Duppee. Tina with the concrete heart?' She remembered the encounter with Tina when her dead brother's wife turned up like a sea-beach coconut and demanded her children. They had not heard from the mother in thirteen years – not a line, a birthday card or the wax from her ear. But one day, breezy bright and brassy she waltzed in, wrapped up in a booming squall of a man and said:

'I come for me children! I run away and lef' dem but now I come back!'

Julia McAbe was stunned. The children were her life. Tina worked and she slaved for them. The girl was congenitally a striver and a coper, the boy learning helplessness and encouraged to leave things to the women in his life. Both children were happy to leave. They suddenly found their old life intolerable. They wanted change!

'You all old enough to know, there can be no coming back here!' said

8

Tina calmly. 'Once you walk out a that door, you never walk in again. For years I work for your back and belly. My Mama slave to keep you clean. Once you walk out, you ain' comin' back! Understand?' The children nodded and went with their mother. Two weeks later, neglected, unwashed and hungry they returned to their grandmother. But Tina chased them off even though her mother, Mama King and many other women pleaded with her. 'Hallelujah,' she said, 'I free. They ain't my children and God set me free!' Two weeks later she disappeared. 'Life is a life sentence,' she wrote. 'I prepare to serve two, one for you and one for me. With them I have to serve four. I won't live that long.'

Julia McAbe never said another word. She went quiet-crazy and ended up in Frangipani House.

◆

'When the baby want come out, you want push. They woosh it come out.'

'You don' remember next day.'

'When you pain start the baby get low.'

'Does the midwife give you pain-killers?' asked Cindy.

'Pain-killers! Who can kill pain! Every baby got its own pain!'

'You got to push saafly, Cindy. Push like this.' Sumintra demonstrated to the obvious delight of the others.

Cindy looked full and ready. One by one they touched her, and spoke to the baby inside her.

'Get brains in you' head not cow-guts.'

'Come easy to your mother, you hear,' one said stroking her. 'Don't cause worries.'

'Be healthy and strong,' said another.

'Good milk will flow for you.'

'Sing to the baby Cindy. Rub you belly when you sing. Call the baby. Talk to it,' said Mama King. 'It will move when you talk.'

Cindy felt strengthened and supported. 'I am so happy,' she said, 'that you are all sharing this pleasure with me. Chuck sure will get the same support from your men. Sure thing.'

'Support! They wouldn't give him support. They will give him rum – white rum, bush rum and five year rum. Shoor ting.'

Extract from *Frangipani House*.

Grace Nichols

Born in 1950 in Guyana, where she grew up and worked among other things as pupil teacher, reporter and freelance writer, Grace Nichols came to Britain in 1977. She has had poems published in journals and magazines such as Frontline, Ambit, Kunapipi, Artrage, City Limits *and* Third Eye. *Her cycle of poems,* I is a Long Memoried Woman, *won the 1983 Commonwealth Poetry Prize. She is also the author of three children's books published by Hodder & Stoughton:* Trust you Wriggly, *a collection of stories;* Baby Fish and other stories, *a collection of folk stories; and* Leslyn in London. *Virago has produced a second collection of her poems,* The Fat Black Woman's Poems *(1984) and her first novel,* Whole of a Morning Sky *(1986). A performer of her own poetry, Grace Nichols lives in England with poet John Agard and a small daughter.*

Whole of a Morning Sky *tells the story of a family's move from a Guyanese village to the capital, Georgetown, and of the dramatic political events in which they become caught up as Guyana, racially split between blacks and East Indians, struggles towards independence. A poet's craft with language is evident throughout the book. As is clear from the extracts, 'Archie' and 'Ivy', she does not sacrifice her characters for the sake of her story.*

Archie

As a child Archie was very devoted to his mother. He was her one child, born and raised on the country's windswept Essequibo Coast. His mother was a tall, dark woman, full of the qualities of the women at that time, faith and forbearance, cut and contrivance. She had a little East Indian blood in her, maybe a little Amerindian too, according to her friends. She wore her long, thick black hair in a fat roll at the back of her head.

Archie's father was a carpenter, an African man who already had a child by a wealthier coloured woman when he married Archie's mother. The wealthier woman's family, it appeared, didn't want him to have anything to do with their daughter.

Like most of the earth's people, they were very poor and after school Archie would work in a blacksmith's shop to bring in a little extra. He received twelve pence a week. But in spite of the poverty, his mother insisted that he should wear shoes to school, unlike the other schoolboys his age. Archie did his best to care for them for her sake. He restrained himself from kicking the bricks along the bricky public road and walked on the smoother parts. This and the shoes made the other boys feel he was a mother's boy, a sissy.

They taunted, provoked and pushed him. This went on for quite a while. Archie knew that complaining to his teacher or mother was useless. So one day he decided to pretend that he was going mad which the boys didn't give him credit for. He pulled out his leather belt from around his waist and began to chase them all across the countryside, lashing them wildly about their heads and backs, lashing and lashing, until all the weeks and months of repressed anger had come out, leaving him completely exhausted.

After that they left him alone. One or two even became his friends. Then his father built a cakeshop under the house and things were a little better, but shortly after his mother died. He was twelve at the time, big enough to feel the weight of his loss.

And when he was in a particular frame of mind Archie would relate what happened to him shortly after his mother died:

One dark rainy night he was doing his homework at the table with the aid of a wicker lamp. He was alone upstairs as his father was still below, building a new counter for the shop. The wind was making all kinds of strange noises, tearing at the flapping zinc sheet on their roof.

He was doing his best to concentrate on his arithmetic when he heard footsteps coming up the stairs. At first he thought they were his father's, but the steps sounded lighter. When nobody opened the door, however, he dismissed it as part of his childish imagination. But a few moments later he became uneasily aware of another presence in the room. He stopped working and sat very still but he could feel the presence behind him coming nearer and nearer.

Then he felt as if his head was getting bigger and bigger. His pen slipped from his clammy fingers and he picked up the familiar body odour of his mother, the odour she had after bathing and rubbing her body with coconut oil. Without seeming to turn his head he saw her face behind him, her long black hair disarrayed. After that he knew nothing else.

The next morning he woke to find himself in a strange room. He was at his neighbour's house. When his father came to see him he told Archie what happened the night before. A beam in the roof of the house had caved in, falling across the chair where Archie had been sitting. His father had come running upstairs when he heard the crash and found him lying in a dead faint on the floor, only inches away from the fallen

11

beam which might have killed him if he had remained in his chair. Somebody had been protecting him.

The story was always a marvel to the children because, as far as they knew, their father never lied. And his mother must have been sorry for having to frighten him for after that he only saw her in dreams and always she was distant and smiling.

But his father died too, only four years after his mother's death and he had no choice but to go to live with his half-brother, Jack, who was older than he and who came to see him from time to time. Jack's mother had never married and still lived with her own parents. They were all ambitious people who were determined to see Jack through a medical career. But they treated Archie kindly and his brother helped him with many things – English grammar, decimals and books – that were to see him to a teaching profession.

When his brother left for the USA to study, Archie was left on the threshold of life, a very lonely and sober young man.

He began teaching at a village school on the Essequibo coast and taught there for nearly ten years. Then he asked for a transfer to a city school, got one, and a few years later met his wife. He was thirty-two at the time. She was eighteen.

That his wife's upbringing was completely different to his was clear to him from the beginning. She was nurtured on love and gaiety.

From the very first time Archie set eyes on her at the home of an old music teacher friend he could tell that. Love and gaiety were there in the soft tendrils that escaped from her two plaits and curled behind her creamy brown neck, in the sleeveless white dress that fell to her knees, in her round arms and laughter-suppressed mouth, in all her slim girlish freshness.

And when he began to visit her home, as he had in mind courting, he understood why she had blossomed the way she had: her father, a jovial, brown-skin major in the Police Force, was openly affectionate with her and her mother, an extremely charming and soft-spoken woman, seemed nothing but love.

They lived in one of the more elegant-looking houses in the Eve Leary compound where the higher officers in the Police Force were housed. The home, which was breezy and spacious, overlooked the Atlantic and the stretch of sea wall that was built to keep it out. It was a happy home, always full of visiting friends and relatives, laughing chattering people who were entertained with fruit cake and home-made ice cream.

But his visits hadn't always been easy for him. At times he felt uncomfortable and stiff. Clara and her girlfriends had a way of bursting into sudden fits of stifled laughter that he couldn't see the reason for most times, and one Sunday afternoon a cousin of hers, a blind young man of about her own age, played a trick on him.

Sonny, as he was called, seemed to have made up for his blindness by acquiring a special sense of direction and touch which he used to play practical jokes on nearly everyone he met. Unknown to the as yet uninitiated Archie, Sonny came across to where he was standing on the veranda and slipped an egg into the pocket of his baggy trousers. Later, when they went back into the drawing room he said to Mrs Harris, Clara's mother, that she had better have a look at her eggs on the shelf as he had the feeling that somebody had stolen one.

Mrs Harris, who was accustomed to his pranks, got up to look and then laughingly admitted that one of her eggs was indeed missing.

Archie, who was puzzled by all this talk of a stolen egg and the laughter that had begun in anticipation of something, was even more astonished when Sonny slid over to where he was sitting on the sofa, pushed a hand in his pocket and came up with the only slightly cracked egg. 'I keep telling you, you must stop this habit of stealing other people's eggs,' Sonny said in an admonishing tone, his round face the picture of innocence and earnestness. They were all laughing so heartily, Clara almost slipping from her chair, that Archie had no choice but to join in.

Yet in spite of the laughter it seemed that she was drawn to the suffering quality in his face and not to the smooth boyish faces of the other easy-going young men she knew.

They were married, a big formal event which only a few of his relatives attended, and shortly after he was offered the post of headmaster at a school back in Essequibo. They went there with three weeks of the long August holidays still to go.

In those early days of marriage they went for long walks along the pitch-black coast road at nights, with their only light the huge stars that clung close to the earth, and the only sounds those of the mysterious Goat Sucker birds with their uncannily human cries of 'Ah-who-you Ah-who-you', and the pounding of the Atlantic on the shore.

Sometimes he would suddenly release her hand and run ahead a little, laughing in the darkness and trying to scare her. When a few moments later he jumped out at her she would pretend to be a bit annoyed, just to please him.

In the hot, slow, breezy days they lazed around the house eating their fill of oranges, mangoes and pineapples. He was surprised at himself for following her movements around the house, almost fearing that she would disappear.

It seemed as if they did nothing but sleep, eat and make love. His long limbs felt too reluctant and heavy to do anything else. He felt a bit ashamed of the glow on his own face. That she should see it. His body reached for hers with a silent intensity.

And she, having come with no preconceived notions, undressed for him unashamedly, and accepted his thrusting hardness like the savouring of some strange exotic fruit, its full flavour eluding her. It was only after the birth of her first child, Dinah, that she began to fully savour the taste. It was as if her little daughter had touched some tiny hidden secret spring as she made her way down, saying, 'Here mother, a little gift to compensate for all the pain. A gift, a gift, the unfolding of your own fount of pleasure.'

And Archie, so obsessed was he by his passion that one morning, a couple of years after their marriage, he sat at the breakfast table staring at her. Staring more than usual, at her face, her neck, her bosom. Then he said in a sudden voice, 'What would you do if I was to hit you, eh?' For he badly wanted to hit her. To slap her cheeks hard. To slap her for her own lovely childhood and his hard empty one. To slap her for the pain and jealousy she was already arousing in him.

They sat there staring at each other for a while, man and woman sizing each other up, testing each other. Different emotions chased across her face, but when her voice came it was very calm, 'Make sure that whenever you hit me you do a very good job of it,' she said. 'Make sure that you don't leave an ounce of strength in my body. Make sure that I can't get up again, you hear.'

Archie knew she meant it.

Ivy

Ivy Payne groaned, turned, lifted herself up, her elbows supporting her body on the hard fibre mattress that lay on a bed of wooden planks. She stayed that way for a few nodding moments, then gently hoisted herself over the sleeping limbs of her children and stumbled, not quite fully awake, into the dark passageway that led to the kitchen. On her way she passed a small bedroom in which her eldest son and his wife and child were sleeping. Her second son, Vibert, had again slept out for she

14

couldn't see his long, awkward frame curled up on the bedding on the drawing room floor.

Ivy didn't feel like going down to the yard bathroom and contented herself with splashing cold water on her face at the back window, scrubbing her teeth with some kitchen salt and rinsing the night away.

Today was Friday and she must hurry down to the abattoir before all the good runners and blood for her black pudding were sold out. She had taken up with the business ever since her trawler fishing husband had died four years ago, leaving her with the six children. After his death she was forced to sell their Broad Street cakeshop and take up residence in one of the Ramsammys' rundown little houses in the Charlestown yard. She supported herself and children with the black pudding money and from what she made at her weekly Saturday night dances. She couldn't depend on her eldest son for anything, now that he had his own family. But she did get some extra help from her manfriend, Cyril.

Cyril, a plumpish middle-aged man, came about twice a week. On these occasions Ivy made up a bed for the other children on the floor outside with Vibert so they would have some privacy. Cyril always came very late at nights, picking his way around the sleeping bodies and left in the morning before they woke up. He himself worked on the waterfront as a stevedore and his contributions to Ivy's family came in useful.

Vibert hated the best bone in Cyril for reasons peculiar to himself. At nineteen he was sullen and brooding and at nights would lie staring at the quiet face of his father's photograph which his mother had carefully hung on the drawing room wall. He could hear the shaking of the bed in his brother's room. He could endure that. What he couldn't stand was the sight of his mother's locked door and the knowledge that Cyril was inside there with her.

The thought of Cyril's smooth body and slick hair next to his mother's healthy darkness aroused such a fury in him. He felt she had no shame. He remembered the way she had carried on at his father's funeral, throwing herself across the coffin, but that was like a woman all over, he thought, quick to forget. Now he had to restrain himself from kicking the shaky door in and dragging the man out of the house, down the steps and right through the passageway. Also the way his mother had of putting aside Cyril's food first in the glass bowl made him sour inside.

Ever since the night that Vibert had ripped away her nightdress Ivy felt that some indefinable thread in the relationship between mother and son had been severed. That was the last time she had tried beating him.

Vibert would always remember the look of outraged astonishment on her face, her tears afterwards. He didn't know what had possessed him that night. It had nothing to do with her shouting that he had no ambition or the blows she rained about his head and neck. In the act of deliberately ripping her nightdress he thought he was showing her the complete disrespect which he felt he now had for her.

Ivy lit the kerosene stove in the kitchen, then hurried back to the bedroom to dress. When she came out she added three heaping potspoons of sugar to the water on the stove, unplugged two tiny balls of paper from a tin of evaporated milk and poured a little in. She didn't trust her biggest girl, June, with the milk. She lifted down a basket of bread which she had baked the day before and placed a tin of margarine beside it. June would give the others their bread and tea later. Ivy helped herself only to a cup of the hot thin tea as she didn't want to get wind in her stomach, then she tied her head with a blue headtie, picked up her red shopping bag and hurried out of the house.

She picked her way along the passageway, stepping on the odd pieces of board precariously laid down. Apart from the clanking of pans which came from Mrs Lall's hut and which only reinforced Ivy's belief that she was haunted, the yard was still asleep. Ivy passed the remaining range rooms, patches of black crouching in the softening dawn, and stepped out into the cool streets.

She walked like a woman filled with sweet life, the red shopping bag with two large brown bottles fitted snugly into the crook of her arm, her cotton shift of red and yellow flowers blowing gently at the knees of her sturdy polished legs. A pale half moon still hovered in the skies and the streets had hardly begun to stir. Passing a rumshop, Ivy spat at the scent of urine that would dissipate itself in the sunshine later in the day.

She liked to start a day like this, untouched by the hungry, peevish faces of her children or the bawling of her son's baby. On days like this she felt strong, basking in her ability to cut and contrive and to make a living for her children. It wasn't good to depend on any man and, even though she appreciated Cyril's help, she intended to make life her own way.

Ivy's thoughts continued to flow in serene contentment until she neared the Stabroek Market with all the buses lined up from the night before. Then it all came back. The news about the general strike last night.

Ivy stopped in her tracks, the red bag slipped down her arm to her fingers. 'Oh Christ! I forget everything bout dis kiss-me-ass-strike,' the words broke involuntarily from her lips in a strangled kind of way. 'Shit,' she went on, sucking her teeth, 'don't tell me dis going mean I kyant get no runners and blood to buy.' Ivy looked around in agitation as if seeking someone to tell her just what the strike would mean.

When she had heard the news from her eldest son, Marcus, last night, the thought that it would affect her black pudding had never entered her head for some reason. Now realisation was beginning to dawn.

Ivy stood there in a fit of indecision for a full five minutes. Across by the market she could see a few vendors standing uncertainly around their boxes of produce. Then she decided that she wouldn't turn back. She would go down to the abattoir and beg someone there to help her. There must be someone there, one of the men she joked with week after week. She didn't mind waiting the entire morning just as long as she got some blood and runners. She had come to depend too much on it, not only the money which made things stretch far into the week, but on the activity itself, the stuffing and the boiling and the cutting in a kitchen full of the scents of thyme and peppers, while every few minutes someone came around to the back door for a 'fifty cents black pudding' or 'a dollar black pudding.'

Ivy was just in time to see the night watchman rolling his bicycle away from the faded government abattoir building as she swung the corner into the street. He was moving away from her and she raised her arms and began to clap frantically, calling, 'Hee-ooo, hee-ooo.'

He heard her and turned his bicycle around. 'Is what you doing here, girl? You en hear bout de strike?' he asked as he came near her.

'Jesus Christ,' said Ivy.

'Is where you living girl?' he chided her.

'But I must get mih blood and runners,' said Ivy. 'You kyant help me?'

'Me!' he exclaimed, 'Sista, I would advise you to go home. You wasting yuh time waiting here. Nobody coming to work here dis morning. You see me. Is home I going home. No more nightshift till I hear dis strike call off. I would advise you to go home. When dem abattoir people come down here they en coming to work. They coming fuh demonstrate like de union say. I been at the meeting yesterday an I know what I talking bout.'

Ivy was only half listening to him. Already she could visualise how hard the coming week would be if she failed. But when the watchman suggested slyly that she meet him later that afternoon, her eyes returned swiftly to the present, and with a 'haul yuh ole tail', she sent him riding slowly away.

Extracts from *Whole of a Morning Sky*.

17

Janice Shinebourne

Janice Shinebourne was born in Canje, Guyana. She lived there until the late 1960s when she moved to Georgetown to work and attend the University where she read English. She moved to Britain in the early 1970s, completed a BA degree, qualified as a lecturer and taught in colleges in Brixton and Southall. In the mid-1980s she left lecturing to work as a community activist in Southall and co-edit the Southall Review. *Ms Shinebourne began to write fiction in Guyana in the early 1960s and her literary and journalistic writing has been broadcast on BBC radio and appeared in several Caribbean and London newspapers and journals. One of her early stories won the Guyana National History and Arts Council Prize. Her first novel,* Timepiece, *was published by Peepal Tree Press in 1986 and won the Guyana Prize (1987) in the category of first novel. Her second novel,* The Last English Plantation, *also published by Peepal Tree Press, appeared in 1989.*

Timepiece *addresses a variety of themes: the interplay of race, class and gender; individuality and community; rural and city life; education and social development. Above all,* Timepiece *has a strong sense of history, both as the shaping past and the present in the making. 'This is Modern Times', short though it is, touches on aspects of all of these.*

This is Modern Times

Ben closed the shop on Sunday afternoons and went to sleep in the hammock under the guinep tree. On one of those afternoons, when Helen was cleaning the shop, she had found his aging accounts. They were stacked a dozen high, each a thick foolscap book. Their spines fell away easily, the threads melted loose. His handwriting hadn't changed over the years. Customers' unpaid debts dated back seventeen years, carried forward to the current books, uninterrupted by sub-totals, under lengthy columns headed 'Items' on the left, 'Prices' on the right. Many accounts were crossed out with the word DECEASED, in large block letters. When she totalled the accounts, the accumulated debts ranged from sums of one hundred to a few thousand dollars.

Helen commented, 'Your Daddy in' no businessman.'

Deep in sleep, his left leg dangled over the side of the hammock. His

18

arms were crossed on his stomach. He lay in a twisted position, his head almost touching his shoulder. His mouth was half-open, and the breeze played with his thinning hair. The sunlight finding its way through the leaves of a tree, flecked the length of his body with drops of light.

'I weary quarrel with him,' Helen said. 'Them ladies only got to smile with him, and he would hand them the whole shop. And when I talk about it they call me a virago. He like to give them credit. It is not business, is pleasure.'

Ben had come to the kitchen. He saw his books brushed clean, she still at work on the figures. He was resentful. He demanded bitterly, 'Who gave you permission to interfere with my books?'

He wanted no apology. He was hurt. Instead of being pleased, he felt betrayed. Later, he burnt the accounts. Before that, he sulked for days, and wouldn't speak to them.

At home, Ben and Helen were not like individuals, but combatants in a battlefield. They fought over their beliefs. Their friends took sides. Helen was pro-Georgetown and all that implied. Ben was pro-Pheasant and all that implied. No quarter was given. Helen was pro-education, Ben anti. He loved the village and the people. Apart from her close circle of friends, Helen hated the village. Their friends were not so much involved in their quarrels as concerned with protecting them from each other, each group close, loyal and indivisible.

Helen, Nurse, Miss K, Noor and Zena bound themselves together. They prided themselves on their independence of mind. Had they had opportunities, they felt, they would have done better. Their postures were bold. With each other, they let down their guard and were subtle and humorous. They lived in a world of their own, shutting out and barricading their lives against the reality that they lived in a place where their fates were confined by poverty. Restless, they built little rebellious dramas into each day.

As a girl, Nurse Nathaniel had worked at the village hospital. When it was shut down she went to the town hospital. She was now retired, but served the village. Whenever she visited, her laughter rang deep and frequent through the house. In the grip of mirth, she threw her head back, and let it rock her body. On Christmas days, at christenings and weddings, she would accept a shot of rum, asking the Lord to forgive her before she downed it. In her presence, the men took off their hats, and the women watched their tongues. Whose children she had delivered, who she had seen to death's door: this was their regular source of conversation. She was a large woman who liked to wear striped and check dresses with small round collars, reminiscent of her nurse's uniform.

19

Nurse, like Noor, was the kind of woman who, it seemed to Sandra, possessed the kind of strength she would like to have. Yet they were different on the outside. Nurse was Afro-Guianese and Noor was Indo-Guianese. Nurse was an Anglican and Noor was a Hindu. Nurse was a trained nurse out in the world, up and down the road on her cycle every day, in and out of each home, giving advice, prescribing cures and treatments, and Nurse did not distinguish between the races. If you were sick and in need, she came at any hour, however large or small, physical or mental the problem. Noor exerted the same influence though she was uneducated, without Nurse's sort of training. Noor was especially skilled at settling severe family and marital conflicts. Husbands and wives in crisis went to her for advice. In her gentle presence they became humble and tolerant. Daughters who threatened suicide and violent sons were taken to Noor who invariably adopted them in some form or other, became a surrogate mother. Noor and Nurse exchanged experiences when they met. Nurse's husband had died many years ago and her only son, James, had grown up and gone to live in Georgetown where he was now working as a male nurse in the Public Hospital. Noor was childless. Her husband, Muniram, was a boiler at the factory. Each afternoon, Noor and Muniram could be seen sitting together on their landing, sipping a cup of tea and chatting in a relaxed way, like old friends.

Miss K did people's washing for a living. She travelled from Forest to Corentyne to the town, to various homes, spending a day in each, and while doing the washing and ironing, impressing with her sharp wit and sarcasm. She hated men; when not belittling them, she was subtle and soft-spoken. She wore headcloths which she wrapped in various fashions, and chewed tobacco discreetly. She was always thanking the Lord for the shelter over her head and her daily plate of food, which, she said, were all a woman needed, as long as she 'di'n bother with no foolish man'. People said that Miss K was married once, but the man had gone away and never come back.

Zena's husband had a woman in town. She was also childless. Like Miss K, she hated men. Her husband's unfaithfulness was a constant source of pain which only rum, aspirins and occasional rage-letting appeased. She tracked the woman down once and administered a beating, which only hardened her husband's attitude to her. Ben said she was the only woman in the village who knew how to cook. She was always bringing him small morsels to sample, and this caused a few rows between Zena and Helen.

These women formed a maternal council. They met in Helen's kitchen to solve not only each others' problems but also the problems of the women who sought their advice, with Miss K and Zena adding wit and cynicism for good measure.

Ben and his friends let their individual personalities flow easily into group camaraderie. Some of their friendships dated back to their schooldays. Their conversations were a reaffirmation of belonging to each other and their places of work and male authority. The women's talk too was a form of binding, but also a release from their confinement not only as plantation people but also as women at home. They talked to clear a larger place where they could bask in their individuality, briefly, before the demands of family claimed them again.

Apart from Helen, they deemed Ben kind. Men and women from the other villages came to tell him their troubles. That, said Helen, was because they could get things from him, because they knew he was happy to give away what he had. He knew no other life but Pheasant. The men stopped in on their way to the factory and canefields to get a packet of cigarettes, and they stopped in again on their way home, but lingered for talk and companionship.

In Ben's and Helen's battles, ends were never spoken of, only means: the ways of doing things, of living. Sandra overheard these quarrels, and thought them futile. It achieved nothing, only set them further apart.

Ben's friends were his clients, and they had devised, over the years, a system to accommodate their dual relationship. He never kept a written record of their credit. 'Ben, ah take a beer. That make twenty this week.' Or, 'Ben, that make twenty pack a' cig'rette this week, and eight four cents loaf bread, an' about five stout.' To this kind of rough estimating they assented, and settled at the end of the month to their mutual satisfaction. Helen said it used to drive her crazy when she first came to live in Pheasant, but she had got used to it. It did not mean she accepted it; it was madness; he didn't do it to make a living, only to pass the time of day. Ben had his retorts ready, some as sarcastic as Helen's. He told her to mind her own business and keep her place; her job was to keep the children fed and house clean, clothes washed and food cooked; how he ran his business was his business; he provided the children's school fees; when Christmas came he could hand her money to buy new curtains and new furniture if she wanted these; he bought her clothes; so why did she want to tell him how to run his business; she should count her blessings, go down on her knees and thank God – instead of harassing him night and day; as if he wasn't good enough for her; let her leave him and find another man. The invitation to leave and find another man always silenced Helen, though inwardly she raged.

They had the ability to make their children feel they were the cage which forced them into cohabitation; yet, they put them first, in their different ways. To Ben, his children's happiness was important. They must live at peace with themselves, their conscience must be clear, no one must insult them; the law of life was learning to live with people according to the rules of conscience. This made no sense to Helen. Her classic reply was: could one eat and drink these things; did it keep away starvation, pay the doctor's bills? She was ambitious for her children, but Ben undermined her aims. For Helen, their redemption lay in education, but Ben called them away from 'the damn homework' to help him with a chore he thought more important. He cut himself off from them unless they did what he wanted them to do. As the children grew older, moulded by school, they found themselves cut off from him, and therefore from the village itself, stranded in their own orbit where they had to find their own way, pushed by Helen towards a vague 'better future'. To grow was to fight her parents' battles. Sometimes Sandra was afraid of it, more often, she could not imagine anything else. She had to swim her way through their turbulence.

'I could have become a nurse,' Helen always reminded him. 'I always had ambition. You have none. You are more like my mother, like Sarah. I see people come from poverty and make good. But not you. You think you can do better than people like that. The Roman Catholic priests and nuns use to beg Sarah to let me become a nurse. They say they would pay my way, look after me, but Sarah say no. I dared not open my mouth to tell her I want it. I use to pray she would agree, but no, when I finish primary school, she drag me to her stall in Stabroek every day to help her. If I had power over my life, I wouldn't be here behind God back with you. I would be living in a civilised place, like Georgetown.'

When Ben had no answer to her tirades, he resorted to stony silence, and sought out his friends for consolation. They had the power to give him peace. Only goodwill flowed between them. They had no secrets, trusted each other and were proud of it. Helen did not understand how these things could make a person happy. She said he and his friends fitted each other like a hand in a glove, that she didn't know why they didn't marry each other then they could sit and talk whole day and whole night. One of these friends reappeared after an absence of ten years. He was a short grey-haired man. When Ben saw him get off the bus, he'd exclaimed:

'Well, what is this I seeing? Is Reuben I seeing?'

Reuben was amused by Ben's surprise. They couldn't get enough of shaking hands and hugging each other.

'Man Reuben,' Ben said, 'I thinking all this time that tiger done eat you out in the interior. Remember when you lef'? Tellin' me you goin' porkknockin'? An' I ask you if you in' frighten, li'l piece man like you goin' an' porkknockin' – that dem Amerindian people chase you with bow and arrow. . . ?'

'Man Ben,' Reuben replied, 'I married an Amerindian gal.'

'What! Well now I know why you like the place! Congrats man, congrats . . .'

'An' I have three children, jus' like you.'

'Well yes, I never thought you would marry and settle down. You was always such a serious fellow.'

'An' I in' still serious?'

With each exchange, they laughed deeply. Ben introduced Helen to Reuben, and he complimented him on his choice. He stayed all day. He talked about the interior.

'You never see so much land,' Reuben said. 'Cattle fat fat fat.'

Reuben spoke with contentment about the interior. With his hands he described the size of the pumpkins that grew on his farm. Ben described the changes in Pheasant, and Reuben replied that he had noticed: more people, more houses, cars, buses, a police station, and he had seen an electricity generator in someone's yard.

They talked like ancient men, referring to the vanished world of their childhood, not the recent past. It was the first time Sandra heard Ben criticise Pheasant, confess to someone that changes he felt apprehensive about were taking place: mechanisation on the estate, the growing influence of the Georgetown unions and hints of conflict spreading from the capital unlike anything before. She saw it was the very distant past his values were based on, not the present.

Ben, Reuben and Joe Bachan, who still lived in Good Land, had been schoolboys together in Canefields. Their parents were indentured labourers and the children of freed slaves. Their parents did not survive to be middle-aged. Lacking contact with the towns, the modern towns, centres of business, education and colonial power, where the influence of the English was strongest, living in such a deeply rural area, so close to their own past, submerged in the life and landscape of the plantation and the forest, completely segregated from the English overseers, wedded entirely to their own ragged community, they were men who preferred to hold back from the future. They did not trust it at all, did not like it, the brashness, ignorance and arrogance of it, although their instinct for freedom was as fierce and strong as anybody else's. Cactus, who still lived in the forest, belonged to their parents' generation, and their stand resembled his. This rush to the town, the rush to be modern without understanding what it meant – men like them treated the future

23

like a plague. It was typical of Reuben not to go to town but to the interior.

Days after Reuben left, Ben repeated everything he said, word for word. It all vindicated his philosophy. 'You see how Reuben does live?' he told Helen. 'I in' tell you a man could live without hustling, fighting an' losing he pride?'

When Sandra had finished primary school, sat and passed her high school entrance examinations, it had brought on their worst quarrel. Helen asked him to make provision for her school fees. Ben declared he was against the idea of her going to high school. It was not money, he said, but principles; he thought education was a waste of time; besides, she didn't consult him about it; she just went ahead and made plans for the children without him; he was just a money-making machine; now she wanted money for the school fees, only now was he to be involved.

They quarrelled for days. The tension mounted. Their exchanges grew more fierce, until, one night, Helen threw an ice-pick at him. It barely missed him, landing in the wall a few inches from his head. It happened quickly. In the instant it took Helen to realise what she had done, all their blood-boiling fury went. Sandra saw, for the first time, the purest look of intimacy pass between them. They saw, at its deepest, their capacity for destruction. In that second, the distinction between the attacker and the victim blurred. Both were guilty, and saw it. Their faces mirrored one conscience. But it couldn't last. Their natures could not alter shape and direction now, after a lifetime of battles. Ben recovered from the shock. He shook with rage. He gritted his teeth and clenched his fists. Helen said nothing. She only turned and fled the house, leaving him without means to vent his rage. Then he too stormed from the house, leaving them to complete the chores, light the lamps and shut the shop. He returned when they were asleep. When he was settled in bed, Sandra rapped on his door and asked after Helen. He said she was in New Amsterdam, spending the night with the Shepherds. Mr Shepherd was headmaster of the primary school, another old friend of his, the only one Helen approved of, the one who lived for the future.

Next afternoon, Helen returned with Mr Shepherd. Sandra saw them get off the bus, and ran to tell Ben. But when she approached him, her confidence left her: she had to stay out of it, these were adult passions. She withdrew, but watched from the doorway. Ben, sitting near the counter, did not see them until Mr Shepherd loomed over him.

'Good afternoon, Ben,' Mr Shepherd said.

When Ben was hurt, he carried his wound visibly. He gave Helen a bitter look as she lifted the counter flap and entered confidently, as if she had committed no crime.

'Good afternoon, Shep,' Ben replied, reluctant.

Mr Shepherd wore his grey suit, with the jacket open, so his suspenders could be glimpsed. He had the habit of clearing his throat and baring his teeth before speaking. He did so now.

'Man Ben,' he said. 'What Helen telling me now?'

Ben sat rigid. He was struggling to control himself. He kept his eyes on Helen. She chatted with the customers and straightened the sweet bottles on the counter.

'Ben, we have to talk about this thing, man,' Mr Shepherd insisted. 'Helen tell me you don't want to send Sandra to high school.'

Ben broke his silence. 'I don' believe in education.'

'What?' Mr Shepherd was shocked. 'You don't believe in what?'

The customers, hearing the alarm in Mr Shepherd's voice, pricked up their ears.

Mr Shepherd sighed. 'Ben, I know you pride yourself on being a self-made philosopher, but sometimes you go a li'l too far . . .'

'Don' worry criticise me . . .'

Mr Shepherd waved his arms, and interrupted sharply, 'No no, man, we in' talkin' 'bout you, we talkin' 'bout Sandra. Don' be so damn selfish. . . !'

'Selfish?' Ben retorted. 'Who bein' selfish? I should know the meaning of the word better than any man. I always put my children first. Don' come to me with "selfish", Shep. When you use that word, it depend on what a man talkin' 'bout wanting . . .'

'Ben, don't complicate and confuse this story! You know very well what we talking about. We talking about education! Let us talk education, not philosophy. Don' shake up the two things in one bottle. Everything belong in it place. Now you hear me out! Listen, this is not our time. This is modern times. In our days you lucky if you got the chance to get an education. Now, all our children could get an education. You could be excused for turning your back on it. It was too bleady hard in those days. You and I went to school together. You had to mind your family when your father died. I admire you for it, at fourteen starting a business and succeeding in building one. I went on to teach and study some more, and I had was to starve just like you. By the sweat of our brow we two survive and make good.

'But things have changed in this country. We couldn't dream of what these children today could dream of. The children of today are the leaders of tomorrow. And for the first time, it is our responsibility to prepare them for this task. You and I could ever think of running country? Awright, we di'n have that privilege, but we can have it through the children . . .'

'Girl children run country?' Ben retorted scornfully. 'Girl children must stay home and mind children and their home.'

Mr Shepherd's face fell. 'Ben, you make me shame. Think! Think! Use the brains God give you. Educate your child and let her be a pride to you. When it come to education, all that matter is brains. I don' see the difference between boy and girl children. Education is pride, man. Is not something you could eat like a plate a' food, is something higher in satisfaction. Man, when I go to church to pray, is the pride I does thank God for that I get from education.'

Ben was outraged. 'Pride! Education! What about Care? I mus' send my child 'way from her home whole damn day? Look man, if something happen to her in town, who would care? Not a damn soul! Town people don' care 'bout one another. Is pure dog eat dog does go on in town. Besides, nobody don't have interest in a child like it own parents! I know them primary school teachers here, I know their parents, the kind of homes they come from, whethe' they is decent people or not. I mus' entrus' my child to town people I don't know?'

Mr Shepherd's feelings were hurt. 'Awright, Ben. So much for me. I is town people. Now I know what you think about me.'

Ben repented. 'I in' talkin' 'bout you, man. Shep. You is different. You live among us. Your spirit here. I talkin' 'bout these young people I see put here. I talkin' 'bout these young people I see them put here to teach, with no full experience of life and no maturity. Ol' time teachers that teach me and you was mature, reliable people.'

The talk exhausted them both. Mr Shepherd turned to chat with the customers. Helen, bold now, was moving freely about the shop, passing close by Ben, brushing him with her skirt. He seemed to have forgotten their quarrel. When Mr Shepherd left, he went to the kitchen, and sat alone near the window for a long while. She followed him there, and tried to distract him from his thoughts. He resisted stoically.

Extract from _Timepiece_.

BELIZE

Zee Edgell

Zee Edgell was born in Belize and grew up there in the early 1950s. Her first job was as a reporter for The Daily Gleaner *in Kingston, Jamaica. From 1966 to 1968 she taught at St Catherine's Academy in Belize. During that time she was also editor of a small newspaper,* The Reporter, *in Belize City. She has travelled extensively and lived in several countries including Britain, Bangladesh, Nigeria, Afghanistan, Somalia and the USA. Since returning to Belize, she served as Director of the Department of Women's Affairs and lectured at the University College of Belize. In 1982 Heinemann published her first novel,* Beka Lamb, *which is also the first Belizean novel. It took her ten years to write. She is currently working on her second novel, also set in Belize. Zee Edgell is married and has two children.*

Beka Lamb *uses its account of Beka's growing up to explore the dimensions of ethnicity, class, colour, religion and politics as they affect the consciousness and determine the life possibilities of young women growing up in a small colonial society. The fate of Beka's friend Toycie, for whom the recollections which are in the book stand in lieu of a wake, is a kind of adumbration, a shadow against which Beka's own choices for the future will play themselves out.*

Beka Lamb

What Beka recognised in herself as 'change' began, as far as she could remember, the day she decided to stop lying. Things were getting almost beyond her control. She sat on the top step of the back porch that April Friday, seven months earlier, eating crayfish foot left over from tea and contemplating her latest, worst lie. The sun was going down, and a cool breeze from the Caribbean, several streets away, blew now and then reminding her that it was 'Caye Time' once again.

Popping the last scrap of fish into her mouth, she tossed the shells

27

between the railings and watched as they fell amongst the red bells and green crotons, dappled yellow, growing in the dry earth alongside the bottom of the stairs. Her parents had sat at the table finishing tea when Beka told them she had been promoted to second form. Without looking up from the report card he held between thumb and forefinger, Bill Lamb said, 'It says here that anyone failing more than three subjects at the end of the school year must repeat the class. You failed four subjects, Beka.'

The brown mulatto crust on her mother's cheek bones became extremely dark against the paleness of her skin. She said to Beka, perched on a chair opposite, 'Answer your father, girl.'

'I pass in truth, Daddy!' Beka almost shouted. 'Sister Virgil read my name off a list.'

'Well, all I can say is that Sister Virgil must be helping you out, which for her is unusual. You are a lucky girl. Excuse me.'

The chair scraped against the wooden floor as he pushed himself away from the mahogany table. Stalking into the living room, he sat down in his easy chair, and snapped on the radio that stood on a high cabinet alongside one wall, and the radio announcer said, 'This is the British Honduras Broadcasting Service.'

Lilla put her cup slowly down on the wet saucer, and with the forefinger of her right hand drew beads of sweat off her forehead. Beka opened her mouth, but before she could speak, her mother said quietly, 'Clear the table and wash the dishes now if you are finished, Beka. Your Gran and the boys ate before you came home from school. Change your uniform first.'

Lying was one of the things about Beka that her parents detested most. When they discovered the truth about this latest one, her Dad was going to shout and holler, and definitely beat her till she couldn't stand up. She looked up at the blue sky and rosy clouds. Maybe there'll be a hurricane this year, she thought hopefully. If one came, the school records would all 'wash way' and then her parents would never know she'd failed.

'Let's see,' she murmured. 'How does that rhyme go again? June, too soon; July, stand by; August, come it must; September, remember; October, all over.' A hurricane couldn't come in time to rescue her then. School reopened in June. In any case, Sister Virgil, the American principal, would remember every girl that failed.

Beka shuddered at the thought of the leather belt her Dad wore. Sometimes Bill Lamb would come home from work, the tensions of the work day raging within him, and Lilla, filled with the frustrations of her own day, would sit down to tell him of Beka's insolence, her laziness, and her ingratitude. The story invariably concluded with Lilla saying, 'And the worst thing of all, Bill, is that she lied to me. I could see she hadn't swept the attic properly. Why did she lie to me?'

Because he was in a hurry at those times to have his tea before going for an hour's relaxation at the club, Bill Lamb would say impatiently, 'I don't want to hear a word from you, Beka. Get upstairs. I am going to put an end to this once and for all.'

His felt hat askew on his head, Bill Lamb would follow Beka upstairs stamping his feet with emphasis. On the landing, Beka would begin to scream at the top of her voice before the belt touched her skin, 'No, Daddy! No, Daddy!'

Between lashes, Bill Lamb paused to ask, 'Do you know why I am beating you?'

'No, Daddy,' Beka would reply.

'Not because of the thing you did, but because you lied!'

On one such occasion, the buckle end of the belt escaped accidentally from Bill Lamb's clenched fist and cut Beka on the left corner of her mouth. The next day at school, Beka told anyone who asked that she'd fallen down the back steps and cut her face on the concrete slab at the foot of the wooden stairs.

When her Dad returned from the club that night, he came up to Beka's bedside in the attic where Lilla was rubbing Beka's head and saying, 'It was all my fault, Bill. I can't understand why I complain so much to you about Beka. She had such a pretty smile, Bill, such a pretty smile. That was the nicest thing about her face.'

Looking down at Beka's lip, Bill Lamb said, 'She still has a pretty smile. Smile, Beka! Show your mother what a pretty smile you still have.'

Beka smiled as naturally as she could manage, because her parents always seemed to suffer for such a long time after Beka herself had forgotten the beating, and it was a rare child in the community that didn't get a whipping now, then, or more often.

Turning to go downstairs again, Bill Lamb said, 'Don't worry, pet. Your Gran will rub it with cocoa fat when it heals and then it won't scar.' But although Granny Ivy rubbed it every night for a long time with cocoa fat, the scar browned over but remained visible, and Beka eventually gave up all hope that it would completely disappear.

After that, Lilla tried to keep her annoyance at Beka's shortcomings mostly to herself. She didn't talk much about them to Granny Ivy either, for Granny Ivy nearly always 'took up' for Beka. Beka wondered if her Dad would be able to help himself from beating her when he found out about this latest, most provoking lie.

'O Toycie, Toycie O, I bring the note,' Beka called.

Dropping her brush, and flinging the dirty cloth into the bucket, Toycie ran across a series of planks, put down for easier passage during the wet weather, leading from the steps to the gate where Beka stood waiting.

'We are still going? We are still going, Beka?' she asked in uncertain excitement. The waves in Toycie's hair, parted in the middle, rippled back into a rough bun at the nape of her neck; and the concern in her eyes as she looked at Beka made them coal black against her skin, the colour of cinnamon.

'I was sure Mr Bill would cancel the whole thing, and I didn't dare drop by . . . you tell them yet, Beka Lamb?'

'Ahahangh,' Beka answered making a guttural sound in her throat.

'What happen?'

'Nobody is talking much, and Daddy cut down the bougainvillea bush.'

'For what?'

'It was breaking down Miss Boysie's fence, but it was to punish me somehow or other.'

'Because you fail?'

'Not that so much, though he's sad about that too.'

'Then for what?'

'I told them I passed early on, then later that I fail.'

'You are lying, Beka!'

Beka looked at Toycie's frightened, incredulous face and said right into it, 'I swear by Jumby's block!'

Toycie clapped her hand to her forehead, 'Why you lie on top of failing, Beka?'

'I don't know *why* Toycie, but it wasn't for fun.'

◆

'Hello, Beka gial,' Toycie said, moving over so Beka could also sit in the shelter of the tree.

'Feeling any better?' Beka asked.

'I'm still feeling queasy, but at least I didn't throw up my lunch. Aunt Eila is watching me.'

'No walk today, then?'

'Well,' Toycie replied, looking up at the sunlight shifting on the undersides of the cashew tree leaves, 'I'm going to Mass at St Joseph's this evening. Can you come with me, Beka? I haven't been to that church before, and I might feel shy by myself.'

'I went to Mass at Holy Redeemer this morning, Toycie. Why are you going all the way back there?'

'Beka, girl, I haven't seen much of Emilio since we came home from the caye. All I get is a quick hail and a wave when he flashes by here on his bicycle. He goes to church at St Joseph's and I must speak to him.'

'Why do you want to see him so badly?'

'He's got to marry me, Beka, because I am pregnant.'

'Pregnant? Pregnant?' Beka sprang off the planks as if she'd been bitten by a scorpion.

'Shut up and stop squawking like macaw parrot. Aunt Eila will hear you!'

'How do you know such a thing?' Beka pleaded, looking into Toycie's eyes, black as the seed of a mamey apple; noticing how thick eyebrows touched over her nose, watching pink lips trembling against the rich brownness of her skin. Mama Lilla always said Toycie's fingers were made for music they were so tapered and strong. Beka usually felt overgrown and overfed beside Toycie's slenderness.

'How do you know such a thing?' Beka asked again.

Toycie licked her lips.

'Well, I feel sick in the mornings, sometimes *all* day, and I haven't had my periods for the second month. I was reading about it in a doctor book at Bliss library.'

'Why don't you tell Miss Eila?' Beka whispered fiercely into her friend's face. 'Maybe you read wrong!'

'I can't tell. I can't, Beka. Aunt Eila thinks I'm a queen.'

'What do you think Emilio will do – marry you – Toycie gial?'

'He'll marry me . . . he always said if anything happened he would marry me.'

'But he's in school.'

'So am I!'

'What about graduation?'

Toycie put her head down on her knees and her shoulders were shaking.

'What to do, Beka? What to do?'

'Maybe it's not true, maybe it's not true. Maybe it's some other kind of sickness. I hear about plenty of ladies who think they're pregnant, and it turns out to be only a tumour. Let's talk to Granny Ivy then?'

Toycie grabbed Beka's wrist and held on tight. Her fingers were cold.

'Don't you tell Miss Ivy or anybody, Beka, you hear me!'

'Do I ever back story, Toycie?'

'Are you coming to church with me or not?'

'Yes, Toycie, yes. But we'll have to take the boys, and wait outside until Mass is finished. Mama wouldn't send me out today without Chuku and Zandy.'

◆

'Have a piece of cane, Eila,' Granny Ivy was saying. 'What's up then, gial?'

'Toycie's not eating much, Miss Ivy,' she said, her voice unnaturally high. 'Course, she never was what anyone could call a big eater, but I bought hot corn and pork tamales for tea this evening, and most of it is still sitting on her plate.'

'She's got to begin thinking of the child,' Granny Ivy replied.

'Hardly says a word all day long. Works a bit in the house, or sits in my chair rocking back and forth. I try to tell her it's not judgement day and she isn't the first and she isn't the last. If she would talk, we could plan!'

'Is Nurse Palacio still seeing her?' Lilla asked.

'Oh, my, yes, Miss Lilla. Nurse comes by twice a week with tonic, pills, and books, but Toycie just listens and it's hard for me to get her to take the medicine regularly. Nurse tells me she's anaemic and what they call depressed, and I must get her to the doctor, but Toycie's turned stubborn on me.'

'Let me come over there tonight, Eila,' Granny Ivy said. 'I will try and talk to her. Tomorrow I will get Bill to compel her see Doctor Clark.'

'All right, Miss Ivy,' she answered moving off the steps. 'But I am getting tired, and not a word from her mother. Right now I am going to see an old woman living on Southside they tell me knows about conditions like Toycie's.'

'Why not wait until *after* she's seen Doctor Clark?' Lilla asked placing a restraining hand on Miss Eila's arm.

'I have to try everything, Miss Lilla,' Miss Eila said, dark eyes anguished.

'Miss Eila! Miss Eila!' Beka called, running down the steps, 'Please give Toycie this note for me. I dropped by again after school today but she wouldn't open the door!'

'All right, pet. But those other notes and things you give me, I give her, but she just leaves them on the table till I have to clear them away they are so much.'

'Why is Toycie vexed with me, Miss Eila?'

'Toycie's not vexed with a soul, pet. I think she's gone someplace so far inside herself she forget us back here, that is all.'

'Did you hear any more from the Villanuevas?' Lilla asked.

'Mrs Villanueva comes by for a minute or two, off and on. And one evening Emilio came by himself. He offered to marry Toycie after he graduates, but I don't think Toycie can understand anything much anymore, and if she did understand what that Villanueva boy was saying, I don't think she believes he really intends to marry her, nor do I if the truth be known.'

◆

Granny Ivy tucked a handkerchief, folded into a dainty triangle, in the belt hidden by her bosom. She had her bag, and was preparing to leave, when there was a frantic banging on the back door. Daddy Bill, Mama Lilla, Chuku and Zandy were on the way to the Villanueva house, so Beka tore down to the kitchen hoping it was Toycie come to visit at last. She pushed her whole weight against the door which always jammed. It flew open unexpectedly and Beka shrieked. National Vellor stood in a pool of moonlight, sopping wet, clad in a blouse and skirt instead of the velvet gowns she wore at night.

'Come quickly,' she said, grabbing Beka's wrist. 'Miss Eila not at home!'

She wouldn't let go but pulled Beka down the stairs, through the yard, across Cashew Street, into the lumber yard and down towards the creek. Their feet squelched in the muddy sawdust, and Granny Ivy shouted from the verandah, 'Bekaaaaa! Beka!'

'Help me, help me with Toycie,' National panted.

In the moonlight, Beka saw her friend spread-eagled in the mud, beneath the rickety bridge leading to the latrine over the creek.

'Toycie! Toycie O!' Beka screamed. 'What happened to you? What happened, Toycie?' Stooping beside her friend, she put her arm under her neck and shoulders watching the ugly cut ooze blood onto her nose, mouth and throat. How Toycie's stomach had grown! The moans she uttered were too much for Beka's self-control. Whimpering with fright, she looked at National who ordered, 'Lift her!'

Toycie was so heavy, and Beka, remembering her grace and slenderness, wanted to kneel in the mud and bay mournful remonstrances at the moon. In National's shack, they laid Toycie gently on the blue chenille spread. National turned up the kerosene lantern and Beka watched in panic as the blood trickled onto the pillow from Toycie's forehead. National pushed Beka, sobbing with fright, through the door and she ran full tilt to find help. At the edge of the lumber yard, she saw Granny Ivy hurrying across. As she reached Beka, an army truck screeched to a stop inches from where they stood.

'Bloody British!' Granny gasped to the soldier who hopped down from the cab of the huge truck.

'Toycie drownded, Granny Ivy, Toycie drownded!'

'My sweet Jesus Christ!' Miss Ivy exclaimed, breaking into a swift walk, pushing Beka along the path in front of her. The soldier, his blonde hair slicked flat on his head, picked his way behind them asking repeatedly, 'What's oop then? What's *oop*?'

Inside the shack, National was holding a cloth tightly over Toycie's forehead, fanning her ashy face with desperation. The soldier, without saying a word to anyone, grabbed the cloth, tying it tightly around Toycie's forehead. He lifted her off the bed and began stumbling with her in his arms toward his truck. Granny Ivy rushed after him shouting, 'I am going with Toycie to hospital. Find Eila first, then get Lilla and Bill. Tell them to hurry!'

'Yes, Gran, yes,' Beka said, hovering uncertainly at the doorway. She was stunned. National removed her wet, muddy clothes. Blood had made a bib on her blouse. The room stank of creek water. Her hair hung in tendrils onto her shoulders. Above the bed of rough sawmill planks, hung an old, fly-stained calendar showing a giant tree, its roots above the ground. Behind the tree, flowed unending fields of what looked to Beka, like emerald grass. Women, resembling National, wearing veils on their heads, walked through the fields, pottery vessels on their heads or in the crook of their elbows.

Beka glanced around swiftly noticing the velvet dress lying in readiness across a chair beneath a window overlooking the creek. National poured water into an enamel basin and then turned her palms upward, following Beka's gaze around the room.

'You see,' she said. 'No mother, no father, no school. What can I do?'

'Toycie,' Beka said, swallowing her spit. 'Toycie had school.'

National flung her wet clothes over the window ledge and stood looking across the lighted creek to the other side of the town, then she came over and pushed Beka gently through the door.

'Please,' she said, 'you go now and run!'

Extract from *Beka Lamb*.

CUBA

Omega Agüero

Omega Agüero was born in Camaguey, Cuba, in 1940. She has worked as an actress and a teacher. Her first book La Alegre vida campestre *(The Good Life in the Country: Havana, Unión de Escritores y Artistas de Cuba) won the David Prize for short stories in 1973. 'A Man, A Woman' (Un Hombre, una mujer) is taken from her collection of short stories* El Muro de medio metro *published in 1977 by the same publisher. Another volume of stories,* Mujer flotando en el tiempo, *and a collection of poetry,* Después de Muerta tronarán mis huesos *are in preparation. Her works have been included in anthologies in East Germany, Bulgaria, Czechoslovakia and The Ukraine.*

Omega Agüero's stories deal with a range of situations. Her early stories focus largely on peasant life and the problems of the women in Cuba before the revolution. In her latest work she explains themes of remembrance and the world of dreams.

A Man, A Woman

'I'll kill you.'

Her voice said, soft and sweet by her lover's side. He smiled the smug smile of a man who knows he is loved. And anyway, she said it so gently that despite the strange shadowy glint in her eyes it sounded like a caress.

'I'll kill you if you leave me.'

This time her voice was more assured, as she stroked the man's hair and bare shoulders.

'So you want to force me to love you?'

'I hate you.'

'Why do you hug me then?'

'Because when I don't hate you, I love you.'

'You don't hate me.'

'I've told you, I'm crazy . . . if I weren't, how come I go on hugging you. . . ?'

'That's not being crazy.'

'What is it then?'

'It means you're too hot-blooded, that's all.'

She kissed him. He smiled his almost female smile and said: 'Let's go to sleep; I have to get up early tomorrow.'

'You should find yourself a stone.'

'Why, am I a stone?'

'Yes.'

'What you said scared me.'

'What was that?'

'That you'd force me to marry you. It wouldn't do you any good. Even if you succeeded, I'd divorce you straightaway.'

'I know that from the last time, and I haven't forced you into anything.'

'But if you say it, it's because you're thinking it.'

'I don't want to force you to love me . . . I said it to see what you're made of.'

'What I'm made of? The same as ever. Why do you want to know what I'm made of?'

'Because I can't live with a man who abandons me when I'm pregnant. Last time you didn't come back until . . .'

'Tell me . . . are you pregnant now?'

'No.'

'Sure?'

'Sure.'

'Let's go to sleep.'

He turned his back to her.

'You used to sleep in my arms.'

He gave no reply. Realising how tired he was, she kept silent, feeling tenderness and pity for him. 'He's just a poor kid who won't accept any responsibility in life,' she thought as she fell asleep, not wanting to explore her thoughts any further.

As usual, she woke up late; she couldn't bear to watch the time go by, stretching out endlessly until he came back. She would wake up and lie in bed listlessly, filled with regrets. When she thought of her mother, the knot of emotion in her chest swelled until it took her over completely, choking her so she could scarcely breathe.

'How good mothers are!' she had said to him two nights earlier.

'Why's that?'

'I don't know . . . but they are good.'

'Maybe it's because they forgive us everything.'

'It could be.'

That was the frightful thing: mothers forgave everything, but that did not stop them suffering.

'Graciela, don't go with that man. If you do, you'll never set foot in this house again.'

She did go off with him, and when she came back her mother said not a word. She cooked her favourite dishes for her, scurried about for things to offer her. She looked after and spoilt her just like when she had been a child. That was the dreadful thing: she had forgiven her, but went on suffering. When the telegram arrived: 'If you have sorted everything out as you say, come back,' she ran after the man even though she was still weak. She had lost a lot of blood and the doctor had told her to rest. Her mother did not cry, pretended she knew nothing, but she did know. Her eyes seemed to be saying: 'What are you doing with a man who doesn't want your children?'

They met; back in bed again, he begged her forgiveness, but by now there was nothing left to forgive. His repentance left her feeling sorry for him because he was a coward, because he was so selfish, such a tiny child, as small as an amoeba. She felt for him what mothers feel for their problem child: pity. She said 'my baby' to him, 'it's nothing, my baby'; every time she spoke to him she called him 'my baby.' But when she was all alone she knew she had not forgiven him, and that she felt two contradictory emotions for that man. They argued, they fought, and then said the sweetest things to each other; their bodies exchanged the softest caresses. But it was Hell. 'Today I'm finishing with him.' She would pack her bags, spend the whole afternoon folding and packing her clothes ready to leave; but then he knocked on the door, she opened it, they kissed, and she forgot everything, devouring him in bed, in his bed.

Someone knocked at the door. It was noon, time for the cleaner to come and do the room. The room . . . if only they lived in a house . . . then she could clean, could put up lace curtains and so perhaps no longer think about . . .

'May I clean the room, madam?'

The men who did the cleaning said 'madam' to her face, but behind her back called her the 'mistress' and uttered obscenities which made them laugh.

She went out to the balcony of the reception room. 'Why not throw myself from here?' The balcony was on the fifth floor, with a view of treetops, some terraced roofs and the long, white street lying there lifeless, steaming, unbearable. 'Why not throw myself from here?' She saw a boy ride past on a bicycle. What did she matter to that boy? What did she matter to anyone? She felt the same nausea she had been feeling for the past few days, the same nausea as the previous time. It made her eyelids droop so that the daylight became no more than a line where the treetops, the roofs, the lifeless street merged into one; simply a line of light. Inside her body, she could feel her blood and all her cells stirring as new streams flowed through her. 'What if I kept the child and fought for him?' The light grew more intense, more rounded. 'What if I were capable of digging in the earth with my bare hands to find him food . . . if I were capable . . . I'd take him through parks and streets to show him all the beauty that exists in things and people. All that I have never found for myself, but would be capable of finding through him and for him.'

When the lover returned, she had gone.

Translated by Karin Wilson
From the collection *El Muro de medio metro*.

Mirta Yáñez

Mirta Yáñez is from Havana, Cuba, where she was born in 1947. After completing her studies in Spanish language and literature in 1970, she won a prize for poetry for her volume Las Visitas *(Visits: Havana Comisión de Extensión Universitaria, 1971) which was published the following year. Mirta Yáñez has taught Spanish–American literature and has collaborated on and authored many publications both within and outside of Cuba. Her interests include children's literature and cultural history and she has been director of the Department of Cultural Activities in the University Extension service. 'We Blacks All Drink Coffee' (Todos los Negros tomamos Café) is from a volume by the same name (Editorial Arte y Literatura Instituto Cubano del Libro, Havana, 1976) which won honourable mention in a short story competition in Cuba.*

We Blacks All Drink Coffee

Tell me with what flowers
you greased your plough
so the fragrant land
smells of spikenard?

JOSÉ MARTÍ

She says that I don't even know how to wash my own clothes and yet I want to go off. What is a mother's child going to do in a place like that? Just imagine what my grandmother would say if she knew, if she were to rise from the grave and see what the apple of her eye wanted to get into. It's a good thing she is dead, because if she weren't . . . There's a lot of talk about irresponsible mothers. But not about her.

And so my mother goes grumbling on and on from the end of the corridor where she has gone to take refuge so that her voice will be lost, will slip in between the furniture, so the neighbours will not hear one word sounding louder than another, what would they think of this family, of this child of fifteen wanting to go off to pick coffee?

Things were different in her time. What would a well brought up girl be doing in the middle of the bush? Who would have thought of such a thing? Going where there are so many dangers. At least that's what the books say. Right into the heart of a titanic forest, a girl from a good family. Luckily there are no wild animals in this country.

For my mother the only safe place is my room with its four walls, a roof, a floor of the most ordinary sort. And not even then is it completely worthy of her confidence.

What do I care about the neighbours? But she does. And she closes the windows so that the argument will not go beyond this castle which is the protective shell of my family life. And when the room is the way she would have it, like the cell of a cloistered nun, she rushes forward from the other side of the corridor, she claps her hands. She shouts carefully. I am what is known as a girl who was given everything she ever wanted. If I asked for a flying bird, a flying bird I would get. Now look how ungrateful I was.

She says I think of no one but myself. I don't think of anyone, she says. One of my grandmothers is in the grave. If I insist on going off I'll be sending the other one to the edge of the grave. With a sudden collapse. All the catastrophes that could occur because of my pigheadedness. As the eldest, who has led a very sheltered life I should accept my

39

responsibilities. The blood pressure of grandmothers and aunts can fall precipitously because of a *brigadista* who picks coffee.

There are so many dangers out in the country. My mother does not have a list on hand. A paper which she could unfurl from her chest like a banner, a string of familiar words, the first of which would be diseases. Who is going to look after you? When something goes wrong with your lungs I am the one, she is the one, who will be responsible for you. A daughter at death's door for the rest of her life, kept in a room with its windows closed to keep the early morning dew from coming in and the reproaches from going out, a daughter without any vital signs, without a will of her own, how wonderful. Withering away like a flower, filled with remorse to her last gasp for the folly of her adolescence. A trip to the coffee fields, and then a heroine dependent on the charity of a self-denying mother, always at her post with a load of comments such as, 'it happened just as I warned you', 'listen when you're told, or you'll never grow old', 'that's what you get for disobeying your mother who wants the best for you', for ever and ever. What more could she want?

In the mountains where they pick coffee, or so she has heard, she has never seen it with her own eyes, eyes the worms will soon be picking at thanks to all this heartbreak, the mountains are slippery and treacherous. They slip from under the feet and leave the *brigadistas* hanging in mid–air, from a branch. The plants of the red and green coffee beans are like waves sweeping over a little girl of fifteen who knows nothing of life.

And if afterwards her period, her menstruation, is one, two months late, what will the family think of this child who has risked losing her honour going to do voluntary work? For though it is not actually said, honour is not something you can touch, or see, it is only something you lose. And where will they look for her, where will they go, where would they complain? She will not be the first to have left home a good little girl and to have returned, at best, pregnant. And then, how awful it would be. The whole family having turned its back on her; the neighbours revelling in the gossip; the little girl the talk of the town.

What argument can counter this? How can I know in August if my period will be right on time in October, in December and in all the months to come? What guarantee can I give my mother that I will safeguard the family's precious honour? What a strange agreement to have to sign just to go to pick coffee. Breaking my back at work for forty-five days, and still having to make sure that all my functions are in place, with every gland responding on time. No defect in my body to provoke the anger of such a decent family as mine. Having to contend with the suspicious glances of my mother's fearsome neighbours. What a way to screw up someone's life, I tell myself.

And who knows if the coffee–picking mightn't turn your head so much that you even fall in love with a Negro, she says in a powerless rage.

You know what it means to be a nice white girl. As white as the paper daisy that my mother is crushing nervously between her hands in my birthday photograph, its yellow heart overflowing with innocence. For a white girl must receive maximum care, must be brought up according to all the rules of good health and hygiene. She cannot go alone out onto the street. She must go with her father to the movies. She goes to school holding her mother's hand. She must not play with others. And never, never get into mischief.

How times change.

You are, I am, she says, the one who stands to lose. If my mother would only let me explain to her. If only there were some way of getting out of her head those visions which she is hurling at me from every corner of the room, as she moves about, her voice louder and fiercer with every minute. In this room of white people living together as a family. Where the ancestors have most certainly been white. Where I tell her, who knows what kind of blood anyone has? That in the mother country, there had been dark-skinned Moors for centuries, no-one can avoid it. That those who do not have the Congo in them somewhere . . .*

My mother raises her hands to her bosom so as not to hear me, so as not to let another sentence in. So as to separate me from her breath. So as not to listen to me saying I am not a white paper daisy which she keeps between perfumed handkerchiefs. What's the point? What if I fall in love with a Negro? This is important, I learn for the first time in my life. The colours, shades, the tones of voice which show me for what I am, within these four walls, in the bush I am going to, or on the street corner, this little lily-white girl, carefully watching a man with his fly shamelessly open.

Still clasping her breast, my mother retreats along the corridor, saying, 'do as you think best'.

Translated by Claudette Williams
From the collection Todos los Negros tomamos Café.

---

*A reference to a popular saying that all Cubans have some African ancestry.

JAMAICA

Erna Brodber

Erna – 'Lixie' or 'Stick' – Brodber was born in Woodside, St Mary, Jamaica in 1940. She went to school there and in Kingston, attended the University of the West Indies (when it was the University College of the West Indies) and obtained one of the first MSc degrees in Sociology. After working as a caseworker in private and public children's services, she was awarded a National Institute of Mental Health Ford Foundation pre–doctoral fellowship to the University of Washington in 1967, where she studied psychiatric anthropology. Having gained a PhD in history at UWI, she worked there as Research Fellow in the Institute of Social and Economic Research (Mona). She has published many articles and monographs including 'Abandonment of children in Jamaica', 'A study of yards in the city of Kingston' and 'Perceptions of Caribbean women.' Her two novels, Jane and Louisa Will Soon Come Home *(1980) and* Myal *(1988) were published by New Beacon Books. Brodber has been a member of the (Rastafarian) Twelve Tribes of Israel since 1976. She is currently managing director of Black Space Ltd (Ja) and is based in Woodside. She has a son, Timothy, aged four.*

Her first novel – revolutionary in its structure – celebrates aspects of the life of the small Jamaican country community as it focuses on the problems associated with the growing up of a girl child in the Caribbean. The extract contains an extraordinary evocation of two people dancing at a country fair and demonstrates Brodber's control of language and supremely accomplished powers of description.

Into this Beautiful Garden

But our minds hatched and set and hatched and multiplied like fleas and chiggers. Like the time we learnt of sex and babies:

–You remember the time when Mama and Papa did bathe in the same pan? Hmmm that's why. That's why her belly did get so big–

–That is not true for she would have did have a baby–

Any bit of information that hinged even slightly on the theme was priceless. We bargained for information, we blackmailed, we peeped:

—If you tell me what you did see on the sheet, I will tell you what Girlie tell me—

—OK then. I will tell you but you must tell me first—

—No Sir. You first for Girlie have a baby already and what I know is more than what you know—

—Well then, I did see blood on the sheet and that mean say . . .—

—All right then, I will tell you. Girlie say is like when your mother have a bottle of honey and she say nobody must touch it. And everybody tief out some but is only you one get catch—

—Oh that is honey moon—

—And she say that she did think that is bad stomach she did have and she was taking castor oil for it but her baby father box the glass out of her hand and she never get to drink it and her father kick her with his water boots and run her out of the house—

Uhhhmmmm. That is that. If there is more, we a grow, we will see. And we allowed another mystery to seduce us.

Now what did Janey and Louise mean? They weren't too cold either for our big people were fidgeting.

—How do they know so much— they were saying but we knew that. We knew that Granny prayed in great detail and loudly. Besides, the partition between their room and hers was very low and they could see and hear anything she did or said. In any case Granny Tucker talked aloud to herself all the time.

◆

Every first of August at about three o'clock Papa Son's bamboo sax bellows out:

> Cum awf a Mattie belly . . .

Oh Jeezaz and I can't get my hair plait fast enough to answer the call.

> Cum awf a Mattie belly . . . ly
> Far Mattie belly is so saaf and tender
> Cum awf a Mattie belly . . .

and it makes your skin itch and makes you feel as if you want to wee-wee and you can't even tell anybody how you feel. You are just miserable because you are not there yet.

> Far Mattie belly is a engine rubber
> Cum awf a Mattie belly . . .

If is not Papa Son, is Kissie Dover. And if it is not Mattie Belly is Peanut Vendor but it still don't matter for is still the same bamboo alto sax. And is the same church fair ground. With the coconut bough shed bigger than anything you ever see. A platform in the middle for the musicians and booths, bamboo enclosures for stalls. Snowball man, fresco man, pattie pan man, toto woman, drops . . . everything but nothing like Kissie or Papa Son standing up straight and pushing out his chest like a cock trying to crow and stretching as if to put the horn through the coconut boughs . . .

Cum awf a Mattie belly . . .

You can see it even if you're not there yet. You putting on your shoes with the cross straps, your patent leather shoes you've been vaselin-ing for days, your organdy dress with puff sleeves and your socks to match. Your big fat hair ribbon sticking off a mile. Your straw handbag and your 'kerchief in your hand still wet at the corner from the nine-pence bottle of khus-khus water which your uncles in Town send you every now and then.

But you're not speaking to anyone for they will not come on and the man is saying:

Cum awf a Mattie belly
and you just left to cry. And you can't go by yourself for Sister have the tickets and all the spending money and though Mass Stanley know you from the day you were born, this is a business day and the church needs the money for the foreign ministry and everybody must present a ticket so they won't let me in.

Pi pananana Pi pananana pananana a dududups dupdups. And you know that a circle has gathered around Miss P and whoever her partner is, that she has just finished trembling her belly and that her partner has just done pushing his leg between her two to signify the end of the dance and you weren't there to see it.

For what seems like centuries, Mass Stanley has kept the fair gate. He does not belong to our church but he has travelled and knows all kinds of behaviours so nobody dares fool with him . . . stranger or district people. So he is the best man to keep the gate. Mass Stanley is round and very black. Everything about him is round. His belly, himself, his chest, his nose, his mouth. His face and head form a round commander coco with valleys dug out for eyes and top lip. His eyes are all brown, pupil and iris are all the same. You don't see him. He doesn't see you. You just see the sparkle like a peeny wally shining by day or by night. He is a favourite of mine and I am a favourite of his. He is the tar baby that cut Nanny Goat down to size. And it more than pleases me that this tar baby and I have a way with each other. I have his ticket, he says and I feel that I can do anything with him except go through that fair gate and up the hill to the fair ground without paying.

My Mass Stanley pleases me most at the last part of the Fair, when he is no longer the gate man but my Mass Stanley. He appears on the Fair Ground. Coming up the hill, under the booth now, the most brilliant peeny wally, and everybody feels him, although jam packing one another, they should be locked down in their own steps. Mass Stanley is coming; it is ten o'clock in the night and late for lesser ones like me. Kissie and Papa Son and everybody know. Is Mass Stanley time now and I know that Aunt Becca woulda give her eye teeth to partner him in the quadrille but he has never danced with anyone else but Miss Elsada. Only when she says:
   —Cho Stan, dance with somebody else this time— and she calls out somebody's name. But that hardly ever happens.

Ten o'clock is Mass Stanley's time and the whole Fair Ground knows this. Peanut man O, Patti pan O, be he Papa Son or Kissie Dover. And I am full of pride. Silence. Mass Stanley in his cut away coat, his panama straw hat with the pin-prick holes, his two-toned shoes with their pin-pricked holes. Mass Stanley O. And Miss Sada in her peplum dress and her upsweep hair. There are others too but they don't matter. If Alexander Richmond was there now, it would be different but my father doesn't dance.

Silence.

You hear me.

Is banjo man time now and old man time now.

Mass John get up like him young and like him been Kissie Dover and Papa Son all day. He hug up that banjo with its white basin and sway her and drag his finger backs against the strings and you 'fraid to draw your breath as the old people stand up like buckram in a bottle, man holding woman round her waist like we never see in ordinary life. She looking up at him like she beautiful and slim and she in the view master machine. Man leaning his head and looking down at his partner like he do that every day for the last century.

45

And they start.

Watch them leaning stiff like starch. O Mass Stanley! Look how him fling him foot from the knee and stick it off like him slim. O Mass Stanley. Again, Quiet there. Again. Watch Mass Stanley foot! Second figure now.

Rock the lady. Rock the lady on your toes. Walk like you going somewhere and yet is only behind her and around to come right back to your space. With one hand behind your back, kick the knee and stick out the heel. O Mass Stanley, toe it. She to the right and you to the left and let that square of a shoe box into a parallelogram and back. O. Look at her cross your shoulder. She pretty eh and she so light and is only Miss Rose in her coarse boots tomorrow. Bring her round. That's right and keep your hand round her til she stand in place and the music stop. Right.

Third figure now and everybody is a soldier and the ladies are waving them off to war. Yes now Charlie, let we hear the rhumba box. We hear it. Now send off the men ladies, send them off. Let them work. Mass Stanley worked in foreign, served in the war so he knows. Right men. Go on by yourselves. Go on. Show off. Hold up your head and smell. Smell him. You better than him but is all right. Yes move round him and let him know that you know but is still all right. You don't hold it 'gainst him. And come back to your women now. Send them up to warm up. Let them know each other. Give them their chance but show them how. That's right. Bow to each other. Mannersable. That's right. Show them your rhythm Miss Lou but gently, that's right. Decent and gentle. Now smell them. See who have on what but be mannersable. Greet them. Let them feel at home but let them know that you are still the best and you know it. Go back to your man and tell him is all right. All of you come together now and say is all right. Is all right. It hot and sweaty but is still all right. Is all right now Charlie. Tie up the rhythm.

Yes.

Cutting wood. You mad now and we understand.

Figure Four. Beat the box Charlie. Rock and stomp. You own the whole world. Rock and stomp. We out here looking but is not we. Is stage audience. Rock and stomp and move off by yourself. Mass Stanley I can depend on you. Slide out by yourself with your back foot. Turn round, kick your leg from the knee and stick out your heel. O Mass Stanley. Find Miss Sada now and lead her out and mek we see her dance. But you not craven. You not selfish. You know how to treat other women even if they not nice like Miss Elsada. Take in the other man wife. Take her in sir. Take her in. Show her courtesy. Lead her up to the rest and introduce her. Miss Sada don't mind. Let her meet Miss Sada. Now take them both in so everybody know that nothing not going on behind her back. Take her. O yes Sir. Yes Mass Stanley. But you can take your medicine. See the other man coming for Miss Sada. Yes. Don't vex. Bow to him nicely. Yes Sir. Mek him know is all right for you did take his wife for a dance too. Smile Sir. He doing well but he can't do well like you. No sir. Miss Elsada know it and the other lady know it too but they trying with the other man. They polite; they don't want him to know. And you polite too, you wouldn't want him to know either but all of we know. Smile sir. She coming back now. Cool off. Simmer down. Give it to Mass John and the banjo. Him is older man, let him simmer it down. Yes Mass John, they need you. Slap your hand back, flash your fingers. Give them pause to let them know that they must simmer down. Flash again and again and stop.

Figure five.

One, two, three pause.

When cow 'kin done.

Ah wey Harry a go do. . . .

Anything goes. Do the lancers. Slide, slide and hop then kimbo and stick; slide, slide and hop, then kimbo and stick. Slide, slide and hop, then kimbo and stick. . . .

I loved Mass Stanley and nobody seemed to mind. There were pimento trees in his yard growing out of rocks. And the rocks were peculiar too. They were full of holes. You had to walk carefully for if you stubbed your toe, it was liable to get stuck and to break off altogether. And the rocks had a smell. Sometimes of coffee and tobacco and sometimes of sweet soap as if Miss Sada washed them. Seems to me though that if she put coffee water or kananga water or any such thing in them to give them that smell, those cupped stones would harbour mosquitoes and it didn't seem that Mass Stanley and Miss Sada had any more mosquitoes than we had. So I don't know how come their yard smelt so sweet.

They liked to have me creeping into their house too. I would walk in and sit at the doorway and Mass Stanley, smoking his pipe in his rocking chair by the door, would crinkle his eyes and start talking to me. Or sometimes, he would say: 'You know Elsada' or 'You know Baba' and I knew that it was me he was talking to for they had all been there before me and he hadn't said a thing to them. He had been rocking and smoking and thinking and because I came, he got brave enough to think aloud because he knew that I wanted to know. He told me about Cuba and cutting canes and driving ox-driven carts, about frutopan and fighting in Cuba and Belgium. Mass Stanley had lived.

He told me about Manalva and how the district was. And how he used to ride a horse with his sword and shield to protect the queen.

–And a bet you couldn't tell me who was the queen eh girl?–

And I would guess and guess. –No you couldn't know. Who now would know what Coolie Gal used to be like–

And I still didn't know.

–Mammy Cool. Coolie Gal. A lovely samba girl every man wanted. Something like your Aunt Becca–

And every time Miss Sada would say:

–You have to bring Rebecca een? Stan is only a chile you know. Mine you let her grow big before her time–

–Cho Elsada, what that can do?– and he would be side-tracked into some other argument.

–My time now one like this working for herself and looking to find herself a husband before trouble take her. But you not going to have no trouble Nellie. You can fight. So much so that people won't even want to fight you. So you won't even see trouble. But now and again you must try to know it; it can trip you and fall you and you wouldn't even know what hit you for you don't know how trouble stay– He would wink at me and I would smile. There was some meaning there but mi ah grow mi wi see.

At other times he would press on to the end before Miss Sada caught him. –Something like your Aunt Becca but not so stocious. Bwoy she did stocious bad! Fellow Pinnock. Poh! Becca have too much juice for him. She never take her match. Thank God Coolie Gal was big woman to me or else I woulda bruk mi neck two times. Chile, woman sweet–

Janey and Lou were right. There was something to know.

Extract from *Jane and Louisa Will Soon Come Home.*

Michelle Cliff

Michelle Cliff was born in Kingston, Jamaica in 1946 and received her early education there. Later she studied in New York and at the Warburg Institute of the University of London. She considers her identity as a mixed–blood Jamaican and the colonial experience as influences on her as a writer, as also the works of James Baldwin, Bessie Head, Ama Ata Aidoo, Virginia Woolf and (especially) Toni Morrison. Her published work includes The Land of Look Behind *(New York, Firebrand Books, 1980),* Abeng *(New York, Crossing Press, 1984) and* No Telephone to Heaven *(New York, Dutton, 1987). She is currently working on* Bodies of Water, *a collection of short stories and a novella. A recipient of a (US) National Endowment for the Arts Fellowship in Creative Writing and a Massachussetts Artists' Foundation Grant in Fiction, Ms Cliff currently lives in Santa Cruz, California where she writes and teaches freelance.*

Among the central concerns in Michelle Cliff's work are issues of race, class and colour. In the extract which follows the three conspire – ironically – to deprive the heroine of community and context.

No Telephone to Heaven

Boy took Clare to a high school. The principal, brass ornament indicating she was Mrs Taylor, a woman with a flushed face and thin body, timepiece dangling on a chain around her neck, greeted the two of them, asked them to be seated. They faced her in heavy oak chairs. Immediately she told them it was a matter of course in New York City schools to have foreign students begin a year behind so they wouldn't get 'lost'. The woman stated this custom perfunctorily, expecting to quell any objection. Boy let her have her say and then suggested an exception might be made for his daughter – after all, she was proficient in Latin and French, was beginning Greek, and had studied algebra and geometry since she was ten. In addition the girl had read many of the classics: Dickens, Shakespeare, Milton. He rested his case.

The woman said this made no difference. None. 'That is all beside the point, Mr . . . ah, Mr' – she glanced at the card in front of her – 'Savage.'

'I don't understand.'

'We are professional educators here. We are talking about degrees of emotional development. Children develop differently. Children from underdeveloped countries develop at a different rate than American children. Believe me, it's for the girl's own good.' She lifted the timepiece from between her breasts, glanced at it, allowing her abstraction to sink in. 'I am sorry, Mr Savage. I am sorry but that is our rule. There are no exceptions.'

'I see.' Boy acquiesced, never once asking where this was written, and could he see the guidelines of the Board of Education.

'Now . . . now that we have an understanding, let me go over the form with you. I will take down the information, to save you any difficulty with our language.' She smiled at the man who spoke to her in the King's tongue.

Boy said nothing at all.

'I will take down the information and send it to the elementary school in your district.'

'I could do that.'

'Not necessary. Our job . . . Race?' She met his eyes over her bifocals.

'White . . . of course.' As soon as it was out of his mouth he realized his grave error in appending the 'of course.' But the woman, the damn virago, he said to himself, had thrown him off. He had expected name, address, telephone to come first. He should have let *white* stand boldly. There was equivocation. And she immediately caught on. The lie colored his face more deeply.

'Are you sure?'

'Yes, quite sure.' Clare felt her stomach twist. Boy barreled on. 'My grandfather – '

'And your grandmother, Mr Savage? Are we to hear of your entire family tree – slave and free?' The specialist smirked at her rhyme.

She did not wait for his reply.

'Well.' She smiled at Clare, the first time she had addressed her. 'You see' – she turned to Boy – 'I am familiar with you island people. My husband and I vacation in Montego Bay occasionally.'

This woman acted as if she had been hired by the government to track down Savages trying to pass for white.

'My family is one of the oldest families – '

'And your wife's family, Mr Savage?'

'My wife and I are separated.' Silly declaration. The first time he had admitted his changed state, but senseless in this context. Would Kitty's blood now be erased?

'Mr Savage, please.' A new sternness was in the woman's voice. She was through with his games. Her time was valuable. 'Mr Savage, my husband is a physician. One of the very few Christian doctors left in this city, if you know what I mean.'

'Oh, yes. Yes, I do.' Boy nodded eagerly. Common ground?

'As such he has had to meet *them* more than halfway. He works for the public health service. In charge of maintaining the obstetrical well-being of Spanish-speaking women in his care.' The euphemisms confused her audience. 'He is a very witty man. Do you know what he would call you?'

'No,' Boy responded, having no idea what was coming next.

'He would call you white chocolate . . . I mean, have you ever seen a child's expression when he finds a white chocolate bunny in his Easter basket? He simply doesn't understand . . . he thinks it strange. I do not want to be cruel, Mr Savage, but we have no room for lies in our system. No place for in-betweens.'

Time passes. Monday, September 16, 1963. Adjusted to America after a fashion, the girl Clare sits in a green room with red geraniums on the windowsill. Dark green shades flap against the glass. Her father calls this their adopted country. They have lived here for three years. Time passes. Her mother continues to write but her letters hold no resonance – she 'keeps in touch'. The cotta remains intact. The two sides stand off. Boy suggests that he and his elder daughter may pay a visit. Yes, Kitty writes, that would be a nice thing. Let me know when and I will arrange a place for you to stay. But, he responds, money is short. They will visit as soon as he can make the fare and buy presents for everyone. Hesitation. What *is* he afraid of?

There is quiet until the next exchange. The two maintain a grace of connection – neither expects things to change.

Boy takes up golf. Trades in the '52 Plymouth for a '61 Chevy. Christmas gifts fly to Mountainview Gardens – unaccompanied. Now he sells televisions in the appliance department of Abraham & Straus. A lot of people seem to have credit – business is good.

Through all this – this new life – he counsels his daughter on invisibility and secrets. Self-effacement. Blending in. The uses of camouflage.

September 16, 1963. The girl Clare sits on a high stool in front of her homeroom, chosen by Mrs Douglass, a Black woman from Americus, Georgia, to read the morning paper to the class. Mrs Douglass believes in keeping her students informed. Today there is a story which should have caused the sun to eclipse the earth – something . . . something in the heavens should have objected.

In thick dark letters, stark: SUNDAY SCHOOL BOMBED – next line, smaller print: FOUR CHILDREN DEAD. A picture accompanies the letters. More pictures inside, they promise. A stained-glass window. Fragments of images dangle from its leaden boundaries. The face of Jesus is ruined. Dark space where the bomb has torn it off. His hands and crook intact. The legend of the window – willing workers – half there, half absent. Clare reads the text, the names, the ages attached to the names.

She monotonizes her voice for she is afraid of being moved – and this news has brought her dangerously close. She is afraid of embarrassing herself in front of this class of children who fidget as she speaks.

'Addie Mae Collins, 14; Denise McNair, 11; Carole Robertson, 14; Cynthia Wesley, 14.'

She is able to hold two things in her head at the same time. To read fluently while her mind is tracing something else. She has a chemistry quiz that morning and reviews, as she reads, the elements in the periodic table – dissolving the immediate like someone in solitary. First column: Hydrogen, H; Lithium, Li; Sodium, Na; Potassium, K. But she is troubled. Her mind recites, of its own accord: Hydrogen, 14; Lithium, 11; Sodium, 14; Potassium, 14. She has already forgotten the names, but the ages persist. She is older than all of them.

Her voice reads on.

'The Sunday School lesson that morning was "Love thy neighbor". It was in the middle of the lesson that witnesses heard a car slow down outside the Sixteenth-Street Baptist Church. Witnesses report that there was a distinct silence, followed by a rush of air, then a deafening explosion. In addition to the four dead, there are twenty-one injured. A man standing in the rubble of the hundred-year-old church was heard to scream, "Love them? Love them? I hate them!"'

Clare's voice stopped. *How could he not?* The class was still in motion. *Had they not heard?* Passing notes. Copying homework. Aligning their books on their desktops spine to spine. She glanced at Mrs Douglass, head up and down as she kept busy with her Delaney cards, recording attendance by sight. There was no rush of air in the room. No explosion. Clare folded the newspaper and returned it to the teacher's desk. She muttered, 'I'm sorry', the phrase she had been taught for people bereft, and felt foolish. Unable to go further.

The next morning, on her way to school, she put a nickel in the blind man's plastic dish at the mouth of the subway and picked up a copy of the *News*. On the front page was the picture she needed to see. A girl in a coffin, open. Girl, coffin, platform, all draped in a fine white cotton, like a delicate mosquito netting protecting her from the tiny marauders of a tropical night. A curtain to protect onlookers from the damage. The veiled girl identified in the caption as 'one of the victims of Sunday's bombing'. There she was – still and whole. As if sleeping, the undertaker might have advertised. Clare wondered what the veil hid, then was ashamed for wondering, confusing the sleeping pose with resting in peace. She cut the picture from the paper and put it in a celluloid pocket in her wallet – to glance at it even when they buried the President and she and her father watched the televison nonstop for three days.

It was during that strange weekend in November that her father caught her glancing at the picture of the dead girl. He asked her what was keeping her attention so. She replied, 'Nothing'. Thinking perhaps a movie star was stealing her mind from American history in the making, he demanded to see the picture. She held her wallet toward his chair. They came to grief over it.

'Girl, do you want to labor forever as an outsider?'

'I don't know, Daddy.'

'You are too much like your mother for your own good.' His voice was ragged, sharp. 'You are an American now. You need to realize what that means.' He slid the picture from the celluloid, casually folding it into his shirt pocket. 'This is for the best,' he told her, in a softer voice. 'You must not ponder these things so. We are not to judge this country . . . they give us a home. Your mother could never understand that . . . she blamed the whole place for a few ignorant people . . . that's why we lost her.'

A soldier at Arlington sounded taps as Boy spoke. He turned from his daughter as his eyes misted.

It did not matter that the picture was gone – it was in her mind. Connecting her with her absent mother.

The picture, and what it represented, like the meeting with the woman principal, the departure of Kitty, encircled a subject which became taboo between father and daughter. Should a newscast refer to the 'burgeoning civil rights movement', her father took care to distract her, and himself, with talk of something else. Not realizing his daughter could hold two things in her mind at once.

When Kitty Freeman Savage died, her brother Frederick telephoned her husband in America, barely able to contain the bitterness in his voice. Then he buried his sister in Kingston, in a cemetery which held no history for her family – burial in her mother's ground was not a question. The ties had been broken. The land was ruinate.

Clare returned home from school – she was a sophomore in college by that time, working three evenings and all day Saturday at Abraham & Straus, a position achieved because of her father's expertise in sales. She returned that particular evening to her father's weeping. He held a glass into which he stared. 'Your mother is gone,' he told his daughter.

At first Clare thought he was confused – reliving Kitty's departure of five years before. Then he raised his red-rimmed eyes at her and she knew. Just like that. 'How?' she asked. She did not cry.

'Your uncle said a brain hemorrhage in the night . . . He said she had been suffering from headaches . . . They asked her to see a doctor . . . begged, he said . . . to go to Miami if necessary . . . but she wouldn't leave . . . Your mother was the soul of stubbornness.' He sat before his daughter, thinking. Yes, that was it, Kitty brought it on herself.

In her last letters to them nothing had been said to indicate to them she was suffering. 'I am glad you are studying,' she wrote a P.S. to her elder daughter. 'I hope someday you make something of yourself, and someday help your people. A reminder, daughter – never forget who your people are. Your responsibilities lie beyond me, beyond yourself. There is a space between who you are and who you will become. Fill it.'

This death came without warning. No dogs howled. Had they done so, the daughter would not have sensed the significance of their noise.

She woke at twenty to find herself a motherless child – plainly.

What would her mother think of her on this truck? Of the task ahead of all of them? Could she love her for it?

At breakfast the morning after the news arrived, Boy pressed her. 'Have you cried for your mother yet?' He spoke behind eyes newly wet.

'No.' Her voice did not break.

In a sudden he was on her. 'You callous little bitch. I suppose you have more feeling for niggers than for your own mother.' Out it slid. The fury he had been holding in him escaped – the cause of his loss. Again, he aligned his daughter with his wife, who had abandoned him to strangers and died without a word.

Clare breathed deep, looked full into his furious face. 'My mother was a nigger' – speaking the word at him.

His five long fingers came at her, as she had expected, marking her cheekbone, making her weep in shock.

'And so am I,' she added softly.

She left the table to splash cold water on her face and get away from him for a moment. When she returned, he spoke to her as if nothing had passed between them, as if they had just joined one another at breakfast. He spoke to her without enthusiasm. 'Your sister will be coming here.'

And so she did. Speaking her mother's language, while Clare spoke her father's adopted tongue. One daughter raised in captivity, the other in the wild – so it seemed to Clare. Jennie came to them as to two strangers.

For her Kitty was vivid. They had slept in the same room in Mountainview Gardens, in the shadow of Wareika Hill. She had heard her mother cry out, 'Jesus! Tek me now!' She was not able to tell these people about it. She sensed that they envied her, that they did not know what to do with her. She existed in an afterlife where her mother surrounded her; she thought her mother could see her every move. Her dreams told her that.

'Did she leave anything behind?' Clare questioned the bluefoot sitting across from her.

'What you mean? She lef' me.'

'No. Did she leave anything behind? I would like to have something of hers . . . a keepsake.'

'Only this ring,' Jennie lifted the wedding band for Clare to see. It hung around her neck on a length of string.

'Did she wear that?'

'Yes. From time to time.'

'You better not let him see it, he'll take it for himself.'

'Him will have to cut me to get it.'

Silence. Then Clare spoke again, tentatively posing the one question she needed answered.

'Did she ever say why she left?'

The girl just stared at the ring around her neck.

'Why she left this place so suddenly? I know she couldn't stand it . . . could not make herself at home . . . and she had just lost Grandma . . . but did she ever say why she didn't take me as well?'

The girl spoke without looking at her sister. 'One time she say she feel you would prosper here. She say is because you favor backra, and fe you Daddy. Don't feel bad, man.'

Silence again. Clare fought herself, not wanting to weep in front of this girl, who meant well by advising her not to regret their mother's choice, as foolish as that was.

'What ever happened to Grandma's place?'

'Oh, it all overgrown by now. Rat live there. None of the family want to business wid it. It possess itself.'

'You ever visit it?'

'Few time we go down fe mango season, and fe drink and wash wid de water. She say is de purest water in de world dat.'

The years with her mother in the sun had rendered the younger sister dead-gold. Clare struggled within her city skin, birthright gone paler, an image of the river with her mother almost breaking her heart.

She left Jennie to her wanderings in the city. Left Boy to his newfound love – not his rediscovered daughter but an Italian-American widow who sold cosmetics on the main floor of A&S. The woman tried to be kind to Jennie, silently wondering when she would lose her tan, bringing her vials of sample scents, tubes of sample lipsticks, discouraging the girl when she returned from suspicious places with strange victuals. It upset her father too much, the woman told her, to smell curried goat after all this time.

As soon as she finished school, Clare left home. She borrowed money from her mother's brother Frederick, pledging to repay him, took a student fare to London, and began to explore. Nothing held her.

Extract from *No Telephone to Heaven.*

Christine Craig

Christine Craig was born in Jamaica and graduated with an honours degree in English from the University of the West Indies. Her first published works were the texts for two full-colour children's books produced by her husband, Jamaican artist Karl Craig, and published by Oxford University Press in 1970 and 1971. She has produced several non-fiction publications and training manuals on feminist and health topics. Her short stories and poems have been published in local, British and American anthologies and journals. Her first collection of poems, Quadrille for Tigers *was published in 1984 by Mina Press, Berkeley, California.*

She lives with her two daughters in Kingston, Jamaica and was recently awarded a fellowship to the International Writers Programme at Iowa University, USA.

In the Hills

Up in these hills the mornings bloom so gently moist, everything so wet with dew and wrapped in pale grey that you want desperately to hold your arms out, to pull it all to you and hold it there for an hour, keep it with you for a space of time. But the sun, busy auntie, rushes out and tidies it all away so quickly you can hardly believe your grey moment was ever there. Later, the busy, rushing sun will spread herself out and reign expansively throughout the hills.

Years before, I had left the heat and the noise and the warring of the city to build my small house here on my mother's land. The land had been new and difficult to work, but now it was yielding up its crops regularly and I had become part of the cycle of planting and weeding and watering and reaping. My nearest neighbour was some few chains away down the hill. A silent old man who kept a few cows and walked the two miles to the village to sell his milk. On Saturday he stayed in the village to get his drinking evening in and on very clear Saturday nights I could hear him singing his way home with unctuous, richly turned psalms.

A few miles further up the mountain lay a forest reserve. Land carefully planted out with firs. I became aware, gradually, that something was going on up there. A coming and a going and sudden noises of jeeps rambling up and down the stony road. The first time I saw them they were clearly city youths. Tight trousers and skinny T-shirts, hair luxuriously uncombed and lazy, slouchy hips, and talking, so much talking all the time. A week later I saw them drilling, soft cat manoeuvres, boys' games played with stony eyes.

Twice a week the big shots came to talk, to stir the blood, to lay strong reasons why they should learn the war game and be prepared to play it out down in the dusty city. These leaders walked like men but their repeated jargon sounded like gun fire under the firs and in silence I watched the scene close up like the stilted figures in a No play.

One of the boys came to my house. He wanted vegetables for the group. I let him have them, making myself sound simpler and more crazy than in the days when I was really ill. Soon they became greedy, they wanted the corn and beans before they were even full. I told them there would be more for all of them if they waited but they said their time was now and they could not wait. One Saturday afternoon a boy came on his own. He asked for nothing but stood silently near my front step and looked around. I took no notice of him and busied myself with my tomato plants, pinching out the first buds so the plant would not bear before it was strong enough. The sun was going down and still he stood there, his dark eyes large and quiet in his thin face. I went inside and made a quick supper for us, bread and plantain and fresh carrot juice to wash it down. We sat on my verandah until eventually I asked him: 'What is it, are you afraid?'

His thin body moved suddenly, jerkily and he looked at me.

'Yes,' he said. 'I can see no way out.'

He spoke for awhile then of his hot, bitter existence in the city. No job, no money for him. When the big ones spoke it had sounded so simple. Stay with me, learn to hate, learn to kill and you will have a job, you will have a house and you will be free. Free from the oppressors.

He sat there, as the evening turned into night, and he said: 'I am

57

afraid to kill another man. It is a sin to kill. And afterwards, what job can I get that will make me forget what I have done. What pride can I take in my house if I have such a sin in my heart?'

I had no answer of course, I could only watch the lines of his thin body aching with pain as he sat there on my small verandah.

'What do the big shots tell you?' I asked. 'How do they make it seem alright to the others?'

He sighed and I saw the shine of tears in his eyes. 'They say,' he whispered, 'that we are all oppressed, that we cannot all be free to enjoy the new society unless all make the sacrifices. They say we will be heroes and our names will be written in the history books.'

I looked out into the starry sky and heard my old neighbour singing his way home up the hill. 'So, that is a good thing,' I said. 'If none of you have anything now you will have to do something together to get what you want.'

The young boy looked at his hands and then folded them round his body, he suddenly seemed very young indeed. He said: 'Perhaps there is another way. This way, they will get what they want. They will always have us then because we shall have to live with what they have made us create.'

I shivered then, on my small verandah and went inside to fetch a shawl. I suggested we make some hot tea and he came inside and helped me light the lamp. The dirty things from supper still lay on the table in the alcove that I call my kitchen. He fetched some water from the big oil drum out back and washed our few things while I waited for the kettle to boil. He was quick and economical with his movements in the small space which only I had moved in for so many years.

We took our tea back out to the verandah and found to our delight that the moon, which had been struggling up over the hill, had made it to the top and lay, flatly gleaming into our verandah. For the first time he smiled and threw back his head to catch the gleam of the light under his half-closed eyelids. But he grew serious again and blew on his tea to cool it.

'You could leave,' I said, testing him. 'Run away.'

'No,' he said firmly. 'I am in the group now and there is no way out. There was no way out when I was in the city and there will never be a way out for me now.'

The warm tea eased its way past the back of my closed throat. I said, 'I used to live in the city. I had access to money, on terms. I too was in a box, a prison. It took me a long time to find my way out, but I did. You will find your way out in your own time.'

He set the cup down and looked carefully at me. 'I used to think that way once,' he said. And then he was walking down the step and out across my garden and off into the hills.

Up in these hills the mornings are so soft and moist that you want, just for one moment, to gather it all to you. To hold, just for that second a soft, new life before that overriding sun burns and dries it flat away.

Previously unpublished short story.

Velma Pollard

Velma Pollard, sister of Erna Brodber, was born at Comfort Hall, Benbow, St Catherine in 1937 and grew up in Woodside, St Mary, Jamaica. She read languages at the University of the West Indies, Mona, when it was UCWI and subsequently did post–graduate degrees at McGill and Columbia Universities and the UWI, Mona where she recently completed a PhD in Language Education. A member of staff of the Faculty of Education since 1975, she has published various articles on the teaching of English and on Caribbean Literature and Language. She has also edited – with Jean D'Costa – Over Our Way (London, Longman, 1980), as well as Anansesem *(Kingston, Longman Jamaica, 1985) and* Nine West Indian Poets: An Anthology for the CXC Examination *(London, Collins, 1980).* Crown Point and other Poems, *her first collection of poetry, was published by Peepal Tree Press in 1988 and the Women's Press published* Considering Woman, *a collection of prose writing in spring, 1989. Velma Pollard has a daughter, two sons, and a granddaughter.*

Velma Pollard is concerned with gender–related issues in a Caribbean still defined by its history, so that race, class and colour continue to complicate the attempt to secure psychic wholeness, personal quiet, a self. Hers is a wry use of language, humour lurking always beside/beneath the perceptions, however painful.

Monologue

'im is a self-made man
im mek imself
das why im no mek good . . .'

59

Masters, who will define what good is?

Tip, tip, tip. Somewhere a recurrent drop of water was sending the whole world mad. It sent a slow, pure, stream of calm through a narrow, endless hole pierced through the chaos in Karl's head and he smiled . . . for if there was heaven after all these months of raging hell, it was this one nail hole leaking icy calm.

–Bredda Man!–
It must be time to eat. This is the supper shift fellow. Always sits and talks after everyone's supper; always talks while he's serving too. But I never answer for I cant hear a single clear syllable with all those loud laughs deafening me as these eternal brown men shake my hands and shake my hands again . . . Funny how they shake my hands and squeeze them as I look in their eyes and look at their black moustaches. Funny how the hand pressure gets to my head and I can feel each hand squeezing my brain and the lines on my brain come together and the grey matter springs through their fingers and the pain is so much I cant even scream and I feel my eyes bulging in anguish and terror and the whole of me becomes one total pain then nothing . . . And now this nail hole clear and pure. Bet I can sleep tonight without trouble and without the needles again. Tonight I wont see Aunti's twisted face as she stands at the bank door watching all this vile shaking and seeing my hurt and hurting to think how much she suffered and how hard she tried, to get me to that hurt.
    –Bredda Man!–
    –Hi–
    –Look, a finish set the table; but you mus want to know what happen outside today–
    –What happen today?–
    –Today is the biggis of all the raids a bin tellin you bout. Di boys dem walk into di bank, you know di big branch, King Street, and wen you hear di count is four dead, three wounded and nearly a thousand pounds in loot. Few more like dat an di whole ting fix–
    This colour story is really something. This fellow is sure I must be grounds. One look at me, short, black and newly scrubbed – somebody's yard boy on a holiday, and he offers me my identification painlessly, pricelessly, in spite of this room and the cost he must recognise. Is a compliment really. This presumption almost that I am too sensible to let them con me into thinking otherwise. I take it gratefully, with both hands, but only because I had taken it myself, unoffered, long before. So I can look up and smile victory with him. One skip step and he sweeps

up the tray in a deft movement pats me on the shoulder with his free hand and smiles.

   –Dat good pardner, congrats–

   –Tomorrow, Bredda Man–

Tonight Aunti frees me. Tonight she leaves that wretched bank door for the last time I'm sure.

There is a painting full of blues and whites and greens, a slightly over-crowded canvas called the 'Dinner Party'; all these men and women over-dressed and sitting straight up grinning toothpaste smiles; collars choking them; faces of idyllic inanity. I can see the corner in the library now. Some honest expatriate trying to tell the blacks to give themselves a chance. Not really blacks noh; reds for me, blacks for him. I'm not too sure he knew the subtle differences.

That final night out there; that's what I was looking at. And when I broke the glass in Fenton-Smith's face, it wasn't really old Fenton I was looking at, much as I hate his guts, poor chap, it was every one of those pale faces grinning on that canvas and every one of them in every bank like that at every do like that – every pair of eyes that told me nothing, not all the scholarships, the trips abroad, the multiplicity of pieces of paper, could ever make me make it.

The ambulance came quickly. But Fenton-Smith's blood had turned his whole white shirt red; and I gritted my teeth and said not a word but kept staring at Aunti's ghost at the door and into her pained face underneath the bandana tie-head with the straw hat on top. Then her eyes held me; and suddenly I started to scream and they rushed me through the door, out of that place with all their eyes looking at me, and into my ages of raging hell . . .

Sunday at Hopeville after service and after everybody greets everybody else, they all go home to their beef and rice and peas and the churchyard gets so still you can hear the fork touching teacher's Sunday plate no matter where in the church-yard you go. Sunday so the brown almond leaves cover the ground and ripe almonds rest on their bellies or on their sides as the slope of the hill controls them. Saturday and Sunday, the church–yard without children's hurried feet and children's hungry mouths. Monday they call it school–yard and every one of those almonds will be gone; but little piles of seeds will wait for recess bell; and groups of three or four will pile around each heap, chiefly girls, for some reason; and the stones will go down in a kind of ritual thumping: bup, bup, crack and the almond shell will yield, and the little white almost coconut will be carefully extracted and put to join its brethren on the

61

large almond leaf lying on its back. Just before the end-of-recess bell rings, the sharing begins . . .

You know the track that runs past the church and curls itself around by the graveyard. You can see it clearly through the church window when big people are taking communion and children and guests are gazing in boredom, through the window. Pass the girls' lavatory, pass the famous sink–hole covered with a whist arbour that always bears blue and white blow–blow; pass where the damson trees meet across the same red dirt track and turn left. Some large stones rise up from the earth, with little holes on their faces. These stones are much bigger than the ones we used to cook on in the yam–seed pot days. This is Hopeville's Stonehenge. It's a place to sit and let time roll through your mind. Nobody comes there on a Sunday afternoon. Monday it becomes a pass for children from Gray's Pen who come to school at Hopeville. But Sunday it is deathly still. And if a little sister tries to use the short-cut, and sees you, she will turn back and run; for you must be a catcher–man waiting to cut her heart out to make black heart/art medicine if her mother is oldish; or you must be a hungry young man waiting to rape her if her mother is youngish. Either way you win . . .

But this Karl can't go there any more. Hopeville won't allow this Karl to go there. Long long ago, when Aunti was alive she put a stop to that and crowd up the silence: Aunti, a taking a walk roun' church.

–Where you going Karl? Let me come with you noh. Then we can call on Miss Madeline and Mass Busha as we passing. A did tell you that Mass Harold and Miss Jo–Ann come back? A don't even think they see you since before you went away but they always asking for you. When saying so a sure they don't know Daphne either for Miss Mellie didn't move out here yet when they leave. So is just as well we all go. Karl! . . . Kaaarl!–

Daph used to make a big thing of this need for silence and a chance to visit yourself sometimes. She used to work at a boarding school in the country once, she told me, and she made this need sound like a lot of pain there. Everybody was friendly, everybody was helpful, everybody was always around everybody else in a small community that was determined you shouldn't be lonely, determined you shouldn't miss the bright lights of the city. But one evening she got away, and rushed down the hill, and over some rocks and opened her heart and her eyes so the old tears could flow for all kinds of nameless sadnesses. . . .

As soon as she sat down and started to cry, little men with tattered hats and with cutlasses in their workmans hands came one by one forgetting their own tiredness and their own anxieties to look with grave concern and to ask what happen to the nice lady. Waterloo, she used to say, had that one thing over country Jamaica; you could cry by yourself for hours, except: that the place was so ugly and friendless that you had to cry and look at ugly things but in country Jamaica you couldn't get a chance to cry but you could look at beautiful things and talk to friendly people. I suppose you can't have it all . . .

But if you can't get your silence and your visit to yourself, you might just run off your mind to find it forever like Mass Clifton and Mr Rinyon at Hopeville who take it by force and block out everybody . . .

'Draaf Porterrrrrrrr! Draaf Porterrrrrrrrr!' That would be Mr Rinyon stepping down the Hopeville main road. To this day I never found out what draft porter was but I believe it was a potent brew like bush rum or something. It looked brown, from far. I don't know what they could have made it from; I'm sure wet sugar was included though . . . that brown colour, almost black . . . Nobody else sold it. Only Mr Rinyon (not Mass anything mark you, oh no) Mr Caleb Rinyon tall, thin well–dressed in his washed–out Khaki suit and his braces – not really holding up anything, not like Gramps' his just hung loosely about his waist and over his shoulders for he was so thin! His hat was an old army hat; the broad–brimmed type, the only one in Hopeville. It was old and light brown as I remember it though it must have been dark brown at birth. The draft porter was in a large tin container with a handle on top and a pouring spout at the side. On the other side of the pan there was another handle. So the pan was a woman akimbo when he set it down and on the kimboed hand, hanging from a short string, were quart, pint, half-pint and gill cans . . . Hi, I haven't heard of nor seen a gill measure since I started buying things for myself! I can't think now what Aunti could fry with a gill oil; half pint sounds like the smallest I ever see in the supermarket . . .

–Draaf porterrrrrrr, draaf porterrrrr! you ask me about the Kaiser– Mr Rinyon would begin although there was no one in sight on the road and I could hear only because I was behind the clump of fever–grass in the pass.

–If you ask the men in the trenches they will tell you what I tell you– then he would pause, get his strength together, twist his mouth to one side so gold teeth showed slightly, half close his eyes in anguish (?) and add with gravity: –I left him there a corpse. A corpse I say!!!!! . . . (or was it corporal?)–

People said Mr Rinyon was shell–shocked. I came to find out that this is a thing they say about most people who went to war and hadn't been able to deal with the experience. One day when I was at school in town I saw an old white woman running as fast as her shaky strength could take

63

her and looking up in the sky . . . I could see nothing spectacular there; a normal aeroplane cruising along . . . someone told me she behaved like that every time a plane passed; something about bombings in Europe . . . She was shell–shocked too.

Late in the afternoon Mr Rinyon would pass our house again. People say he used to drink the last of the draft porter when the day's sale was over and you could hear him coming, his hard boots grating on the loose stones his voice smooth not cracking at all, though he was old:

> All dogs are barking in the trenches
> Barking at the Union Jack . . .
>
> What a disappointment
> When they catch the Kaiser
> All those wars will soon be over
> When you hear the song of old Britannia . . .
> God save the king . . .

There was another one he used to sing too about sending down Rumania, Australia and Canada but 'for God sake don't send me!' Nothing in my experience of history in school helped me clear up that combination of countries. After a time I decided that they sounded good together to Mr Rinyon and that was it. But when I came upon some English twentieth century poem some old woman praying . . . in Westminster I think, asking God or whoever to send the blacks, or at least the colonials and spare 'our' boys. It's just as well the lyrics were too wrong to make sense for the business of fighting to die or get shell–shocked so some other people won't is too heavy to think about; I might even decide that is consciousness shock Mr Rinyon . . .

Mr Rinyon had his silence though it was so loud on the outside . . .

Mass Clifton's silence was simpler; less exotic all together. You see, he hadn't gone abroad. Mass Cliff was young – no more than thirty perhaps. His stride was distinctive; average sized steps, evenly spaced, but with a jerk, as if he meant to march but couldn't really, if he must keep his backless slippers on his feet as well. He was silent except for his step and the slight slurp of the slippers on the gravel. His tight three quarter pants, emphasising his goat-thighs lean and strong, tight with the tightness of a lifetime of hills, was always scrupulously clean. If his head was down, he was mumbling to himself; if it was thrown back (by far the more likely) he was thinking and silent.

–Good morning Mass Clifton–

–Morning–

He always answered as if he resented your interrupting something important for a mere greeting. But I always greeted him as I greeted everybody I was afraid of in Hopeville in those short pants days. You must tell a mad man good morning before he decides to do something about impolite children. Though in truth and in fact Mass Clifton wouldn't harm a soul. Occasionally those out and out bad children who Aunti said had no home training would shout:

–Mad Cliftoooon!– and Mass Clifton would give a considered half turn and respond in slow, deliberate tones:

–Your mother's ass is more mad than I–

In Hopeville you had to be mad to talk English all the time.

They say Clifton was very bright and had gone to Mico to train as a teacher. I can't remember now whether his studies had sent him mad or whether somebody had worked obeah on him through jealousy . . . Aunti would remember. All I know is that all through my childhood he walked down the road counting the stones at his feet and every now and then throwing one behind him.

. . . If I leave this place and go to Hopeville and sit upon a stone and look at the harmless bushes covering the cave they call Daddy Rock; or if I try to sit in the cave in all that cool stillness where they say so many seeds were spilled, you will hear that Miss Elvy bright son study till im tun fool an is same ting dem did tell im madda im shoulda stop study long time for too much book no good. They will say that is book make im siddung a plait im finger an look eena dih cave top like im laas something . . .

Or you will hear dat a smaddy dweem so far a jalous dem jalous dih bwoy fih im brain; dats why dem tell him god mother since him mother pass on, fih tek dem advise and go see if dih man a calabash tree can see fih help him . . .

And everybody would be right. For when you get what you want and stop wanting what you get; is fool you turn fool. And the smaddy who do you so is yourself. And that self keeps fighting the other self for it wants you to stand in the impossible metal coffin leaning on the wall, leaning like bright silver with plenty pretty pretty patterns exactly as the Fenton–Smiths print it. All this time you looking for cool tinkling icy peace . . .

Extract from *Karl* (unpublished).

Joan Riley

*Joan Riley was born in Hopewell, Richmond, St Mary, Jamaica in the 1950s, the
youngest of eight children, six girls and two boys. She received her undergraduate
and graduate degrees from Sussex University and the University of London,
respectively. Currently resident in London with her two children (a boy aged eight
and a girl, aged three), she describes herself as 'action researcher, mother, community
involved'. She sees as influences on her writing, 'the lives and struggle of ordinary
folk and probably . . . the painter Lowry: I wanted to do with words what he did
with brush and canvas, create a permanent tribute to the everyday life of working
people.'*

Joan Riley's works include The Unbelonging *(1985),* Waiting in the
Twilight *(1987),* Romance *(1988) all published by The Women's Press, London.*
The Waiting Room, *a collection of science fiction stories, and* Diaspora under
Twin Suns, *a science fiction novel, are to appear in 1989. She hopes to return to
Jamaica soon. Ms Riley's works address social issues of relevance to the lives of
Caribbean peoples as well as of blacks living in Britain. However, her work goes
beyond narrow concerns.* The Unbelonging, *for example, raises the questions of
sexuality/alienation/child abuse, and the following extract reflects her engagement.*

Closing the Case

'A get a jab, Stanton,' she said, watching for his reaction as he ate, head
bent over the tray of food balanced expertly on his lap.

Stanton's head jerked up. It was fleshier since he came to England,
but still distinguished, with a parting straight down the centre of the
greased–back hair.

'A jab?' he repeated, as if he could not quite believe he had heard her
right. 'Whe yu get jab fram?'

Adella felt a twinge of disappointment at his response. She knew that
he felt she should have gone and begged money from the welfare.
Somebody had told him she could claim money from the government
now that she was a cripple and he resented her refusal. He thought her
pride misplaced. 'Yu doan waan go ask de govament dat have plenty
money but yu keep afta me fa de lickle bit a earn,' he would often say in
disgust. 'Well if is proud yu proud, yu gwine jus haffe eat pride. When yu

66

wante wante bad enough yu gwine run go beg dem.' Now she saw the near anger in his eyes, the resentment he felt at her announcement.

'Is nuting big,' she said hastily. 'Is jus a cleaning jab in a big office. A start Monday. De pay no good, but it will tek de burden off yu if a working too.'

He seemed to swell visibly under the subtle praise. 'A see dat,' he said more sympathetically. 'Is hard fa me to manage, what wid yu getting sick an all an nobady fe help out.'

'Dat true,' she said hastily, seeing the spectre of Gladys rising between them again. Since she had thrown her cousin out he had never forgiven her. And on the rare nights he still slept in the house, he slept on the settee, refusing to share a bed with her. Adella would not admit that it was because of her cousin, insisted on thinking that it was the pressure of her stroke, the fact that she could no longer work to keep his comforts up. 'Once a get inna de swing a might get some overtime work and tings shouldn't stay so tight no more.'

Stanton nodded, biting appreciatively into the succulent meat before digging his fork into the tender red peas and rice.

'An yu might come back to yu own bed,' she ventured, seeing his pleased absorption with the food in front of him.

The fork stopped moving, poised in mid–air. 'Wha yu mean?' he asked suspiciously. 'A tell yu already – dat part a de marriage done.' He paused, finishing the remnants of the food on his plate before adding, 'Fram yu have de stroke, yu change, Adella. A doan recognise yu de way yu get bitta. Doan tink a can fagive yu fa de way yu treat Gladys an dat afta she give up her room an her work fe come look afta de children.'

Adella bit back her anger, the injustice of it running through her. They both knew why she had thrown her cousin out, and a sudden thought occurred to her. 'Yu still go a blues wid Gladys?' she asked casually.

'Yes, man,' he answered, before realising what he had said. 'Well somebady haffe look out fa her, since is yu mess her up.'

She felt the bitterness like a sour thing on her tongue, tasted the pain before it seeped inside her, spreading everywhere. No wonder he stayed out most nights – no wonder he never had any money though he no longer bought the same amount of clothes. She had heard the rumours on the street, in the market. Everybody was whispering about them carrying on, blaming her because she was losing her husband to her own cousin. 'A know bout yu an Gladys, Stanton,' she said sadly, pushing back the raw pain. The tears threatened to clog her throat and shake her voice.

'Who tell you someting a go on wid Gladys an me, dat good fanuting

67

Lisa? Why she doan bring her pickney dem ova or go back to fe her husband stead a fasing in ada people business.'

'Lisa know bout it, but is not she tell me.'

'Is nat?' he was surprised now, interest in the plate forgotten as he reached automatically to balance the tray on the arm of the settee. 'So who tell yu?'

'Everybady talking bout it. A even hear some church brethren sey dat yu an she is sinning togeda.'

'Dem people should mind dem own business,' he said sullenly, a little boy caught out in a lie but not ready to admit to guilt. 'A ongly look out fa de chile tru she is blood. Gladys is a good girl, anybady can see dat.'

Adella looked at him sadly. 'Dat where yu sleep a night time when yu doan come home?'

He could see she did not believe him, had not accepted a word he said. 'A haffe sleep somewhere and Gladys grateful fa de way a treat her.'

She looked at his sullen face, the small moustache he had been trying to grow since those long, half–forgotten days when they had been so happy in Kingston. 'Yu doan even gi me money fa yu own children, but yu pay her rent fa her and keep her. A doan believe is jus tru she related to me. If so ow come yu would a mek yu children starve?'

Stanton was looking at her in surprise. His widened eyes told her that he could hardly believe she was throwing those hard words at him.

'She is a she–devil, Stanton,' she continued, past caring about the anger in his face, the likelihood that he would attack her once again, hit and pound her as if she was to blame for all the things gone wrong with him since he had come to England. 'Yu is not strang. Woman can lead yu if dem have a will.'

She had half–expected the blow when he stood up and came to tower menacingly over her. It sent her sprawling back into the chair, her cheekbone aching where the curled fist had landed with all his anger and his strength. Adella sat up shakily, holding her good hand to her cheek, shrinking away from the anger that radiated from him.

'If yu waan de truth, Gladys an me been moving fram way back. She is more woman dan yu an she faithful at dat. Is a shame yu neva learn anyting fram her insteada try mek me feel small all de time.'

She felt sick deep inside, her mind recoiling from an acceptance of what he was saying. He was only trying to hurt her, had to be. He had not forgiven her for her treatment of the other woman and was trying to get back at her for it.

'Yu tink a waan live like dis?' he asked, opening his hands to include the whole house. 'Yu keep tell me is your house, is yu do dis, is yu do dat.

68

Ow yu tink it mek me feel? Gladys diffrent, she mek me know she preciate what a do fa her.'

'But, Stanton, yu know a preciate what yu do fa me,' she said timidly as the back of his hand swept out, and connected with her face again.

'Doan tell lie. Yu was always de same fram way back, always a cuss bout someting, a wante wante an a breed more pickney. Well yu can have yu house cause a leaving right now. A gwine live wid somebady who undastan me.' He turned and stalked out, and she heard him in the bedroom, wrenching open cupboard doors and drawers, cursing about the noise. She sat stunned, unable to believe he was serious, that he intended to abandon her. Panic clawed at her. What would she do without him? How would she manage with him gone? No! he couldn't go, couldn't live with her own cousin right in the same area. She would never get over the shame, the pity of it. Stumbling to her feet, she moved with clumsy haste, bad foot dragging more than ever with her agitation. She could feel shivers of fear coursing through her and she prayed that he would not attack her again. She told herself it was just anger and he did not mean to carry out this threat, would not leave her after their years together. She clutched at the jamb as she opened the bedroom door, mind screaming rejection of what her eyes could see. He had hauled down his grip from the top of the wardrobe and it lay gaping open on the bed. Clothes and shoes were crammed drunkenly inside. He was pulling shirts, vests and socks out of the drawer, flinging them into the case with angry disregard. It was so unlike him. Stanton was always so neat and tidy. Adella couldn't move. Her mind continued to resist the nightmare in front of her.

'Yu caan leave me, Stanton,' she said finally. 'A sorry a vex yu – but yu caan jus up an leave me wid de five children dem.'

He paused to give her an angry look – hissed through his teeth in irritation when he realised that his grip was overflowing. Climbing on the bed, he pushed the clothes down, leaning on the case so he could snap the catch shut.

The bed was still littered with clothes: trousers and jackets strewn on the floor, and hanging in the wardrobe. Without a pause, he pulled down her grip and started to throw clothes in it.

'A will give it back to yu when a come fe look fa de children. A not teking it, jus borrowing it.'

Adella nodded automatically. She didn't care about the grip. He could take Delores and Mikey's cases as well if he wanted. She just could not bear the thought that he was going to leave them, was going to walk out and leave her without a husband, her children without a father.

'Stanton, do a beg yu, doan left me alone. A gwine get betta, a gwine try fe do what yu want.'

She could feel the tears wet on her face, the slight prickling as they traced downwards, the saltiness at the corners of her mouth.

'Yu doan undastan?' he asked cruelly. 'A doan have no use fa yu no more. A caan live up to what yu want, Adella, an a tink is bes a left yu now fore tings get wussa an wussa.'

'But a get a jab now, Stanton,' she pleaded. 'Tings gwine get betta, a know it will.'

He ignored her and continued to toss clothes into the case as if she wasn't there. Adella felt a surge of anger and resentment bubbling over.

'Well go to her den,' she said bitterly. 'Yu tink is yu she want?' She was breathing hard, feeling the injustice inside, her head aching from the force of her emotions. 'Fram she can tek weh her own cousin man, yu tink yu can trus her? Come to dat she not gwine trus yu? Is not she yu want, Stanton, is yu family yu running fram, tru yu caan responsible fa dem.'

He closed the case on an angry snap, hauling it off the bed to join the other one on the floor; giving her a last spiteful look he picked up a case in either hand after making sure he had not forgotten anything. 'Yu should look pan yuself,' he said nastily. 'Yu get ole and ugly. Yu let yuself go so bad a doan tink any man gwine waan look pan yu much less waan move wid yu.' With that he walked to the door, pushing roughly past her.

Extract from *Waiting in the Twilight*.

Olive Senior

Olive Senior was born in rural Jamaica in 1941 and spent much of her childhood in Trelawny, Westmoreland and St James. She received her high school education in Jamaica after which she went to Carelton University in Canada to study journalism. She subsequently returned to Jamaica where she has worked as a journalist, in public relations, as a freelance researcher and writer, and in publishing. A former Publications Editor in the Institute of Social and Economic Research (ISER), UWI, Mona, Jamaica, and editor of Social and Economic Studies, *she is* currently *Managing Director of Institute of Jamaica Publications Ltd and editor of* Jamaica Journal. *In 1980 she received the Institute of Jamaica's Centenary Medal for Creative Writing and in 1988 its Silver Musgrave Medal for Literature. Olive Senior has published various poems and short stories, as well as scholarly articles, in journals in the Caribbean and overseas. Her books include* The Message is Change *(Kingston, Kingston Publishers, 1972),* The A–Z of Jamaican Heritage *(Heinemann Educational Books (Caribbean) Ltd, 1983), a collection of poetry,* Talking of Trees *(Mona, Kingston, Calabash, 1985), a collection of short stories,* Summer Lightning and Other Stories *(Longman, 1986) which won the first Commonwealth Writers' Prize in 1987 and* Arrival of the Snake Woman *(Longman, 1989). She has also written* Working Miracles, *a book on the roles and status of Caribbean women, in connection with the Women in the Caribbean Project (ISER–UWI, Barbados).*

Do Angels Wear Brassieres?

Auntie Mary is a nervous wreck and Cherry weeping daily in excitement. The Archdeacon is coming. Auntie Mary so excited she cant sit cant stand cant do her embroidery cant eat she forgetting things the house going to the dog she dont even notice that Beccka been using her lipstick. Again. The Archdeacon coming Wednesday to the churches in the area and afterwards – as usual – Archdeacon sure to stop outside Auntie Mary gate even for one second – as usual – to get two dozen of Auntie Mary best roses and a bottle of pimento dram save from Christmas. And maybe just this one time Archdeacon will give in to Auntie Mary pleading and step inside her humble abode for tea. Just this one time.

Auntie Mary is due this honour at least once because she is head of Mothers Union and though a lot of them jealous and back–biting her because Archdeacon never stop outside their gate even once let them say anything to her face.

For Archdeacon's certain stop outside her gate Auntie Mary scrub the house from top to bottom put up back the freshly laundered Christmas Curtains and the lace tablecloth and the newly starch doilies and the antimacassars clean all the windows in the house get the thick hibiscus hedge trim so you can skate across the top wash the dog whitewash every rock in the garden and the trunk of every tree paint the gate polish the silver and bring out the crystal cake–plate and glasses she bring from

Cuba twenty–five years ago and is saving for her old age. Just in case Archdeacon can stop for tea Auntie Mary bake a fruitcake a upside–down cake a three–layer cake a chocolate cake for she dont know which he prefer also some coconut cookies for although the Archdeacon is an Englishman dont say he dont like his little Jamaican dainties. Everything will be pretty and nice for the Archdeacon just like the American lady she did work for in Cuba taught her to make them.

The only thing that now bothering Auntie Mary as she give a last look over her clean and well ordered household is Beccka, dirty Beccka right now sitting on the kitchen steps licking out the mixing bowls. The thought of Beccka in the same house with Archdeacon bring on one of Auntie Mary headache. She think of asking Cherry to take Beccka somewhere else for the afternoon when Archdeacon coming but poor Cherry work so hard and is just excited about Archdeacon coming. Auntie Mary dont have the courage to send Beccka to stay with anyone for nobody know what that child is going to come out with next and a lot of people not so broadmind as Auntie Mary. She pray that Beccka will get sick enough to have to stay in bed she – O God forgive her but is for a worthy cause – she even consider drugging the child for the afternoon. But she dont have the heart. And anyway she dont know how. So Auntie Mary take two asprin and a small glass of tonic wine and pray hard that Beccka will vanish like magic on the afternoon that Archdeacon visit.

Now Archdeacon here and Beccka and everybody in their very best clothes. Beccka thank God also on her best behaviour which can be very good so far in fact she really look like a little angel she so clean and behaving.

In fact Archdeacon is quite taken with Beccka and more and more please that this is the afternoon he decide to consent to come inside Auntie Mary parlour for one little cup of tea. Beccka behaving so well and talking so nice to the Archdeacon Auntie Mary feel her heart swell with pride and joy over everything. Beccka behaving so beautiful in fact that Auntie Mary and Cherry dont even think twice about leaving her to talk to Archdeacon in the parlour while they out in the kitchen preparing tea.

By now Beccka and the Archdeacon exchanging Bible knowledge. Beccka asking him question and he trying his best to answer but they never really tell him any of these things in theological college. First he go ask Beccka if she is a good little girl. Beccka say yes she read her Bible every day. Do you now say the Archdeacon, splendid. Beccka smile and look shy.

72

'Tell me my little girl, is there anything in the Bible you would like to ask me about?'

'Yes sir. Who in the Bible wrote big?'

'Who in the Bible wrote big. My dear child!'

This wasnt the kind of question Archdeacon expecting but him always telling himself how he have rapport with children so he decide to confess his ignorance.

'Tell me, who?'

'Paul!' Beccka shout.

'Paul?'

'Galations six eleven "See with how large letters I write onto you with mine own hands".'

'Ho Ho Ho Ho' Archdeacon laugh. – 'Well done. Try me with another one.'

Beccka decide to ease him up this time.

'What animal saw an angel?'

'What animal saw an angel? My word. What animal . . . of course. Balaam's Ass.'

'Yes you got it.'

Beccka jumping up and down she so excited. She decide to ask the Archdeacon a trick question her father did teach her.

'What did Adam and Eve do when they were driven out of the garden?'

'Hm,' the Archdeacon sputtered but could not think of a suitable answer.

'Raise Cain ha ha ha ha ha.'

'They raised Cain Ho Ho Ho Ho Ho.'

The Archdeacon promise himself to remember that one to tell the Deacon. All the same he not feeling strictly comfortable. It really dont seem dignified for an Archdeacon to be having this type of conversation with an eleven–year–old girl. But Beccka already in high gear with the next question and Archdeacon tense himself.

'Who is the shortest man in the Bible?'

Archdeacon groan.

'Peter. Because him sleep on his watch. Ha Ha Ha.'

'Ho Ho Ho Ho Ho.'

'What is the smallest insect in the Bible?'

'The widow's mite,' Archdeacon shout.

'The wicked flee,' Beccka cry.

'Ho Ho Ho Ho Ho Ho.'

Archdeacon laughing so hard now he start to cough. He cough and cough till the coughing bring him to his senses. He there looking down the passage where Auntie Mary gone and wish she would hurry come back. He sputter a few time into his handkerchief, wipe his eye, sit up straight and assume his most religious expression. Even Beccka impress.

'Now Rebecca. Hm. You are a very clever very entertaining little girl. But what I had in mind were questions that are a bit more serious. Your aunt tells me you are being prepared for confirmation. Surely you must have some questions about doctrine hm, religion, that puzzle you. No serious questions?'

Beccka look at Archdeacon long and hard. 'Yes,' she say at long last in a small voice. Right away Archdeacon sit up straighter.

'What is it my little one?'

Beccka screwing up her face in concentration.

'Sir, what I want to know is this for I cant find it in the Bible. Please sir, do angels wear brassieres?'

Auntie Mary just that minute coming through the doorway with a full tea tray with Cherry carrying another big tray right behind her. Enough food and drink for ten Archdeacon. Auntie Mary stop braps in the dooway with fright when she hear Beccka question. She stop so sudden that Cherry bounce into her and spill a whole pitcher of cold drink all down Auntie Mary back. As the coldness hit her Auntie Mary jump and half her tray throw way on the floor milk and sugar and sandwiches a rain down on Archdeacon. Archdeacon jump up with his handkerchief and start mop himself and Auntie Mary at the same time he trying to take the tray from her. Auntie Mary at the same time trying to mop up the Archdeacon with a napkin in her mortification not even noticing how Archdeacon relieve that so much confusion come at this time. Poor soft—hearted Cherry only see that her sister whole life ruin now she dont yet know the cause run and sit on the kitchen stool and throw kitchen cloth over her head and sit there bawling and bawling in sympathy.

Beccka win the scholarship to high school. She pass so high she getting to go to the school of Auntie Mary choice which is the one that is furthest away. Beccka vex because she dont want go no boarding school with no heap of girl. Beccka dont want to go to no school at all.

Everyone so please with Beccka. Auntie Mary even more please when she get letter from the headmistress setting out Rules and Regulation. She only sorry that the list not longer for she could think of many things she could add. She get another letter setting out uniform and right away Auntie Mary start sewing. Cherry take the bus to town one day with money coming from God know where for the poor child dont have no father to speak of and she buy shoes and socks and underwear and hair ribbon and towels and toothbrush and a suitcase for Beccka. Beccka normally please like puss with every new thing vain like peacock in ribbons and clothes. Now she hardly look at them. Beccka thinking. She dont want to go to no school. But how to get out of it. When Beccka think done she decide to run away and find her father who like a miracle have job now in a circus. And as Beccka find him so she get job in the circus as a tight—rope walker and in spangles and tights lipstick and powder (her own) Beccka perform every night before a cheering crowd in a blaze of light. Beccka and the circus go right round the world. Every now and then, dress up in furs and hats like Auntie Mary wedding hat Beccka come home to visit Cherry and Auntie Mary. She arrive in a chauffeur—driven limousine pile high with luggage. Beccka shower them with presents. The whole village. For fat Katie Beccka bring a years supply of diet pill and a exercise machine just like the one she see advertise in the magazine the lady did give to Cherry.

Now Beccka ready to run away. In the books, the picture always show children running away with their things tied in a bundle on a stick. The stick easy. Beccka take one of the walking stick that did belong to Auntie Mary's dear departed. Out of spite she take Auntie Mary silk scarf to wrap her things in for Auntie Mary is to blame for her going to school at all. She pack in the bundle Auntie Mary lipstick Auntie Mary face powder and a pair of Auntie Mary stockings for she need these for her first appearance as a tight rope walker. She take a slice of cake, her shiny eye marble and a yellow nicol which is her best taa in case she get a chance to play in the marble championship of the world. She also take the Bible. She want to find some real hard question for the Archdeacon next time he come to Auntie Mary house for tea.

When Auntie Mary and Cherry busy sewing her school clothes Beccka take off with her bundle and cut across the road into the field. Mr O'Connor is her best friend and she know he wont mind if she walk across his pasture. Mr O'Connor is her best friend because he is the only person Beccka can hold a real conversation with. Beccka start to walk toward the mountain that hazy in the distance. She plan to climb the mountain and when she is high enough she will look for a sign that will lead her to her father. Beccka walk and walk through the pasture divided by stone wall and wooden gates which she climb. Sometime a few trees tell her where a pond is. But it is very lonely. All Beccka see is john crow and cow and cattle egret blackbird and parrotlets that scream at her from the trees. But Beccka dont notice them. Her mind busy on how Auntie Mary and Cherry going to be sad now she gone and she composing letter she will write to tell them she safe and she forgive them everything. But the sun getting too high in the sky and Beccka thirsty. She eat the cake but she dont have water. Far in the distance she see a bamboo clump and hope is round a spring with water. But when she get to the bamboo all it offer is shade. In fact the dry bamboo leaves on the ground so soft and inviting that Beccka decide to sit and rest for a while. Is sleep Beccka sleep. When she wake she see a stand above her four horse leg and when she raise up and look, stirrups, boots, and sitting atop the horse her best friend, Mr O'Connor.

'Well Beccka, taking a long walk?'

'Yes sir.'

'Far from home eh?'

'Yes sir.'

'Running away?'

'Yes sir.'

'Hm. What are you taking with you?'

Beccka tell him what she have in the bundle. Mr O'Connor shock.

'What, no money?'

'Oooh!'

Beccka shame like anything for she never remember anything about money.

'Well you need money for running away you know. How else you going to pay for trains and planes and taxis and buy ice cream and pindar cake?'

Beccka didn't think about any of these things before she run away. But now she see that is sense Mr O'Connor talking but she dont know what to do. So the two of them just stand up there for a while. They thinking hard.

'You know Beccka if I was you I wouldnt bother with the running away today. Maybe they dont find out you gone yet. So I would go back home and wait until I save enough money to finance my journey.'

Beccka love how that sound. To finance my journey. She think about that a long time. Mr O'Connor say, 'Tell you what. Why dont you let me give you a ride back and you can pretend this was just a practice and you can start saving your money to run away properly next time.'

Beccka look at Mr O'Connor. He looking off into the distance and she follow where he gazing and when she see the mountain she decide to leave it for another day. All the way back riding with Mr O'Connor Beccka thinking and thinking and her smile getting bigger and bigger. Beccka cant wait to get home to dream up all the tricky question she could put to a whole school full of girl. Not to mention the teachers. Beccka laughing for half the way home. Suddenly she say –

'Mr Connor, you know the Bible?'

'Well Beccka I read my Bible every day so I should think so.'

'Promise you will answer a question.'

'Promise.'

'Mr Connor, do angels wear brassieres?'

'Well Beccka, as far as I know only the lady angels need to.'

Beccka laugh cant done. Wasnt that the answer she was waiting for?

Abridged, from the collection *Summer Lightning and Other Stories.*

Sylvia Wynter Carew

Sylvia Wynter Carew was born in Cuba of Jamaican parents in 1928 and was educated at the Universities of London and Madrid. After leaving university, she worked as a writer for radio and television producing, inter alia, *plays for the BBC, and translating Gabriel Garcia Lorca's* Yerma *for the BBC's Third Programme. In 1962 her only novel,* Hills of Hebron, *was published by Jonathan Cape. She began contributing articles on culture, politics and history to the Jamaican newspaper,* The Daily Gleaner, *in that year, and continued to do so for the next 18 years. Her academic career began in 1963 when she joined the Department of Spanish at the University of the West Indies, Mona, Jamaica, as a lecturer. She has held posts at the Universities of Michigan and California (San Diego) and has been Professor in the African and Afro–American Studies and Spanish departments at Stanford University since 1977. Drama has always been a major interest of Professor Wynter and two of her plays, a folk musical,* Maskarade, *and a historical drama,* Ballad for a Rebellion – 1865, *have been produced in Jamaica. As well as being novelist and playwright, she is the author of numerous articles, reviews and critiques published in various Caribbean and international journals on a variety of literary, historical and cultural subjects.*

Hills of Hebron *considers politics, religion (of a small sect), race, class, madness, the role of sexuality, the psychic crippling which physical handicap can cause. 'The Kingdom of Heaven' and 'The Rape' barely represent the achievement of a work broad in its reach, but searching and coherent.*

The Kingdom of Heaven

The time approached for Prophet Moses's flight to heaven. The faithful became restive. They had wound up their affairs on earth – sold their lands, their livestock, furniture, most of their belongings to shrewd unbelievers who did well out of the sales. And for days now the chosen ones paraded about the town in white robes and gold paper crowns. The robes were getting soiled, the crowns losing their glitter. The unbelievers, inured to watching their neighbours try to escape from the circus of destitution into which they had all been born, to search for gods and devils and prophets to set them free, knew that it was best to 'laugh and let live'.

The Brethren Believers celebrated Christmas Day as the birthday of Prophet Moses. Some of the town's idlers joined in the 'freeness', and when they were discovered, fighting broke out. Prophet Moses quelled the riot, reminded his followers sternly that they were men of peace, and decreed that there should be fasting and prayer until December 30th. The Brethren Believers, many of them with blood-stained robes, obeyed their leaders and slunk away to wait. And when the period of penance had passed there was another banquet. No uninvited guests turned up this time. No advance notice was given and the doors were bolted.

Early next morning when the town was asleep and the grass drenched with dew, Prophet Moses led his followers out to the foothills, and to a place where a giant breadfruit tree spread out its broad leaves like an offering to the rising sun. The Prophet climbed to the top of the tree. As soon as the sun came up, he promised, he would take off for the Kingdom. Three hours later he would return with a fleet of golden chariots driven by white angels, dressed in tunics with gold buttons.

The faithful clustered beneath the tree, faces upturned, their eyes bright with hope. From where they stood they could see their Prophet through the dark green leaves, the silver–grey branches writhing like limbs in agony. He looked to them like some strange and magical fruit about to be plucked by a hand from heaven. They sang joyously and tears rolled down their cheeks. They clapped their rough hands together and banished silence from the hills and valleys. They held themselves erect for the first time in their lives. Were they not the dispossessed on earth about to inherit all the vast spaces of heaven? Were they not outcasts, prodigal sons, trekking back home after epochs of homelessness? Their hymns of praise were a benediction over dark hills hunched against the sky:

'Behold the wretch who lust and wine
Had wasted his estate,
He begged a place among the swine,
To taste the husks they ate.

I die with hunger here, he cries,
I starve in foreign lands,
My father's house have large supplies,
And bounteous are his lands . . .'

And as the sun rose above the hills, they fell on their knees. Their singing shook the land and their tears mingled with the dew. The sunrise was the presage of the long–delayed fulfilment of their hopes:

'On Jordan's stormy banks I stand
And cast a wistful eye,
On Canaan's fair and promised land
Where my possessions lie.
We will rest on that fair and happy land
Very soon.
Just across on the evergreen shore
Sing a song with Moses and the Lamb
Very soon,
And dwell with the Father evermore.'

There are garbled accounts of what actually happened to the Prophet that morning. Some said that his fall was an accident, that his foot caught in a branch and he stumbled. Others maintained that he literally spread out his arms and flew off, and when he was half–way up was cast down again by the forces of Satan. Whatever the truth was, Moses became a fallen idol, abandoned by the great majority of his followers. Liza and a few of the faithful carried him home, called in a doctor to set his broken leg, taking turns to nurse him. In the town itself there were empty lamentations amongst 'the chosen ones'. Some, blinded by the rage of losing everything, stood outside Liza's house and abused the Prophet. Liza, bursting out of her house, cowed them with a passionate rebuke. Grumbling, they departed with nothing but their robes and crowns to call their own. They had to start the business of earning a living in a cruel town all over again.

The laughter of the unbelievers echoed through the valleys and over the hills, rolled down to Paradise Bay and reached as far as Kingston. The anger of the Believers passed swiftly and they, too, joined in the laughter.

Aloysius Matthews laughed but little. He was not a man with much time for mirth. He worked hard and liked his work. And Kate's heart was heavy. Many of those who had lost everything were market women. She had seen their lives touched by the magic of new hope. Now she saw them return defeated, heard them quarrelling, fighting, screaming, saw them like scorpions stinging themselves to death, impelled by self–hatred and the bitterness of a broken dream. She was better off than they were, but she was still one of them.

Ambrose chuckled and rubbed his hands. His flock had returned, and ten new members with them. Sister May–May, reaching deeper into the abysses of her own spirit, became more possessed than ever. This was the true way, the only way, for the lost ones, the disinherited in search of God, of themselves, of the Kingdom. And young Sister Beatrice looked on entranced, felt herself drowning in the strange fury Sister May–May scattered around her as her limbs fused with the drumming and she leaped and whirled and reached for the sky, as her body trembled and she wept and spoke in unknown tongues. Ambrose, presiding, would pass by and strike Beatrice with his rod. And she remained still, shivering like a sapling in a high wind until he led her off to his room; and the earth would shake with stamping feet, the drums thunder in her ears as he towered over her, masterful, demanding.

The Rape

Isaac began to tell himself that he only visited the couple to get material for his writing. To bear out his purpose he asked questions about the past in Cockpit Centre. Obadiah answered gladly. But his answers were either bald, bare facts – how many of the New Believers there had been, the date and the hour on which they had set out, the time they had reached Hebron, etc., or were panegyrics about the greatness of Prophet Moses. If, as sometimes happened, Hugh came over and joined them, he would substitute loud praises for Obadiah and himself.

But one afternoon, when Hugh was absent and Rose sat on the steps with them, shelling corn, she asked her husband questions about his life as a small boy in Cockpit Centre. Isaac found himself absorbed in Obadiah's simple, graphic account of his childhood. The next morning he wrote a short story about Obadiah's running away to Paradise Bay, returning to find his mother dead, and thinking that his whole world had been swept away by the sea. He wrote the story in the first person and his identification with the young boy was complete. The young boy was an amalgam, in appearance, of himself and Obadiah. And the young boy's mother looked like Rose. He started off the story by describing her as she looked to the boy. And words came to him new–minted, in their pristine innocence, with all the dross of centuries, the tawdriness and disillusionments, discarded.

He took the story with him to read it aloud to Rose and Obadiah. But on the way it seemed to him that the story would reveal so much of himself that he would never be free of them again. He would be implicated with them in a conspiracy of understanding that, binding him to them, would bind him to Hebron for ever, and to the image that Hebron had made of him. He tore up the story and flung the bits of paper away. He went to see them as he had intended, but all the time his manner was furtive, as if he had committed a crime.

In his last week in Hebron he began staying away from them. He had become afraid. His nights were tormented with dreams. He took long walks, seeking refuge in the thickly wooded hills. His obsession was not only with Rose, but with Rose and Obadiah together. Always, in his dreams they approached him hand in hand, Obadiah naked to the waist, and Rose dressed like the woman who had accosted him in Kingston, her breasts leaping from the tight dress, her mouth reddened like blood, her breath raw with rum . . .

This image remained with Isaac, beset him like furies. When in the light of day he felt ashamed and strove to banish it, his life seemed to become absurd and purposeless. He would even find himself standing at the edge of a sheer drop, trying to calculate whether death would be certain, or whether perhaps he might only end up with the inconvenience of a broken leg, as his father had done when he tried to fly to heaven. Then he would start thinking of his father's reputation with women, and this would become a justification for his desire. After all, like father like son, and the chip never fell far from the block. Suddenly he felt consumed with an overweening arrogance. All the women of Hebron were his to do with as he willed, as his father had done . . .

He found himself singing the dirty songs he had learnt as a boy in Cockpit Centre. He sang and shouted them to the hills and the trees. And the songs dredged up memories of all that he had heard about Rose's birth, about her fourteen–year–old mother and the parson, her grandmother and the Chinese grocer and his father. His knowledge of her past gave him the same sense of dominance that he had felt towards her as a boy, only now it aroused lust instead of pity. As the days passed he expunged from his mind the innocent years when they had been brother and sister, and replaced them with the smell of the sea, of stale urine in a narrow enclosed lane, and a woman's body which had become Rose's, writhing against his.

He drifted through the last days in the grip of an erotic nightmare that drove him to walk miles across the hills, to batter his fists against the rough bark of the tree–trunks. He avoided the New Believers, leaving home early in the mornings and staggering in, late at nights, to sleep. His mother was worried about him. In answer to her anxious inquiry he told her to leave him alone, once and for all, to leave him alone. Confronted with an aspect of her son that she could not understand, she pretended not to see it. He was only a bit overwrought with his studies, she told herself, only a bit overwrought. Still, she was relieved when the day came for his departure. And she would not admit to herself that his manner troubled her, that she had sensed in it a presage of disaster.

It was his last night in Hebron, and he sat across the table from his mother . After they had eaten, she had cleared the table, taken the dishes to the kitchen but returned almost at once. She glanced at him from time to time, waiting for him to speak. But she saw that his spirit was as withdrawn from her as it had always been. His face, under the lamplight, seemed strange to her. The lines were harsh, his chin stubbled with spiky black hairs. She had not noticed before how thin he had grown. They sat on in silence. When she could bear it no longer, Miss Gatha told him of the money that his father had left for him, of the large sum that she, by dint of great frugality, had added to it; told him where she kept it buried, six paces to the right of the single hibiscus plant that grew in the churchyard. She had wanted to win some gesture of approval from him. But he only nodded when she had finished, his face unmoved; and in his heart there was a contempt for her sudden weakness in giving away her secret, her only power over him.

He waited until she began to nod, and as she slept, dreaming her dreams for him, he went out to the kitchen, hoisted the spade over his shoulder, and climbed up to the churchyard. As he expected, she had buried the box deep in the ground. It was some time before the spade rang against it. After he had pulled out the money–box, he shovelled the loose earth back into the hole, and carefully patted it down. Then he cleaned off the spade and replaced it.

At first he was afraid to open the box. He walked with it several miles before he realised that he was on the track leading away from Hebron and down to Cockpit Centre. For a moment he was tempted to continue, not to return. But his habit of caution prompted him to make sure that the money was there, to ensure his escape. He sat down on the verging grass under a mango tree, and felt for the penknife in his back pocket.

His glance fell down the track to the rough post which marked three more miles to Hebron. Seated on the ground with her head resting against the post, Rose was fast asleep. The skirt of her dress had shuffled up above her knee; and a healed scar on her leg shone like a bright coin under the moon.

He stood up, forgetting the box, and walked towards her. A mass of clouds drifted across the moon and Isaac stumbled in the sudden darkness. He thought of Obadiah picking him up when, as a child, he had chased his kite, fallen over, and lain helpless. Obadiah was a fool, he exulted. It was his godfather's stupidity that made him kind, made him trustful, had caused him to take such a vow. Now Rose was like a field left to lie fallow under the sun, a ripe fruit to be plucked by him, Isaac. Soon he would be free of Hebron, would be able to leave it for ever. He was powerful with a certainty he had never known since the night that he had first seen the sea.

Rose heard his dragging footsteps and woke up. As he fell upon her she cried out his name with unbelief. Her body writhed under him as she struggled to break free. Savagely, he forced her elbows behind her back, straddled his legs across hers, imprisoned her thighs. She called out to him again and again but her voice was drowned in the sound of the sea that thundered inside his head. He hardly realised it when she stopped struggling and lay still, her breasts taut in the hunger of his hand, her body arched to his.

It was over. He lay face downwards, his fingers clutching at the grass. He heard Rose's footsteps as she ran hurriedly up the slope, heard her weeping. He wanted to stand up and call out his name to her, to reassure himself as to who he was. For, impersonal like the sea, she had taken him, then left him a castaway, without purpose, without being.

He got up and returned to where he had left the box. He did not wait to open it. Now there was urgency in him to abandon this place, to return to Hebron in search of something he had lost.

Both extracts from *Hills of Hebron*.

Marie Chauvet (Marie Vieux)

Marie Chauvet was born in 1916 and grew up in Haiti. Her novels are among the most explicit pieces of fiction to address the Haitian situation. They are powerful evocations of the complexities and horrors of her homeland. Her earlier works include the prize–winning Fille d'Haïti *(Daughter of Haiti: Paris, Fasquelle, 1954) and* La Danse sur le volcan *(Dancing on the volcano: Paris, Plon, 1957). Her best–known work* Amour, colère, folie *(Love, anger, madness) was published in Paris by Gallimard in 1968. Chauvet's prose is powerful and her insight and vision remarkable. Her third novel,* Fonds des nègres *(Port–au–Prince, Editions Deschamps), won the Grand Prix France–Antilles in 1960. She died in Brooklyn, New York in 1973. Another novel* Les Rapaces *(Birds of Prey: Port–au–Prince, Editions Deschamps, 1986) was published posthumously, under her maiden name, Marie Vieux.*

'Love', the first narrative in the Amour, colère, folie *trilogy, tells the story of Claire, a sensitive, highly intelligent woman. An 'old maid', the frustrations caused by her unmarried state and her black skin are aggravated by a stifling social milieu. Claire's love for her brother–in–law, her fascination with the sadistic military commander Calédu, and her desire to exercise control become the catalysts for a violent political and personal drama.*

Love

I watch the drama unfolding, scene by scene, unobtrusive as a shadow. I, the only lucid one, the only dangerous one, and yet nobody around me suspects a thing. The old maid! The one who has never had a husband, who doesn't know what love is, who has never really lived in the true sense of the word. They are wrong. I am savouring my vengeance in silence. It is my silence, my vengeance. I know just whose arms Annette is going to throw herself into and I have no intention whatsoever of opening my sister Felicia's eyes. She is too blissfully happy and is too proudly carrying the three–month old foetus in her womb. If she was clever enough to catch a husband I hope she will be smart enough to keep him. She is much too trusting. Her serenity exasperates me. She smiles contentedly as she embroiders her son's chemises; for of course it will be a son! And Annette will be his godmother, I can bet on that . . .

I am leaning on my window–sill watching them: Annette is offering Jean Luze her fresh, young twenty–two–year–old body, standing upright, in full daylight. They turn away from Felicia and possess each other without touching. Desire burns in their eyes, Jean Luze struggles with himself but the outcome is inevitable.

I am thirty–nine and still a virgin. A fate not to be envied in the eyes of most women from the Haitian provinces. Is it like that everywhere? Are there other little towns in the world like this one, half buried in ancient customs, where people spy on each other? My town! my country! As they proudly call this dreary *morne* where you hardly see any men apart from the doctor, the druggist, the priest, the district commandant, the local magistrate, the préfet, all new appointees and so typically 'people from the coast' that it is disheartening. The candidates for these posts represent the rare bird, whose parents' greatest ambition had always been to send their son to Port–au–Prince or abroad to make a scholar out of him. One of them has come back to us in the person of Dr Audier who studied in France and whom I examine in vain for signs of the superman . . .

I was born in 1900. A time when prejudice was at its height in this little province. Three separate groups had formed and these three groups were as divided as enemies: the 'aristocrats', to whom we belonged, the petits bourgeois and the common people. Torn apart by the ambiguity of a particularly delicate situation, I began to suffer from a very early age because of my dark skin, whose mahogany colour, inherited from some distant ancestor, stood out glaringly in the close circle of whites and light–skinned mulattos with whom my parents mixed. But all that is in the past, and for the moment at least, I don't feel inclined to turn towards what is over and done with . . .

◆

The leaves fall from the trees, dance and whirl in the air before they fall to the ground. Insomnia has made the living breath of night familiar. I can distinguish the cry of every insect, of every lizard, the movement of every star, each quiver of the earth. I am naked, on my bed, damp with sweat, palpitating with desire. A man's arms encircle my body. I am possessed. How can it be that a moment afterwards, it is all over? Not even a crumb of memory? Ah! How lonely suffering is! I dress and softly approach the door of Annette's room. She is sobbing in the darkness. I knock. A voice hoarse from weeping asks who is there. I answer; she opens. My presence does not embarrass her, I am the silly idiot, the one on whom life has left no marks. She sobs again and then she asks me: 'What do you want?'

I look at her silently and she clings to me.

'If only you knew, Claire . . .'

'Shhh! Don't wear yourself out talking,' I say to her silently: 'I know what you are feeling and I share your feelings. The soul is a millstone, an albatross. It meddles in everything. It creates ties to torture us. Memories mark us, they go deep into our psyches. You are like a flower blown about by the wind. I wish you could be snatched from your ordinary everyday joys and carried away in a huge whirlwind, in danger of your life . . .'

'I want to die! I want to die!' she cries out suddenly, so passionately that it leaves her bewildered. It was not she who spoke, but I. How tired she looks! How draining this love affair is for her! How morally weak she is! Jean Luze is not for her. The feeling he arouses in her is so strong that it is destroying her. Will it kill her? Too bad! I need her to serve as my intermediary. I am old. It is as if I am slowly going sour with my starved virginity locked tight between my thighs.

'Cry with me. It won't be for long, you'll see. Have confidence in your charms. You have all that it takes to seduce him. His armour is only a show. You have already seen that. You must not give up. You are experienced. At fifteen, in full control of your feelings, you were already frolicking in search of a male. I was the first to reap what I had sown. I am going to torture you, torture you both until you cry out for mercy . . .'

'Next month is your birthday, I am going to have a little party for you. Invite whoever you want . . .'

'You are treating me like a child,' she protested.

My offer seems childish, but I want Annette to regain her composure, to dance and laugh as Jean Luze watches. I am going to bring her to the limit of her endurance. Suffering does not excite one, it either arouses pity or annoyance. I, who am so tight–fisted, am determined to sacrifice a lot of money on this reception.

The couple is with us, morning, noon and night, closer than ever. Felicia becomes more and more alive as her stomach swells. She is as tranquil as a statue. Jean Luze is eating heartily. He no longer smokes at the table, he claims the smell of tobacco bothers his wife.

'Pregnancy suits you,' he tells her, putting his arm around her.

Every time I see him being affectionate to her in my presence, I hate

86

her for being so easily contented with this lukewarm, bourgeois feeling she inspires in him.

I swear to shake him out of his tepid contentment. I will load him like a powder keg. He loses nothing by waiting. I will melt his ice. Let him continue to gaze fondly at us, let him smile. I love to see the dimple appear in his chin, his lips curl over his teeth.

◆

Time passes. The wretchedness of the people grows. To each his lot. Our selfishness becomes the rule. We sink deeper and deeper into cowardice and become resigned. I am more in love with my sister's husband than ever and I don't want to think of anything besides this love. It becomes my refuge, my consolation. Once again Felicia is so sure of herself and of her man that she kissed Annette this morning and wished her happy birthday. They gave her perfume and talcum powder.

'Powder and perfume yourself all you want. I am not afraid of anything anymore,' Jean Luze's smile seemed to say. We'll see.

For the past few days, I have watched Annette trying in vain to waylay him, on the landing, in the drawing–room, at his room door! He foiled all her attempts without even seeming to feel superior about it. She does not know what to do now to entrap him. Yesterday she came out of her room in a bathing–suit she had made herself and pretending that she couldn't fasten the bra, she asked Jean Luze to help her. A friendly tap on the shoulder sent her off with these words: 'There you are.'

I hated him for a moment. I feel as if my pains are to no avail. He is more untouched than ever. His attitude, which has become too correct, is all the more offensive for that fact. He wants to make Annette know that: 'You had me where you wanted for a while but you are not going to catch me again.'

And he is not toying with her either. He has completely wiped out everything from his memory overnight. But what is desire if, once appeased, it does not find the strength to renew itself? How could I bear to see myself repulsed? Could it be that life wanted to spare me up till now by keeping me away from certain disappointing realities? Am I tempting fate by becoming hopelessly involved in an affair which leads nowhere? What I feel for this man has become so central to my existence that I can no longer do without it. Nothing seems to move him. It will drive me mad. Annette allowed Bob to kiss her right in front of him and he did not flinch. He gazed at them with a gentle and disinterested look, a pure angelic look, which was like a slap in the face.

. . . It rained last night. A torrential rain which lasted for four hours. And the weather has not improved since. Heavy, dirty–grey clouds hang in the sky like pieces of rags. We wade about through mud–puddles like pigs. The roads, full of cracks, have been transformed into ponds. The boat, indifferent, carries away its cargo of wood piled up on the wharf. Business is booming in this area. Mr Long, as red as a rooster, is directing operations himself. The peasants look like whipped dogs. They stretch out their hands to be paid, resentfully staring into the distance at the devastated mountain slopes. Huge white blotches spread over the mountains like leprosy. Immense rocks protrude from their flanks like tombs. The peasants are there, dressed in work clothes, barefooted, their halfort around their necks, their faces taut with discontent.

'Our land is ruined,' one of them said. 'We have cut down too many trees.'

'I had said no, I had said no,' cried another. 'We should have stuck together, and refused every proposition. But blacks from the hills never stick together for long. They are weak before the whites and the bourgeois. And now the rains are coming and our lands are ruined. The American is getting rich, and he's not the only one. They are all against us.'

The magistrate and the *préfet* go with Mr Long to the office, a small building with a sign 'Long & Co., Export Corp'. That's where Jean Luze spends his days, hunched over papers. He knows all their secrets. An expert accountant, it's his job and he draws up the figures, his handsome face bent over his ledgers.

Nobody is suspicious of him. He is white. And a white man can only be on Mr Long's side. He listens to them talking. And he learns a lot from them. I am waiting for Jean Luze under the shutters of my window. It is four o'clock, time for him to come home from work. I am holding the book and the paper–cutter that he gave me yesterday with the words:

'You spoil me, I am spoiling you too. No, it's true, you are a great girl. Look, it's from Mexico. It's a dagger. One of the best. Keep it as a souvenir of me.'

'Are you going away?'

'One never knows!'

He is not happy. What can I think of to keep him here? If he goes away, what becomes of me? How can the things around us be changed?

For the first time in my life I want to redouble my efforts for a common goal. I would transform this place and make it into a little bit of the paradise which he longs for.

Translated by Betty Wilson
Extract from *Amour, colère et folie.*

Hilma Contreras

Hilma Contreras was born in San Francisco de Macoris and educated in Paris where she studied French, English, literature and archaeology. She started writing in the 1930s. After her return to Santo Domingo in 1933, her stories were published in various newspapers, especially in La Información *in Santiago and in* Cuadernos Dominicanos de Cultura. *She is said to be the first woman from the Dominican Republic to write short stories. A writer of remarkable poetic resonance, she has published three volumes of short stories:* Cuatro Cuentos *(Four Short Stories, 1953)*, El ojo de Dios *(God's Eye, 1962) and most recently* Entre dos silencios *(Between Two Silences) a collection of 16 short stories from which the present story is taken. She has also published a* novella, La Tierra está bramando *(The Raging Earth: Santo Domingo, Biblioteca Nacional, 1986).*

Impossible to classify, Ms Contreras's talent covers a wide range of themes and styles but she particularly excels at the dramatic, psychological, often tragic, tale. Many of her stories have an urban setting and her language is clear, terse, modern.

The Window

I knew it was bound to happen. For a long time, ancient rumours had led me to live in expectation of it.

'His cassock will catch fire at any moment,' I told myself. And it did begin to smoulder.

The night was as clear as a child's gaze. The four of us on a tiny, silent, floating terrace, the sea wafting over us. We were four women in four towers of air. We could hear music, the music of Liszt and our own, carried in our blood, audible only to our own heartbeats. Occasionally, but very rarely, almost never, someone is curious enough to bend and listen to the music beneath our skin, heard by no-one, and then that person is transfixed, dissolving in the overwhelming harmony.

When the lights went out, the terrace began to float on the immense blue pupil of the night. Notes of music – a sonata – drifted from the room . . .

Suddenly a shaft of light sliced through the air of my tower and I began to sway, my eyes on the verge of shattering with the life they drank from the lighted window.

It was a window cut abruptly in the colonial thickness of the wall, a hole halfway between a window and an inverted skylight, out of which spilled gushing light. There he stood. I had been expecting it, as one expects the inevitable. Unbelievably bare-chested, he came to the window and flexed his muscles.

'Ready?' a man's voice asked from outside.

'Yes,' he replied, 'but wait a minute, it's my hour for loving.'

He turned away. This was his hour, like all the hours of his tonsured life. As though a halo cut in his hair could classify a life; the long life of a hairy-chested man!

His back turned to the window and to destiny, he stretched out his arms. I did not want to probe any further into his sin or into his death. It was bound to happen. The two of us would catch fire.

Emotion made me lower my eyes from his white wound.

The sky trembled. The stars began their slow descent, then gradually accelerated into a headlong plunge, a long, endless rain of stars upon the earth.

Bowing to the inevitable, I closed my eyes, my body pierced with stars. I did not have to look to know that in the window, hanging in the brightly silent air, a cassock whose hour had come was burning red.

A flash of light seared my eyelids.

The blondest of the four of us had lit a cigarette. She was staring down at the grimacing curl of the match between her fingers.

'That's real money,' she said.

But I could only shout.

The window had vanished.

The old colonial house still stood there, in among the mango trees of the garden. But the wall was blind, with no skylight, no uncertain opening.

'It looks like the electricity's gone,' Merilinda commented. 'None of the street-lights is on.'

'What a shame,' I protested. 'It was their owl's eyes which shone on the Father's tonsure.'

'So much the better,' said the woman with the cigarette. 'Now we are really alone.'

Translated by Fernanda Steele
From the collection *Entre dos silencios*.

Rosario Ferré

Rosario Ferré, poet and short story writer, is one of Puerto Rico's best–known writers. Born in Ponce, Puerto Rico, she studied English and Latin American Literature in Puerto Rico and the United States. Ferré founded and directed an important review dedicated to the diffusion of the fledgling Puerto Rican literature, Zona de carga y descarga *(Loading Zone). This story is from 'La Muñeca menor' (The Youngest Doll), the first story in Ferré's first collection* Papeles de Pandora *(Pandora's Papers: 1976), which takes its title from the legendary Greek Pandora, the first woman on earth. The collection includes poetry as well as 14 short stories which cover a variety of themes but take as their starting point an ancient legend that the good and evil from Pandora's box spread through the world in the form of writing. Ferré shows the subtle and devastating power of language and examines the effect of human perversity and passion. Ferré has also written critical studies and children's stories. Her other works include* La mona que le pisaron la cola *(1981) and* El medio pollito *(1978), (both books of fables: Huracán, P.R.),* Los Cuentos de Juan Bobo *(Folk tales about the legendary character, Juan Bobo: Río Piedras, Puerto Rico, Editiones Huracán, 1981),* Fabulas de la garza desangrada *(Tales of the Heron Bled Dry: Mexico, J. Mortiz, 1982)* Sitio a Eros *(a book of feminist essays: Mexico, J. Mortiz, 1982), and* Maldito amor *(Mexico, J. Mortiz, 1986; translation:* Sweet Diamond Dust, *US, Ballantine Press, 1989) a novella followed by three shorter pieces.*

The Youngest Doll

Early in the morning the maiden aunt had taken her rocking chair out onto the porch facing the canefields, as she always did whenever she woke up with the urge to make a doll. As a young woman, she often bathed in the river, but one day when the heavy rains had fed the dragontail current, she had a soft feeling of melting snow in the marrow of her bones. With her head nestled among the black rock's reverberations she could hear the slamming of salty foam on the beach rolled up with the sound of waves, and she suddenly thought that her hair had poured out to sea at last. At that very moment, she felt a sharp bite in her calf. Screaming, she was pulled out of the water, and, writhing in pain, was taken home on a stretcher.

The doctor who examined her assured her it was nothing, that she had probably been bitten by an angry river prawn. But days passed and the scab would not heal. A month later, the doctor concluded that the prawn had worked its way into the soft flesh of her calf and had nestled there to grow. He prescribed a mustard plaster so that the heat would force it out. The aunt spent a whole week with her leg covered with mustard from thigh to ankle, but when the treatment was over, they found that the ulcer had grown even larger and that it was covered with a slimy, stonelike substance that couldn't be removed without endangering the whole leg. She then resigned herself to living with the prawn permanently curled up in her calf.

She had been very beautiful, but the prawn hidden under the long, gauzy folds of her skirt stripped her of all vanity. She locked herself up in her house, refusing to see any suitors. At first she devoted herself entirely to bringing up her sister's children, dragging her monstrous leg around the house quite nimbly. In those days, the family was nearly ruined; they lived surrounded by a past that was breaking up around them with the same impassive musicality with which the dining—room chandelier crumbled on the frayed linen cloth of the dining—room table. Her nieces adored her. She would comb their hair, bathe and feed them and when she read them stories, they would sit around her and furtively lift the starched ruffle of her skirt so as to sniff the aroma of ripe sweetsop that oozed from her leg when it was at rest.

As the girls grew up, the aunt devoted herself to making dolls for them to play with. At first they were just plain dolls, with cotton stuffing from the gourd tree and stray buttons sewn on for eyes. As time passed, though, she began to refine her craft, gaining the respect and admiration of the whole family. The birth of a doll was always cause for a ritual celebration, which explains why it never occurred to the aunt to sell them for profit, even when the girls had grown up and the family was beginning to fall into need. The aunt had continued to increase the size of the dolls so that their height and other measurements conformed to those of each of the girls. There were nine of them, and the aunt would make a doll for each one every year, so it became necessary to set aside a room for the dolls alone. When the eldest turned eighteen, there were one hundred and twenty—six dolls of all ages in the room. Opening the door gave the impression of entering a dovecote, or the ballroom in the Czarina's palace, or a warehouse in which someone had spread out a row of tobacco leaves to dry. But the aunt did not enter the room for any of these pleasures. Instead, she would unlatch the door and gently pick up each doll, murmuring a lullaby as she rocked it: 'This is how you were when you were a year old, this is you at two, and like this at three,' measuring out each year of their lives against the hollow they left in her arms.

The day the eldest turned ten, the aunt sat down in her rocking chair facing the canefields and never got up again. She would rock away entire days on the porch, watching the patterns of rain shift in the canefields, coming out of her stupor only when the doctor paid a visit or whenever she awoke with the desire to make a doll. Then she would call out so that everyone in the house would come and help her. On that day, one could see the hired help making repeated trips to town like cheerful Inca messengers, bringing wax, porcelain, clay, lace, needles, spools of thread of every colour. While these preparations were taking place, the aunt would call the niece she had dreamt about the night before into her room and take her measurements. Then she would make a wax mask of the child's face, covering it with plaster on both sides, like a living face wrapped in two dead ones. Then she would draw out an endless flaxen thread of melted wax through a pinpoint on her chin. The porcelain of the hands and face was always translucent; it had an ivory tint to it that formed a great contrast with the curdled whiteness of the bisque faces. For the body, the aunt would send out to the garden for twenty glossy gourds. She would hold them in one hand, and with an expert twist of her knife, would slice them up against the railing of the balcony, so that the sun and breeze would dry the cottony guano brains out. After a few days, she would scrape off the dried fluff with a teaspoon and, with infinite patience, feed it into the doll's mouth.

The only items the aunt would agree to use that were not made by her were the glass eyeballs. They were mailed to her from Europe in all colours, but the aunt considered them useless until she had left them submerged at the bottom of the stream for a few days, so that they would learn to recognise the slightest stirring of the prawn's antennae. Only then would she carefully rinse them in ammonia water and place them, glossy as gems and nestled in a bed of cotton, at the bottom of one of her Dutch cookie tins. The dolls were always dressed in the same way, even though the girls were growing up. She would dress the younger ones in Swiss embroidery and the older ones in silk guipure, and on each of their heads she would tie the same bow, wide and white and trembling like the breast of a dove.

The girls began to marry and leave home. On their wedding day, the aunt would give each of them their last doll, kissing them on the forehead and telling them with a smile, 'Here is your Easter Sunday.' She would reassure the grooms by explaining to them that the doll was merely a sentimental ornament, of the kind that people used to place on the lid of grand pianos in the old days. From the porch, the aunt would watch the girls walk down the staircase for the last time. They would carry a modest checkered cardboard suitcase in one hand, the other hand slipped around the waist of the exuberant doll made in their image and likeness, still wearing the same old–fashioned kid slippers and gloves, and with Valenciennes bloomers barely showing under their snowy, embroidered skirts. But the hands and faces of these new dolls looked less transparent than those of the old: they had the consistency of skimmed milk. This difference concealed a more subtle one: the wedding doll was never stuffed with cotton but filled with honey.

All the girls had married, and only the youngest niece was left at home when the doctor paid his monthly visit to the aunt, bringing along his son who had just returned from studying medicine up north. The young man lifted the starched ruffle of the aunt's skirt and looked intently at the huge swollen ulcer which oozed a perfumed sperm from the tip of its greenish scales. He pulled out his stethoscope and listened to her carefully. The aunt thought he was listening for the breathing of the prawn to see if it was still alive, and she fondly lifted his hand and placed it on the spot where he could feel the constant movement of the creature's antennae. The young man released the ruffle and looked fixedly at his father.

'You could have cured this from the start,' he told him.

'That's true,' his father answered, 'but I just wanted you to come and see the prawn that had been paying for your education these twenty years.'

From then on it was the young doctor who visited the old aunt every month. His interest in the youngest niece was evident from the start, so the aunt was able to begin her last doll in plenty of time. He would always show up wearing a pair of brightly polished shoes, a starched collar, and an ostentatious tiepin of extravagant poor taste. After examining the aunt, he would sit in the parlour, lean his paper silhouette against the oval frame of the chair and each time hand the youngest an identical bouquet of purple forget–me–nots. She would offer him ginger cookies, taking the bouquet squeamishly with the tips of her fingers, as if she were handling a sea urchin turned inside out. She made up her mind to marry him because she was intrigued by his sleepy profile, and also because she was deathly curious to see what dolphin flesh was like.

On her wedding day, as she was about to leave the house, the youngest was surprised to find that the doll her aunt had given her as a wedding present was warm. As she slipped her arm around its waist, she looked at her curiously, but she quickly forgot about it, so amazed was she at the excellence of its craft. The doll's face and hands were made of the most delicate Mikado porcelain. In the doll's half–open and slightly sad smile, she recognised her full set of baby teeth. There was also another notable detail: the aunt had embedded her diamond eardrops inside the doll's pupils.

The young doctor took her off to live in town, in a square house that made one think of a cement block. Each day he made her sit out on the balcony, so that passers–by would be sure to see that he had married into high society. Motionless inside her cubicle of heat, the youngest began to suspect that it wasn't only her husband's silhouette that was made of paper, but his soul as well. Her suspicions were soon confirmed. One day, he pried out the doll's eyes with the tip of his scalpel and pawned them for a fancy gold pocket–watch with a long, embossed chain. From then on the doll remained seated on the lid of the grand piano, but with her gaze modestly lowered.

A few months later, the doctor noticed the doll was missing from her usual place and asked the youngest what she'd done with it. A sisterhood of pious ladies had offered him a healthy sum for the porcelain hands and face, which they thought would be perfect for the image of the Veronica in the next Lenten procession.

The youngest answered that the ants had at last discovered the doll was filled with honey and, streaming over the piano, had devoured it in a single night.

'Since its hands and face were of Mikado porcelain,' she said, 'they must have thought they were made of sugar, and at this very moment they are most likely wearing down their teeth, gnawing furiously at its fingers and eyelids in some underground burrow.' That night the doctor dug up all the ground around the house, to no avail.

As the years passed, the doctor became a millionaire. He had slowly acquired the whole town as his clientele, people who didn't mind paying exorbitant fees in order to see a genuine member of the extinct sugarcane aristocracy up close. The youngest went on sitting in her rocking chair on the balcony, motionless in her muslin and lace, and always with lowered eyelids. Whenever her husband's patients, draped with neck-laces and feathers and carrying elaborate canes, would seat themselves beside her, shaking their satisfied rolls of flesh with a jingling of coins, they would notice a strange scent that would involuntarily remind them of a slowly oozing sweetsop. They would then feel an uncontrollable urge to rub their hands together as though they were paws.

There was only one thing missing from the doctor's otherwise perfect happiness. He noticed that, although he was aging, the youngest still kept that same firm porcelained skin she had had when he would call on her at the big house on the plantation. One night he decided to go into her bedroom to watch her as she slept. He noticed that her chest wasn't moving. He gently placed his stethoscope over her heart and heard a distant swish of water. Then the doll lifted her eyelids, and out of the empty sockets of her eyes came the frenzied antennae of all those prawns.

Translated by Rosario Ferré and Diana Vélez
From the collection *Papeles de Pandora*.

Magali García Ramis

Magali García Ramis is Professor of Journalism at the University of Puerto Rico. Born in Santurce, Puerto Rico in 1946, Magali García Ramis comes from a very close–knit middle class family. She describes herself as a 'second generation Puerto Rican', (her great–grandparents and two grandparents were originally from Spain). She is single, with a large extended family who are very important to her. Influenced by 'comics, films, especially François Truffaut,' and writers as diverse as Tolstoy, Fuentes, Woolf, Dostoevsky and Vonnegut, her publications include a short story collection, La Familia de todos nosotros *(Our Family: 1976) and a novel,* Felices días, Tio Sergio, *(Happy days, Uncle Sergio: 1986) as well as numerous short stories published in anthologies and magazines in Puerto Rico and the United States. A Guggenheim Fellow, Ms García Ramis is currently working on a second novel,* Las Horas del sur; *a second collection of short stories is also in preparation. The extract which appears here is from her first short story, 'Every Sunday', which won first prize at the Ateneo Puertorriqueño's Annual Contest in 1970.*

Every Sunday

None of us has ever died, so I have to answer no.

'No ma'am no, no—one in my family has died, at least not since I was born.' Her deep black eyes delve into my sleepy gaze. The feeble early morning light filters through the cracks of the hut. *Doña* Amparo closes her eyes again. She is in a trance, I think.

'I see it there, next to you. It's the spirit of a girl who died, you know. She was about eighteen, you know, but I don't know how she died. It's always next to you. You say that no sister of yours has died . . .'

'I have no sisters.'

'Or a girl–friend?'

'I have no girl–friends.'

'It's someone who is very close to you, you know, like from your house.'

Yes, it could be from my house, I think. *Doña* Amparo's constant 'you knows' distract me. She tries to look inside me, to that part of me that not even I know, and I feel myself clamming up.

'I can't see any more. Something is blocking my way. Take three baths and put flowers in the water, you know, so the spirits won't control you.'

So that I don't control myself, yes, yes, ma'am I say to her. I am about to tell her that spirits bore me, but as with many other things, I say it in silence and store it in my memory. I get up from the small wooden bench and make to give her a dollar bill. I try to remember my cousin's instructions: 'You put it in the small can she has on the desk.' *Doña* Amparo looks at me without saying a word and I get nervous. I toss the dollar in the first can I see, without noticing it has water inside.

'No, not there,' she says, alarmed.

I look into the rusty blue can. For a second I see my reflection in the water. I see myself double. My spirit and I, I think, and I smile to myself. I am sorry, I say, and I take out the wet bill and give it to her. Then, I remember that spiritualists are supposed to be able to feel spirit vibrations in water. I'm about to lift the old curtain to leave the room, but she calls out to me once more.

'Listen, be careful, be careful of your house and of things that push like the wind.'

Of my house. So she has looked inside me. No–one pushes me, not even the wind, only I, but it isn't worth explaining to her.

'Yes, yes, OK. Good day and thank you.'

Be careful, always be careful. Be careful of my house. Be careful of the wind. Be careful of the world. Live carefully, keep out of trouble, people repeat every day; that is why they don't understand. Out front a dozen people are waiting their turn. To know what the future will bring. To know if it's worth marrying him although he drinks a lot. And to know who has cast an evil eye on the child. And who the husband's lover is. To know everything that witchcraft has known from time immemorial and mankind has searched for – to know.

The humidity, the tropical humidity, the humidity of December in summer, the morning humidity that announces a sweltering Sunday, runs through the nearby fields and touches my neck and face as I leave *Doña* Amparo, the spiritualist's house. I take a gulp of fresh air. In the distance I see the mountains undressing, taking off the cloak of mist that covered them through the night. My cousins are waiting in the car. They are bursting, with faith and incredulity; hoping that it might be true and doubting if it will be, talking excitedly about what *Doña* Amparo said to them.

'Did you like it?'

'Yes, tell me what she said to you!'

'She told me that everything will come out OK with Jorge! She told me that . . .'

I get comfortable in the back seat. I let them talk. Today is Sunday. I would also let them talk if it were Saturday or Monday. I'm not interested. I only want to get home. Today is Sunday, and every Sunday my family, where no—one dies, gather in their country house, while I, if I don't go to my house, I die of boredom. I hate Sundays, but if it were not for Sundays I would never go to my house. As we drive I'm in a daze as I look at the mountains. Mountains, a mountain, any mountain is the strongest force there is. The wind blows in through the window and kisses my eyes. I look at the mountains again; in a few hours I will be among them.

The sign, the sign of the cross. Everyone makes the sign of the cross. The dark-moustached husband to the tiny wife. The godmother to the godchild. The elder brother to the younger, as he sprinkles holy water over his face. The grandmother to the impatient grandson. The mother to the babe in arms. The entire town, generation upon generation, wet their fingers in the same font of yellowish water and all make the sign of the cross when they leave the old church for the hot Sunday awaiting them outside. And I, as usual, out of habit, as I enter the church that smells of melted wax and small town dust, I too make the sign of the cross.

Next to me, at the door, the idiot makes the sign of the cross, without rhyme or reason. During the entire mass I look at him instead of at the altar. He peers out of the corners of his green, watery eyes at all the church—goers, who shy away from him. He stinks like a chicken, like a chicken house during a drought, from the grime that eats at his clothes. While, from the altar, the American priest, blond and extremely tall like the angels on religious cards, sweats out his *Our Father* in an American accent: *padreí nuestro que estais en lous cielous* . . . the town idiot, maimed from the waist down, staggers towards the corner and scatters holy water and signs of the cross that remain floating in the air.

'Hail Mary . . .' is the first thing I hear when my mind returns to the mass. It is almost over; either the priest is breaking a speed record, or I was distracted by the idiot for a long time. It is better to attend mass in a village church than in the parish church in Santurce, to hear the sermons of the Spanish priest, but today it has gone by so fast!

'For God's sake, child, why didn't you take Holy Communion with the rest of the family?'

This is the first thing I hear when I leave the church. Here comes Aunt Pía with one of her nagging sessions. Her real name is Elena, but I call her Pía for her piety . . .

'Today we all took Holy Communion together because it is your father's name day. Even your younger brother went with him to the altar, but you as always . . .'

And as always, I invent an excuse.

'I forgot we were all going to take Communion and I ate a banana a little while ago . . .'

It's a cheap excuse but she would not understand if I were to tell her that I was looking at the idiot making signs of the cross in the air, because she would say: it's you who are the idiot. I move away from her and greet grandparents, uncles, aunts, everyone. We get into the cars and we go by the cockpit to pick up Papi and Uncle Gustavo. They do not have to go to mass. They are the family heretics, according to Aunt Pía. I would like to be a heretic but I don't dare.

We arrive at the country house. It's Sunday. Everything is familiar to me. My cousins' and brothers' laughter in the yard. The view from the balcony with San Juan tiny in the distance. The smell of rice and chicken, a chicken just killed by Aunt Pía's chubby hands. The rum stink of Uncle Alberto's breath. Grandpa and Grandma's obsessions with mini–skirts. My cousins' gossip about dances and boyfriends. The only thing that changes is the colour. Sundays in the countryside are blue and green or gray and green. Today is a blue and green Sunday.

Translated by Carmen C Esteves
Extract from the collection *La Familia de Todos Nosotros*.

Carmen Lugo Filippi

Carmen Lugo Filippi is Professor of French Language and Literature at the University of Puerto Rico, Río Piedras. She holds a doctorate in Comparative Literature from the University of Toulouse and a Masters in French Literature from Columbia University, New York. Carmen Lugo Filippi has done extensive work in foreign language teaching, literary criticism and women's writing, particularly in Puerto Rico. She is co–author, with Ana Lydia Vega, of Vírgenes y mártires *(Virgins and martyrs: Editorial Antillana, Puerto Rico, 1981), which won the P.E.N. Club of Puerto Rico National Literature Prize (Short Story category) in 1982. She has also published many other short stories in magazines and anthologies including the one here, 'Recetario de incautos' (Recipes for the Gullible), which won first prize in the* Revista Sin Nombre *short story competition.*

Carmen Lugo Filippi is currently working on a comparative study of the modern short story as well as writing a novella. Ms Lugo Filippi's work moves freely from personal, domestic concerns to wider, more general social and cultural issues.

Recipes for the Gullible

> 'I write: more than just singing, I tell stories.'
> GLORIA FUERTES

When she began to rummage through the pile of clippings, five huge cockroaches rushed frantically along the edges of the dusty shelves. How revolting! She would have to fumigate that corner of the storage room at once if she didn't want to be devoured by those proliferating armies. She would happily have started the extermination that very instant, but the urgency of the situation forced her to reconsider: she had to find a recipe that was both exotic and easy to prepare. She was sure that if she examined the clippings and the magazines calmly she would find what she was looking for, she just had to be patient and control her growing anxiety, since, after all, the guests she was expecting that evening were not so important as to warrant such a commotion . . . or were they? She did not want to deceive herself, and knew in fact that she was determined to impress them if it was the last thing she did. She couldn't bear the thought of them finding her not only recently divorced, fat, middle–aged, and, to top it off, with money problems. It was so humiliating to have to face none other than her sister and Paco in such circumstances. She would have to pull herself together and appear happy, jolly as usual; she would conceal her flab with a Playtex girdle and cover up her most obvious wrinkles with Maybelline. She would follow the advice of *Vanidades* for drooping eyes and lids: light eye shadow dusted up towards the brow bone, then a firm line of shadow along the lash line, drawn upward and outward, the eyebrows well arched, and, of course, the magic touch of a bit of eyeliner just below the lashes.

Oh well, Paco himself would be showing some wrinkles and a paunch – eleven years don't go by without a trace – you well remember that Doris loved to cook copious pasta dishes with Parmesan cheese (the perfect diet, according to *Cosmopolitan*, to fatten up even a scarecrow).

You smile as you picture Doris, plump–cheeked and double–chinned, and the thought brings such a great feeling of relief that you return enthusiastically to the recipes you have been collecting for years, in anticipation of occasions like this, or imagining important guests to bewitch with your exquisite cuisine, your impeccably–set table and the melodies of your 'Thousand Violins of Love' softly piercing the semi–darkness of the small living–dining room lit only by two candelabra. There is Paco, smiling nostalgically, looking at you through the tiny wavering flames, softly stroking his moustache:

'I didn't know you could cook so well! How come you never told me?'

At that, you would have to arch your eyebrows higher, lift your chin, lean over slightly and reply with something truly witty:

'I was, am, and always will be full of surprises.'

But no. Perhaps it would be better to smile enigmatically and avoid his gaze; this is no time for regrets over what might have been, as Moneró used to sing in his nasal twang, especially when Doris would be on her guard, like a scorpion with its poisonous sting, ready to charge at the slightest false move. No. It was Doris she would have to impress, to show her that man does not live by lasagna alone; she would have to teach Doris – who after all those years in New Jersey had not learned to prepare a meal worthy of a Hollywood film – that spaghetti and canneloni were commonplace compared to her own dinner worthy of a twilight soap opera.

A prawn cocktail to begin with? It was easy to prepare, if she followed the recipe from that issue of *Good Housekeeping* which offered 'easy dishes for buffet dinners'. She searched avidly through the magazines: the scattered covers offered the promise of uniform variety. Faces, faces and more faces in close–up; perfect oval faces with enormous blue, blue–green, deep–green, hazel or slightly violet eyes.

ARE YOU UNFORGETTABLE?
A MAGIC FORMULA TO LOSE WEIGHT WITHOUT DIETING
TRIUMPH SEXUALLY WITH YOUR HUSBAND
PRINCESS LEE RADZIWILL'S PERFECT DINING ROOM
INSIDE THE DUKE AND DUCHESS OF ALBA'S HOME

The settings of dreams began to appear in the glittering photographs. A growing sense of lassitude forced her to lie down on the drab sofa. All of a sudden she burst into that house of wonders and little by little felt a surprising transformation as the rooms grew larger, the lights brighter, as she discovered – what a wondrous thing! – the cushiony depth of an armchair, the fine carvings of a sideboard, the pure whiteness of embroidered linen draperies, the warm hues of a plush rug . . . She went from one room to the next listening in rapture to the swelling sounds of a regal waltz; she dreamed herself a duchess in this new forest of tapestries inhabited by nymphs pursued by satyrs, winged horses and unicorns; she admired herself in quicksilver mirrors, which, facing each other, multiplied to infinity the misty vases filled to overflowing with so many azaleas, lilies, hydrangeas, heliotropes and roses.

Oh! how she would have liked to prolong indefinitely her giddy wandering among the Limoges porcelain, madly piled on heavy mahogany sideboards, to continue to whirl gracefully around the dusky piano, reflected in melancholic bevelled mirrors, to stroke the velvet cushions, the crystal and the shining silverware, to admire the blackened roasting trays laden with pheasants and quails . . . Yes, she would have loved to return to the dining–room, pausing on the way in the picture gallery, where beautiful harlequins showed off their carnival clothes and timeless still–lifes slept their peaceful siestas. Oh! To be able to reach the Victorian–style dining–table without disturbing that roundly perfect moment in the slightest! She would have sat down discreetly with the condescending amiability, the cool deference of a Parisian model, tinged with a sadness that was skilfully heightened by a dark dress and a seemingly careless hairstyle. She would have been wryly amused by contemplating the extravagant display of silver candelabra and sumptuous china; she would have witnessed the ceremonious procession of trays laden with fowl splendidly dressed in artfully prepared sauces; she would have feasted her eyes on the profiteroles, the pastries, the fillings of truffles and brandy.

But she never reached the table . . . The appalling ventilation forced her to get up; she came out of the dream unwillingly, gathered her bundle of magazines and clippings, and headed for the kitchen. She spread the most appealing recipes on the pink formica top, and painstakingly set

104

herself to read the list of ingredients for succulent sauces. It was like fishing in the troubled waters of thousands of words of all sizes and colours, exotic spices which slid like eels between her busy fingers, fragrant herbs which reminded her, she didn't know why, of the plant–life of distant shores, sensual condiments, the mere sound of which aroused sleepy caliphs and maharajas. Such a lustful profusion of names – tarragonsesamifennaniseturmerawaycardaoregano – struggling to attach themselves to her memory, overwhelmed her, leaving her with the terrible inadequate feeling she had so often felt during the thirty-six years of her life. But no. She had to overcome her foolish inhibitions and dare to explore those foreign aromas, she had to be capable of achieving the subtle nuances of taste, the magic alloy of herbs and spices, the happy delivery of meats dripping with voluptuous nectars. Resolved to take stock of her provisions, she opened the cupboard doors. Her eyes glided in a hopeless pilgrimage past the cans of symmetrically–lined Campbell's soups, past the cans of tomato sauce and beans cooked in water and salt. She turned around, quickly gathered together the magazines, and closing her eyes for an instant, she saw Doris, plump–cheeked and double–chinned, inspecting the freshly–set table with open guile, and Paco, now leaning towards you, softly stroking his moustache – an Arturo–de–Córdoba gesture that still bewitches you – especially as he whispers to you: 'What marvellous succulent beans!'

Suddenly you burst out laughing as you throw the magazines into the bin one by one, repeating to yourself the newly discovered refrain: 'You fool, you perfect fool!'

Translated by Lizabeth Paravisini
From the collection *Vírgenes y mártires*.

Ana Lydia Vega

Ana Lydia Vega was born in Santurce, Puerto Rico in 1946. Currently Professor of French and Caribbean Literature at the University of Puerto Rico, Ana Lydia Vega is also one of Puerto Rico's best-known writers. Educated in Puerto Rico and in France, Vega holds a doctorate in Comparative Literature from the University of Provence. She has written numerous reviews, articles, essays and a foreign language textbook as well as fiction: children's literature, a film script and the short stories for which she is so well known. Vega is fluent in English and French, as well as her native Spanish. Her work is characterised by an innovative and liberating use of language: she mixes metaphors, registers, colloquialisms and classical allusions, slides between linguistic codes, even switches languages mid-sentence, with exciting and challenging effect.

Her works include the prize-winning Vírgines y mártires *(Virgins and Martyrs: Editorial Antillana, Puerto Rico, 1981), co-authored with Carmen Lugo Fillipi which won the P.E.N. Club of Puerto Rico National Literature Prize Short Story category, 1982. Another collection of stories,* Encancaranublado y Otros Cuentos de Naufragio *(Cloud cover and other stories of shipwreck) won the prestigious Casa de las Américas prize in 1982 as well as the P.E.N. Club of Puerto Rico award for 1983. Her short story 'Pasión de Historia' won the Juan Rulfo International Short Fiction Prize in 1984. A third collection of short stories,* Pasión de Historia y Otras Historias de Pasión, *was published in 1987 (Buenos Aires, Argentina, Ediciones de la Flor). In 1985 Vega was named author of the year by the Casa del Autor Puertorriqueño.*

Ana Lydia Vega's works reflect a preoccupation with the struggle for women's rights and human rights in general and a commitment to exposing exploitation and oppression. Her stories also address the question of Puerto Rican and Caribbean cultural identity. With satire, wit and humour, Vega continues to challenge the canon and bring new dimensions to the Caribbean vision.

Cloud Cover Caribbean

September, the *agent provocateur* of hurricanes, has declared war, filling the seas with urchins and men o'war. A suspicious breeze swells the guayabera, makeshift sail for this makeshift vessel. The sky is a conga drum stretched tight for a bembe ceremony.

An ugly thing, this muscled arm of sea that separates Antenor from the pursuit of happiness. Compared to the real dangers lurking, the sharks are no more than a pimple on a mosquito's ass. But Antenor must pull through. This is his second day deep in monotonous waves that seem to roll down from the clouds. Since leaving Haiti he has not sighted so much as a fishing boat. It is like playing the discoverer while secretly wondering if the world really is round. Any minute now, he might reach the edge and plunge headlong into the fabled chasms of the monsters.

The putrid mangos, emblems of diarrhoea and famine, the macoutes' war-cries, the fear, the drought – all are behind him now. Seasickness and the threat of thirst once his meagre water rations run out – this is the here and now. For all the menace, this wretched sea adventure is a pleasure cruise compared to his memories of the island.

Antenor settles in beneath the sky's broiling cauldron. Between the boat's rocking merengue and his own weary body he would have sunk into slumber like an island village, had it not been for the Dominican's shouts. You didn't have to know Spanish to understand that the man was shipwrecked and needed a hand. Antenor helped him aboard as best he could. As he did so, a mocking, derisive spirit, the type that dwell in Caribbean trade winds, blew over the little skiff. It was so violent it nearly tipped the two men overboard. At last they managed to quell it.

'Thanks, brother,' the man from the Dominican Republic said, with a sigh of relief that moved the sail to pity.

The Haitian passed him the canteen, then almost had to tear it from his hands to keep him from gulping it down in one. After exchanging long looks, mutually impermeable words and exhausting gestures, they reached the cheerful conclusion that Miami couldn't be far away. Then each told the other, without either understanding, what he was leaving behind – which was very little – and what he was seeking. They told of the endless pain of being black, Caribbean and poor; of deaths by the score; they cursed clergy, the military and civilians; established an international brotherhood of hunger, a solidarity of dreams. And as Antenor and the Dominican, whose name was Diogenes, a neoclassical baptismal flourish, reached the height of their bilingual ceremony, fresh cries rang out beneath the forbidding vault of the heavens.

The two raised their eyes to the waves, and there descried the kinky hair of a Cuban, bobbing along beside the proverbial plank of the shipwrecked sailor.

'A house full of screaming kids, and now grandma has a baby,' Diogenes frowned. As if he had been born on the Dominican side of the border river, the Haitian understood what he meant. Another passenger: another soul, another stomach, to be exact.

But the Cuban howled so mightily, and was so obviously from Santiago, that they yielded at last and pulled him aboard, muttering a quintessentially Caribbean 'what the fuck' as they did so, and the boat began to rumba.

Despite the urgency of the situation, the Cuban had the good sense to ask: 'Anybody going to Miami?' before he grabbed the Dominican's hesitant hand.

The litany of woes started up again. Diogenes and Carmelo, for such was the name of the restless Cuban, raised an unearthly ruckus. From time to time, Antenor chipped in with a meek '*Mais oui*', or a '*C'est ça*', when the fury of the moment seemed to call for it. But he was beginning to resent the monopoly the language of Cervantes was enjoying in a vessel which, destined for exile or not, was after all sailing under the Haitian flag.

With Diogenes as counterpoint, and with a discreet touch of Haitian maracas for backup, Carmelo related the misadventures which had driven him from the shores of the Greater Antilles.

'I'm telling you, friend, it was work, work, work, day and night, no matter where you turned your head . . .'

'Hey, in Santo Domingo there wasn't any work to be had . . .'

'It was cut that cane, boy, day in, day out.'

'Hey, man, where I'm from they bring in all the madamos from Haiti to do the cutting. The rest of us can lie there and rot for all they care.'

The Haitian twitched. The Dominican had mentioned his half of the island, albeit at supersonic speed. He said nothing. Better not to rib-tickle the boat any further; it was already giddy with the slap happy rocking of the waves.

'I'll tell you, boy, there is always a stirfry of trouble somewhere,' said the Cuban, initiating with this unhappy choice of words a search for food.

In a shoebox inherited from a trashbasket in a rich neighbourhood, Antenor had put some cassava bread, two or three ears of corn, a pack of tobacco and a bottle of rum, staples which he had gathered for the voyage with the greatest of difficulty.

Lest one charitable act overshadow another, he had taken the precaution of sitting on the box. But a specialization in black marketeering had given the Cuban a keenly developed sense of smell.

'Nigger, come up off that box,' he said, eschewing formality and eyeballing the shoebox as if it were the very Ark of the Covenant.

Antenor pretended not to hear, though Carmelo's intentions were plainly polyglot.

'Get your black ass off there, madamo, 'cuz it stinks of rum and tobacco,' Diogenes translated, quickly forgetting the vows of mutual aid spoken with his fellow islander prior to the Cuban's arrival.

Still Antenor played dumb. Our undisputed world record illiteracy rate might pay off here, he thought, assuming the most vacant expression possible in the face of his brothers' demands.

They finally became so impatient and indignant at Antenor's passive resistance that they gave him a tremendous shove that nearly sent him overboard on an underwater excursion. They fell upon the box as they might have upon the fabled Horn of Plenty.

After polishing off the cassava bread and the corn, the two rogues renewed their comparative socio-economic analysis of the Caribbean nations. Carmelo chewed tobacco while Diogenes bent his elbow, relishing the rum as though he were ogling the Statue of Liberty's charms under her threadbare tunic.

'I plan to go into business in Miami,' Carmelo said. 'I have a cousin who started out as a lowly pimp and now has his own . . . well, dating service.'

'The land of opportunity,' the Dominican concurred, his rum–fogged breath hot in the Haitian's face.

Antenor had not let out a peep since the others had put him in quarantine. But his eyes were two black dolls pierced through by enormous needles.

'In Cuba,' Carmelo continued, 'dating services are banned. Tell me, how can a man get on with so many restrictions?'

'Hey, in the Dominican Republic we have so many whores we have to export them,' Diogenes replied with such a loud guffaw that it scared a shark that was trailing like a lit fuse in the water behind the boat.

'*Tout Dominiken se pit*,' Antenor grumbled from his tiny Fort Dimanche, which remark Diogenes fortunately did not hear, immersed as he was in weightier concerns.

'The problem,' Carmelo said, digging deeper, 'is that in Cuba the women think they are equal to men and so they don't want to get out and work the streets.'

'That may be true now, but Cuban women used to put out with the best of them,' his friend said, remembering the internationally famous backsides of the island's beauties.

This nostalgic reference to the Batista era was not to Carmelo's liking, and the drift of the Dominican's conversation was getting under his skin. Out of nowhere he parried with: 'Anyway, how is Santo Domingo looking after the hurricane? People say no–one can see any difference.' He capped his dubious joke with a laugh that could be heard back in Guantanamo.

The Dominican went pale, no mean feat for him, but chose to contain his wrath in deference to the Cuban's formidable biceps, the result no doubt of all that cursed cane–cutting.

Masking his change of mind he reached for the canteen. The sea was in open revolt, the boat rocking like a mambo's hips in a Dambala ceremony. The canteen rolled to Antenor's unfortunate feet. The Dominican lunged for it. Antenor grappled with him. The Cuban smiled, following the struggle with the benign condescension of an adult watching children squabble.

109

A fine rain began to fall. The wind, waves and this great Caribbean brawl in the ill-fated boat rekindled the shark's hopes. Miami was as far off as China.

The Haitian threw the canteen into the water. Sooner die than quench the thirst of a Dominican cur. Diogenes started up, aghast. That's so you'll remember we invaded you three times, Antenor thought, baring his teeth to his fellow islander.

'Trujillo was right,' the Dominican roared as he charged at the Haitian's belly like a raging bull.

The boat was swaying like a saint's day float on the loose. Carmelo finally shrugged off his indifference to warn them: 'Easy does it, gentlemen; c'mon, goddammit, we're going to capsize the boat.'

And capsize it they did, exactly as the future Miami businessman had prophesied. Capsized, soaked by the rain, with wind and thunder for background music and the healthy enthusiasm of the sharks.

But just as our heroic emigrés were about to succumb to the perils of the Bermuda Triangle, there came the rasping wail of a horn, like the chant of a priest at a politician's requiem.

'A boat!' Carmelo shouted, waving his arm wildly in the air like a sadist with a cattle prod.

The three unfortunates joined their voices in a long, shrill, hopeful cry for help.

Some time later, and don't ask me how in hell they kept the sharks at bay – it must have been a miracle jointly organised by the Virgin of Altagracia, the Caridad del Cobre, and the Seven African Powers – they lay exhausted but happy on the deck of the rescue boat. On the deck, that is, of an American boat.

The captain, an Aryan, Apollo-like seadog of ruddy complexion, golden locks and the bluest of eyes, came over for a quick check on the disaster and said: 'Get those niggers down there and let the spiks take care of 'em.' Words which our untutored heroes did not understand as well as our more literate readers will. Whereupon the Caribbean brothers were taken, *sans* tender loving care, down to the ship's hold. There amidst wooden crates and mouldy trunks, they exchanged their first post-wreck glances: a mixture of fright and relief, sautéed in some lightly browned hopes.

Moments later, the Dominican and the Cuban had the pleasure of hearing their mother tongue spoken. A little fractured, but unmistakeable. Even the Haitian welcomed the sound. He seemed to recall it from tenderest childhood, and was beginning to suspect he would hear it for the rest of his days. The parched lips of each of the trio were curving upwards into a smile, when a Puerto Rican voice growled through the gloom: 'If you want to feed your bellies here you're going to have to work, and I mean work. A gringo don't give nothing away. Not to his own mother.' Then a black arm thrust through the crates to hand them dry clothes.

Translated by Mark McCaffrey
From the collection *Encancaranublado y Otros Cuentos de Naufragio.*

ANTIGUA

Jamaica Kincaid

Jamaica Kincaid was born in St John's, Antigua in 1949, and spent her early years there. Her mother, a woman who loved books, came originally from Dominica; her father was a carpenter and joiner. She came to the United States in her teens to continue her education, and worked initially as a freelance writer, publishing articles in the New Yorker, Ms, Rolling Stone *and* The Paris Review. *A staff writer for the* New Yorker *since 1976, she is the author of* At the Bottom of the River *(Picador, 1983), a collection of prose fiction which won the Morton Dawwen Zabel Award of the American Academy and Institute of Arts and Letters, and* Annie John *(Picador, 1985), a novel. Her third book,* A Small Place *(New York, Farrar, Straus, Giroux, 1988) is a witty, provocative, searing critique of her birthplace. She lives in New York with her husband and children.*

There appear to be strong autobiographical elements in her first two books. As the first extract demonstrates, Annie John *is a powerful evocation of the island place, an exploration of the mother–daughter relationship and a celebration of growing up in the Caribbean. In the second extract the surrealist quality is more pronounced. It is also unusual for its positive portrayal of the father figure.*

Marbles

One afternoon, after making some outlandish claim of devotion to my work at school, I told my mother that I was going off to observe or collect – it was all the same to me – one ridiculous thing or other. I was off to see the Red Girl, of course, and I was especially happy to be going on that day because my gift was an unusually beautiful marble – a marble of blue porcelain. I had never seen a marble like it before, and from the time I first saw it I wanted very much to possess it. I had played against the girl to whom it belonged for three days in a row until finally I won all her marbles – thirty–three – except for that one. Then I had to play her and win six games in a row to get the prize – the marble made of blue porcelain. Using the usual slamming–the–gate–and–quietly–creeping–back technique, I dived under the house to retrieve the marble from the special place where I had hidden it. As I came out from under the house, what should I see before me but my mother's two enormous, canvas–clad feet. From the look on my face, she guessed immediately that I was up to something; from the look on her face, I guessed immediately that everything was over. 'What do you have in your hand?' she asked, and I had no choice but to open my hand, revealing the hard–earned prize to her angrier and angrier eyes.

My mother said, 'Marbles? I had heard you played marbles, but I just couldn't believe it. You were not off to look for plants at all, you were off to play marbles.'

'Oh, no,' I said. 'Oh, no.'

'Where are your other marbles?' said my mother. 'If you have one, you have many.'

'Oh, no,' I said. 'Oh, no. I don't have marbles, because I don't play marbles.'

'You keep them under the house,' said my mother, completely ignoring everything I said.

'Oh, no.'

'I am going to find them and throw them into the deep sea,' she said.

My mother now crawled under the house and began a furious and incredible search for my marbles. If she and I had been taking a walk in the Amazon forest, two of my steps equaling one of her strides, and after a while she noticed that I was no longer at her side, her search for me then would have equaled her search for my marbles now. On and on went her search – behind some planks my father had stored years ago for some long–forgotten use; behind some hatboxes that held old Christmas and birthday cards and old letters from my mother's family; tearing apart my neat pile of books, which, if she had opened any one of them, would have revealed to her, stamped on the title page, these words: 'Public Library, Antigua.' Of course, that would have been a whole other story, and I can't say which would have been worse, the stolen books or playing marbles. On it went.

'Where are the marbles?' she asked.

'I don't have any marbles,' I would reply. 'Only this one I found one day as I was crossing the street to school.'

Of course I thought, At any minute I am going to die. For there were the marbles staring right at me, staring right at her. Sometimes her hand was actually resting on them. I had stored them in old cans, though my

113

most valued ones were in an old red leather handbag of hers. There they were at her feet, as she rested for a moment, her heel actually digging into the handbag. My heart could have stopped.

My father came home. My mother postponed the rest of the search. Over supper, which, in spite of everything, I was allowed to eat with them, she told him about the marbles, adding a list of things that seemed as long as two chapters from the Old Testament. I could hardly recognise myself from this list – how horrible I was – though all of it was true. But still. They talked about me as if I weren't there sitting in front of them, as if I had boarded a boat for South America without so much as a goodbye. I couldn't remember my mother's being so angry with me ever before; in the meantime all thoughts of the Red Girl vanished from my mind. Trying then to swallow a piece of bread that I had first softened in gravy, I thought, Well, that's the end of that; if tomorrow I saw that girl on the street, I would just act as if we had never met before, as if her very presence at any time was only an annoyance. As my mother went on to my father in her angry vein, I rearranged my life: Thank God I hadn't abandoned Gwen completely, thank God I was so good at rounders that the girls would be glad to have me head a side again, thank God my breasts hadn't grown and I still needed some tips about them.

Days went by. My mother kept up the search for the marbles. How she would torment me! When I left for school, she saw me out the gate, then watched me until I was a pin on the horizon. When I came home, there she was, waiting for me. Of course, there was no longer any question of going off in the late afternoon for observations and gatherings. Not that I wanted to anyway – all that was finished. But on it would go. She would ask me for the marbles, and in my sweetest voice I would say I didn't have any. Each of us must have secretly vowed to herself not to give in to the other. But then she tried this new tack. She told me this: When she was a girl, it was her duty to accompany her father up to ground on Saturdays. When they got there, her father would check on the plantain and banana trees, the grapefruit and lime and lemon trees, and check the mongoose traps. Before returning they would harvest some food for the family to eat in the coming week: plantains, green figs, grapefruit, limes, lemons, coffee beans, cocoa beans, almonds, nutmegs, cloves, dasheen, cassavas, all depending on what was ripe to be harvested. On one particular day, after they had loaded up the donkeys with the provisions, there was an extra bunch of green figs, and my mother was to carry it on her head. She and her father started off for their home, and as they walked my mother noticed that the bunch of figs grew heavier and heavier – much heavier than any bunch of figs she had ever carried before. She ached, from the top of her neck to the base of her spine. The weight of the green figs caused her to walk slowly, and sometimes she lost sight of her father. She was alone on the road, and she heard all sorts of sounds that she had never heard before and sounds that she could not account for. Full of fright and in pain, she walked into her yard, very glad to get rid of the green figs. She no sooner had taken the load from her head when out of it crawled a very long black snake. She didn't have time to shout, it crawled away so quickly into the bushes. Perhaps from fright, perhaps from the weight of the load she had just gotten rid of, she collapsed.

When my mother came to the end of this story, I thought my heart would break. Here was my mother, a girl then, certainly no older than I, travelling up that road from the ground to her house with a snake on her head. I had seen pictures of her at that age. What a beautiful girl she was! So tall and thin. Long, thick black hair, which she wore in two plaits that hung down past her shoulders. Her back was already curved from not ever standing up straight, even though she got repeated warnings. She was so shy that she never smiled enough for you to see her teeth, and if she ever burst out laughing she would instantly cover her mouth with her hands. She always obeyed her mother, and her sister worshipped her. She, in turn, worshipped her brother, John, and when he died of something the doctor knew nothing about, of something the obeah woman knew everything about, my mother refused food for a week. Oh, to think of a dangerous, horrible black snake on top of that beautiful head; to think of those beautifully arched, pink–soled feet (the feet of which mine were an exact replica, as hers were an exact replica of her mother's) stumbling on the stony, uneven road, the weight of snake and green figs too much for that small back. If only I had been there, I would not have hesitated for even a part of a second to take her place. How I would have loved my mother if I had known her then. To have been the same age as someone so beautiful, someone who even then loved books, someone who threw stones at monkeys in the forest! What I wouldn't have done for her. Nothing would ever be too much. And so, feeling such love and such pity for this girl standing in front of me, I was on the verge of giving to my mother my entire collection of marbles. She wanted them so badly. What could some marbles matter? A snake had sat on her head for miles as she walked home. The words, 'The marbles are in the corner over there' were on the very tip of my tongue, when I heard my mother, her voice warm and soft and treacherous, say to me,

'Well, Little Miss, where are your marbles?' Summoning my own warm, soft, and newly acquired treacherous voice, I said, 'I don't have any marbles. I have never played marbles, you know.'

Extract from *Annie John*.

At the Bottom of the River

Look! A man steps out of bed, a good half hour after his wife, and washes himself. He sits down on a chair and at a table that he made with his own hands (the tips of his fingers are stained a thin chocolate brown from nicotine). His wife places before him a bowl of porridge, some cheese, some bread that has been buttered, two boiled eggs, a large cup of tea. He eats. The goats, the sheep, the cows are driven to pasture. A dog barks. His child now enters the room. Walking over, she bends to kiss his hand, which is resting on his knee, and he, waiting for her head to come up, kisses her on the forehead with lips he has purposely moistened. 'Sir, it is wet,' she says. And he laughs at her as she dries her forehead with the back of her hand. Now, clasping his wife to him, he bids her goodbye, opens the door, and stops. For what does he stop? What does he see? He sees before him himself, standing in sawdust, measuring a hole, just dug, in the ground, putting decorative grooves in a banister, erecting columns, carving the head of a cherub over a door, lighting a cigarette, pursing his lips, holding newly planed wood at an angle and looking at it with one eye closed; standing with both hands in his pockets, the thumbs out, and rocking back and forth on his heels, he surveys a small accomplishment – a last nail driven in just so. Crossing and recrossing the threshold, he watches the sun, a violent red, set on the horizon, he hears the birds fly home, he sees the insects dancing in the last warmth of the day's light, he hears himself sing out loud:

> *Now the day is over,*
> *Night is drawing nigh;*
> *Shadows of the evening*
> *Steal across the sky*

All this he sees (and hears). And who is this man, really? So solitary, his eyes sometimes aglow, his heart beating at an abnormal rate with a joy

116

he cannot identify or explain. What is the virtue in him? And then again, what can it matter? For tomorrow the oak will be felled, the trestle will break, the cow's hooves will be made into glue.

But so he stands, forever, crossing and recrossing the threshold, his head lifted up, held aloft and stiff with vanity; then his eyes shift and he sees and he sees, and he is weighed down. First lifted up, then weighed down – always he is so. Shall he seek comfort now? And in what? He seeks out the living fossils. There is the shell of the pearly nautilus lying amidst coloured chalk and powdered ink and India rubber in an old tin can, in memory of a day spent blissfully at the sea. The flatworm is now a parasite. Reflect. There is the earth, its surface apparently stilled, its atmosphere hospitable. And yet here stand pile upon pile of rocks of an enormous size, riven and worn down from the pressure of the great seas, now receded. And here the large veins of gold, the bubbling sulfurous fountains, the mountains covered with hot lava; at the bottom of some caves lies the black dust, and below that rich clay sediment, and trapped between the layers are filaments of winged beasts and remnants of invertebrates. 'And where shall I be?' asks this man. Then he says, 'My body, my soul.' But quickly he averts his eyes and feels himself now, hands pressed tightly against his chest. He is standing on the threshold once again, and, looking up, he sees his wife holding out toward him his brown felt hat (he had forgotten it); his child crossing the street, joining the throng of children on their way to school, a mixture of broken sentences, mispronounced words, laughter, budding malice, and energy abundant. He looks at the house he has built with his own hands, the books he has read standing on shelves, the fruit–bearing trees that he nursed from seedlings, the larder filled with food that he has provided. He shifts the weight of his body from one foot to the other, in uncertainty but also weighing, weighing . . . He imagines that in one hand he holds emptiness and yearning and in the other desire fulfilled. He thinks of tenderness and love and faith and hope and, yes, goodness. He contemplates the beauty in the common thing: the sun rising up out of the huge, shimmering expanse of water that is the sea; it rises up each day as if made anew, as if for the first time. 'Sing again. Sing now,' he says in his heart, for he feels the cool breeze at the back of his neck. But again and again he feels the futility in all that. For stretching out before him is a silence so dreadful, a vastness, its length and breadth and depth immeasurable. Nothing.

◆

Is life, then, a violent burst of light, like flint struck sharply in the dark? If so, I must continually strive to exist between the day and the day. I see myself as I was as a child. How much I was loved and how much I loved. No small turn of my head, no wrinkle on my brow, no parting of my lips is lost to me. How much I loved myself and how much I was loved by my mother. My mother made up elaborate tales of the origins of ordinary food, just so that I would eat it. My mother sat on some stone steps, her voluminous skirt draped in folds and falling down between her parted legs, and I, playing some distance away, glanced over my shoulder and saw her face – a face that was to me of such wondrous beauty: the lips like a moon in its first and last quarter, a nose with a bony bridge and wide nostrils that flared out and trembled visibly in excitement, ears the lobes of which were large and soft and silk–like; and what pleasure it gave me to press them between my thumb and forefinger. How I worshipped this beauty, and in my childish heart I would always say to it, 'Yes, yes, yes.' And, glancing over my shoulder, yet again I would silently send to her words of love and adoration, and I would receive from her, in turn and in silence, words of love and adoration. Once, I stood on a platform with three dozen girls, arranged in rows of twelve, all wearing identical white linen dresses with corded sashes of green tied around the waist, all with faces the colour of stones found lying on the beach of volcanic islands, singing with the utmost earnestness, in as nearly perfect a harmony as could be managed, minds blank of interpretation:

> *In our deep vaulted cell*
> *The charm we'll prepare*
> *Too dreadful a practice*
> *For this open air.*

Time and time again, I am filled up with all that I thought life might be – glorious moment upon glorious moment of contentment and joy and love running into each other and forming an extraordinary chain: a hymn sung in rounds. Oh, the fields in which I have walked and gazed and gazed at the small cuplike flowers, in wanton hues of red and gold and blue, swaying in the day breeze, and from which I had no trouble tearing myself away, since their end was unknown to me.

I walked to the mouth of the river, and it was then still in the old place near the lime–tree grove. The water was clear and still. I looked in, and at the bottom of the river I could see a house, and it was a house of only one room, with an A–shaped roof. The house was made of rough, heavy planks of unpainted wood, and the roof was of galvanised iron and was painted red. The house had four windows on each of its four sides, and one door. Though the door and the windows were all open, I could not see anything inside and I had no desire to see what was inside. All around the house was a wide stretch of green – green grass freshly mowed a uniform length. The green, green grass of uniform length extended from the house for a distance. I could not measure or know just from looking at it. Beyond the green, green grass were lots of pebbles, and they were a white–gray, as if they had been in water for many years and then placed in the sun to dry. They, too, were of a uniform size, and as they lay together they seemed to form a direct contrast to the grass. Then, at the line where the grass ended and the pebbles began, there were flowers: yellow and blue irises, red poppies, daffodils, marigolds. They grew as if wild, intertwined, as if no hand had ever offered guidance or restraint. There were no other living things in the water – no birds, no vertebrates or invertebrates, no fragile insects – and even though the water flowed in the natural way of a river, none of the things that I could see at the bottom moved. The grass, in little wisps, didn't bend slightly; the petals of the flowers didn't tremble. Everything was so true, though – that is, true to itself – and I had no doubt that the things I saw were themselves and not resemblances or representatives. The grass was the grass, and it was the grass without qualification. The green of the grass was green, and I knew it to be so and not partially green, or a kind of green, but green, and the green from which all other greens might come. And it was so with everything else that lay so still at the bottom of the river. It all lay there not like a picture but like a true thing and a different kind of true thing: one that I had never known before. Then I noticed something new: it was the way everything lit up. It was as if the sun shone not from where I stood but from a place way beyond and beneath the ground of the grass and the pebbles. How strange the light was, how it filled up everything, and yet nothing cast a shadow. I looked and looked at what was before me in wonderment and curiosity. What should this mean to me? And what should I do on knowing its meaning? A woman now appeared at the one door. She wore no clothes. Her hair was long and so very black, and it stood out in a straight line away from her head, as if she had commanded it to be that way. I could not see her face. I could see her feet, and I saw that her insteps were high, as if she had been used to climbing high mountains. Her skin was the color of brown clay, and she looked like a statue, liquid and gleaming, just before it is to be put in a kiln. She walked toward the place where the grass ended and the pebbles began. Perhaps it was a great distance, it took such a long time, and yet she never tired. When she got to the place where the green grass ended and the pebbles began, she stopped, then raised her right hand to her forehead, as if to guard her eyes against a far–off glare. She stood on tiptoe, her body swaying from side to side, and she looked at something that was far, far away from where she stood. I got down on my knees and I looked, too. It was a long time before I could see what it was that she saw.

I saw a world in which the sun and the moon shone at the same time. They appeared in a way I had never seen before: the sun was The Sun, a creation of Benevolence and Purpose and not a star among many stars, with a predictable cycle and a predictable end; the moon, too, was The Moon, and it was the creation of Beauty and Purpose and not a body subject to a theory of planetary evolution. The sun and the moon shone uniformly onto everything. Together, they made up the light, and the light fell on everything, and everything seemed transparent, as if the light went through each thing, so that nothing could be hidden. The light shone and shone and fell and fell, but there were no shadows. In this world, on this terrain, there was no day and there was no night. And there were no seasons, and so no storms or cold from which to take shelter. And in this world were many things blessed with unquestionable truth and purpose and beauty. There were steep mountains, there were valleys, there were seas, there were plains of grass, there were deserts, there were rivers, there were forests, there were vertebrates and invertebrates, there were mammals, there were reptiles, there were creatures of the dry land and the water, and there were birds. And they lived in this world not yet divided, not yet examined, not yet numbered, and not yet dead. I looked at this world as it revealed itself to me – how new, how new – and I longed to go there.

◆

I stood up on the edge of the basin and felt myself move. But what self? For I had no feet, or hands, or head, or heart. It was as if those things – my feet, my hands, my head, my heart – having once been there, were now stripped away, as if I had been dipped again and again, over and over, in a large vat filled with some precious elements and were now reduced to something I yet had no name for. I had no name for the thing I had become, so new was it to me, except that I did not exist in pain or pleasure, east or west or north or south, or up or down, or past or present or future, or real or not real. I stood as if I were a prism, many–sided and transparent, refracting and reflecting light as it reached me, light that never could be destroyed. And how beautiful I became. Yet this beauty was not in the way of an ancient city seen after many centuries in ruins, or a woman who has just brushed her hair, or a man who searches for a treasure, or a child who cries immediately on being born, or an apple just picked standing alone on a gleaming white plate, or tiny beads of water left over from a sudden downpour of rain, perhaps – hanging delicately from the bare limbs of trees – or the sound the hummingbird makes with its wings as it propels itself through the earthly air.

Yet what was that light in which I stood? How singly then will the heart desire and pursue the small glowing thing resting in the distance, surrounded by darkness; how, then, if on conquering the distance the heart embraces the small glowing thing until heart and glowing thing are indistinguishable and in this way the darkness is made less? For now a door might suddenly be pushed open and the morning light might rush in, revealing to me creation and a force whose nature is implacable, unmindful of any of the individual needs of existence, and without knowledge of future or past. I might then come to believe in a being whose impartiality I cannot now or ever fully understand and accept. I ask, When shall I, too, be extinguished, so that I cannot be recognised even from my bones? I covet the rocks and the mountains their silence. And so, emerging from my pit, the one I sealed up securely, the one to which I have consigned all my deeds that I care not to reveal – emerging from this pit, I step into a room and I see that the lamp is lit. In the light of the lamp, I see some books, I see a chair, I see a table, I see a pen; I see a bowl of ripe fruit, a bottle of milk, a flute made of wood, the clothes that I will wear. And as I see these things in the light of the lamp, all perishable and transient, how bound up I know I am to all that is human endeavour, to all that is past and to all that shall be, to all that shall be lost and leave no trace. I claim these things then – mine – and now feel myself grow solid and complete, my name filling up my mouth.

Extracts from *At the Bottom of the River*.

GUADELOUPE

Maryse Condé

Maryse Condé was born in Guadeloupe, where she now resides, but has spent long periods in West Africa, in France and more recently in the United States. She studied in Paris and earned a doctorate in comparative literature from the Sorbonne in 1975. A novelist, playwright, critic and scholar, her works have been published extensively in translation as well as in the original French.

Maryse Condé's work ranges widely in subject matter, historical period and geographical setting. Her novels include Heremakhonon *(1976),* Une Saison à Rihata *(Paris, Laffont, 1981) and the monumental works:* Segou I *(1984) and* Segou II *(1985), set against the background of an ancient African kingdom in the nineteenth century.* Segou *was on the best-seller list in France for several weeks.* Moi, Tituba, sorcière . . . Noire de Salem *(I, Tituba, Black Witch of Salem, 1986), the fictional reconstruction of the life of a black woman burnt as a witch in Salem, Massachusetts, in the eighteenth century, won the Grand Prix Littéraire de la Femme. In her latest novel,* La vie scélérate *(1987), Condé writes the saga of a Guadeloupean family over several generations. She has also written short stories, including the collection* Pays Mêlé *(1985).*

Maryse Condé's talent as a storyteller combines with a keen sense of irony, a skill for meticulous historical documentation and a gift for evoking place and character, to make her one of the most important contemporary writers from the French Caribbean. Maryse Condé is married to Richard Philcox, a professional translator, who has done the English translations of several of her works, including the novel, A Season in Rihata, *from which this extract is taken. In the novel, Marie–Hélène, a Guadeloupean living in virtual exile in the sleepy African town of Rihata with Zek, her African husband, and their six daughters, becomes caught up in a personal and political conflict which centres around Madou, Zek's younger brother. Maryse Condé paints a vivid picture of destructive personal relationships against the backdrop of a fictitious African state, torn by intrigue, corruption and power struggles. The birth of Marie–Hélène's baby, a boy, seems to signal a change in family fortunes, but perhaps it is too late both for the couple and their community.*

Elikia

It was almost eleven when Marie–Hélène left the maternity ward and began pacing the grounds with her new–born son in her arms. Zek had promised to be there at nine, but his lateness, which in other circumstances would have exasperated her, left her indifferent. She did not pay any attention to the baby either. Usually she adored the moment when she finally took possession of her child. Up until that time the nurses, the paediatricians, the orderlies and the auxiliaries had come between the two of them. Suddenly they were alone, recalling those long months they had been together without ever seeing each other. That morning she could only think of Madou. She had only learned of the attack from Zek the day before and had remained stupefied. Madou hurt, Madou in a coma – she could not believe it. He was there a few steps away in that modest ward and she could not go to him. She regretted their last incomplete meetings during which nothing had been said. Unfinished words. Embarrassed looks. Memories withheld. She refused to think he could die. Yet she surprised herself as she sifted through her memories like a miser counting his wealth. Memories which she had resolutely put out of her mind came flooding back.

When they had lived in N'Daru, they had taken advantage of Zek being away one weekend and had gone to the beach at Prahima. Oh, it had been nothing compared to the beaches in Guadeloupe! A meagre fringe of coconut palms crowned the dun–coloured dunes, covered with the remains of fish. Yet the sea had been wonderful. If you looked at it long enough it slowly lost its pale, slight anaemic blue and turned green. And then an islet rose up out of the spray.

The motor launch had been called *Espère–en–Dieu* but she had forgotten the name of the fisherman who had, amid much swearing, ferried them across. Their mother had never accompanied them. Official reason: she was a child from the hills and was afraid of the sea. Their father had never accompanied them either. Official reason: business. So they would set off with three servants and Pierre, as naked as a little satyr. One of Siméon's sisters had lived there with a dozen chickens, as many rabbits and a dog called Balika. It was the only time they could escape from the Des Ruisseaux. Aunt Coralie, whom everyone called Man Keleman, had a large bosom in her loose–fitting dress and could not speak French. She treated her nieces like little princesses. Yes, in Prahima she had relived the delights of childhood.

When Madou took her by the hand she felt she was capable of loving this land and putting down roots. She felt bitter now when she thought of what it could have been like and what Zek had not bothered to achieve.

Madou between life and death. Did she still love him? Why bother to ask? She had been happy with him, because of him, even if for the others her happiness had been a crime. It was unthinkable that he would die, that they would never see each other again and put right those last meetings. She was reminded of the baby by a weak gurgle and stroked his tiny fist. She asked him to forgive her for being so distant. They had a whole lifetime to get acquainted and to love each other. It was possible that Madou, who was lying in that small pavilion, did not have much longer to live.

They had often used to go to the cinema, too. The films were not much and she could not remember any of them. But she had loved the ride through the town in its nocturnal frenzy. Hoodlums transformed by the night crowded in front of the discos; perverse yet childlike prostitutes wiggled inelegantly on the pavements, turning their painted faces towards the light of the bars. They had held hands with the innocence of children.

All these moments she had tried to forget were flooding back. He must not die. No, he must not die.

At that moment she saw Zek coming towards her followed by two of the beggars who frequented the neighbourhood of the hospital. He stopped to get rid of them by throwing them a few rais and, once again, she thought how much of the pharisee he had about him: 'God, I thank thee that I am more generous than other men.'

Where had it led them, his generosity? Come now, she was not going to sink into self–pity. She held it against Zek for being so naively happy to have a son and imagining that a male baby would wipe away years of misunderstanding, sulking and failure to communicate. She blamed him for feeling so little grief at Madou's attack and secretly considering it a just revenge of fate.

In fact, Zek was torn between conflicting feelings. Although the attack proved that nobody was invincible and had given Madou a good lesson, he did not want the outcome to prove fatal. What about his plans for the future? The visit to the *marabout* had cost him thirty thousand rais, part of which he had borrowed from his mother. Now that he had a son, he would have to change his life and make something of himself. He remembered how proud and happy he had felt when at every ceremony he had looked at his father, sitting in the front row of dignitaries, draped in a heavy woven toga with a chieftain's sandals on his feet. Founder of the first planters' union in the country, perhaps in all West Africa. And yet illiterate! Having all his correspondence written by a young primary–school teacher. What sort of mettle had the man been made of? He had listened in earnest to the applicants who constantly filed into his compound. At mealtimes there had been no counting the number of parasites who appeared from every corner of the village and made the women grumble. He should have lived then. When a man relied on his personal assets and not on intrigues, relations or his wife's family connections with Toumany. This brought him back to Madou. No, he certainly did not feel happy about his condition. He did not want him to die. God forbid the thought. But he was not unhappy to see him learn at his own expense that the regime was hated throughout the country. There was not a word of truth in the official version of this counter-revolutionary plot designed to block the Government's process of liberalisation. Liberalisation or hoax?

He walked towards Marie–Hélène thinking how lovely she was with her figure back to normal; how attractive women were when they breast–feed. Whether she liked it or not she was his wife and nothing would prevent him this evening from reminding her of it. Besides, he knew her well enough to know she would not need reminding. He took the baby in his arms and to annoy her, said jokingly: 'I'm sorry, Muti I was held up at the office.'

How poignant! Marie–Hélène realised in amazement that the attack on Madou gave Rihata a fairground atmosphere. Never had there been so many people strolling the streets or sitting on the terraces of the two or three cafés. Small–time traders took advantage of this unexpected tourist boom to sell local crafts: river clay statuettes, reed mats and rafia tapestries, while the Lebanese traders put on show all the bric–a–brac and stuff they had trouble selling. Suddenly Zek put his hand on hers. 'There is one visit we have to make this afternoon. His wife is here with his mother–in–law.'

For a moment, Marie–Hélène did not understand. She had never thought of Mwika, Madou's wife, since he himself seemed to attach so little importance to her. Suddenly she came to life. But curiously Marie–Hélène felt no jealousy towards this unknown girl who was young enough to be her daughter, and whom fate had dealt such a hard blow. What did she know of her husband's past? Probably nothing.

The children were waiting impatiently in the garden for their darling little brother whom only Christophe and Sia had been able to see at the hospital. But they were beaten to it by Sokambi who had abandoned her daily job of dyeing *pagnes* and was dressed in a sumptuous costume to welcome her first grandson. What was this power the birth of a male child had over these people? Marie–Hélène, who was only sporadically possessive, delivered up Elikia to his grandmother. The neighbours were already coming to the gate, anxious to welcome this seventh child, first son, who would surely have a brilliant future. A future minister? Why not a future president? They peered into his adorable little face as he lay fast asleep.

Once all the customary compliments had been made, the guests turned to the subject of conversation that could be heard all over town: the attack on the Minister. Zek noted with some annoyance that nobody contested the official version, the counter–revolutionary plot, and Madou from his bed took on the figure of a liberator and martyr. Régis Antoine, who up until then had ridiculed the pseudo–reconciliation, vehemently defended it. Who, until Madou, had bothered to moderate the whims of Toumany and introduce a little humanity and justice in his behaviour? Nobody, nobody. What about the opposition? They were made up of exiles who sat drinking in their Paris homes before going out to dance with local blondes. The assembly joined in unison. How illogical they were! Zek was tempted to reply that, if Madou were the victim of counter–revolutionaries bent on blocking liberalisation, it was very surprising that only progressives were being arrested who should be only too glad that things were opening up, and probably felt the changes were not fast enough. Then he decided against it. What would be the use? How easy it was to become a hero! All you had to do was die. With the bullets of a madman lodged in his body, Madou no longer represented the arrogance and arbitrariness of a hated regime. He had been given a new face. New features. Zek realised in disgust that whatever he did his brother would always be the winner. If he recovered from his wounds the whole country would persuade Toumany to propel him to the very top – unless he became peeved with his right–hand man's popularity and had him shot. Zek who had never had a head for politics, started imagining a thousand complex possible outcomes.

In the meantime, Marie–Hélène climbed the stairs turning her back on the noisy assembly of visitors. In her opinion, all the events of African community life were devoid of meaning and paid lip–service to a past of which nothing was left. She was bored to death. The same greetings were recited every time. The same exclamations were made. The same jokes repeated. The same gestures. She knew nobody was shocked by her behaviour any more. For years they had been used to the strange habits of the 'foreigner'. In her room she scrutinised herself in the old wardrobe mirror. Still too much fat around her middle and thighs, but that would soon go. How wrinkled her hands were! And her neck had started to be the same. She could still make an impression. But she would shortly be one of those old wrecks about whom people would say, 'My God, she must have been lovely.'

The poison of old age was circulating in her veins.

If Madou died she would have no chance of leaving Rihata before it was too late, before her finest years had flown. Suddenly she began turning his attractive offer over in her mind, yet she was afraid it might be an act of pity. Zek, commercial attaché! She had no inclination to go back to Paris, but she had nothing against London, Montreal and New York, especially New York. They would be close to black people, close to their tragedies and mediocre victories. Olnel used to describe the city, and closing her eyes believed she was there. Harlem, the bleeding heart, the humiliated heart.

Then she regretted the selfish turn her thoughts were taking while Madou was dying. She had not prayed for years. She had not even prayed at Delphine's death. So how could she find the words now?

When there was a knock on the door she knew it was Christophe. She guessed what he must be thinking. Wouldn't this new–born son subtly remind Zek that Christophe was merely an illegitimate child admitted to the family out of indulgence? Perhaps soon made to feel out of place? She knew Zek well enough to know that such thoughts would never cross his mind. Christophe was his child, the only one he had chosen to have. He had been the first to love him and nothing was going to change that.

Translated by Richard Philcox
Extract from *A Season in Rihata*.

Simone Schwarz–Bart

Best known for her novel Pluie et vent sur Télumée Miracle *(Paris, Editions du Seuil, 1972; translation:* The Bridge of Beyond, *Heinemann, 1982), Simone Schwarz–Bart is also author of several other works. With her husband, the Jewish writer André Schwarz–Bart, she wrote the very moving* Un Plat de porc aux bananes vertes *(Pork and Plantain: Editions du Seuil, 1967). She has also written the narrative/mythical,* Ti–Jean l'horizon *(Editions du Seuil, 1983), and most recently, a play –* Mon beau capitaine.

Born in France in 1938, Simone Schwarz–Bart went back to Guadeloupe with her mother at the age of three. Like many other writers of her generation she studied in France and lived abroad, in Europe and in Africa, for many years. However, her subjects and preoccupations remained firmly rooted in the Caribbean. Simone Schwarz–Bart's novels are complex, rich in images and noted for the poetic quality of their prose. The creole voice with which she evokes landscape, character and the isolated world of rural Guadeloupe is striking. Schwarz–Bart's female characters achieve a mythic level of spiritual marronage *and attest to their author's belief in the resilience and defiance of Caribbean people.*

Queen Without A Name

Woe to him who laughs once and gets into the habit, for the wickedness of life is limitless: if it gives you your heart's desire with one hand, it is only to trample on you with both feet and let loose on you that madwoman bad luck, who seizes and rends you and scatters your flesh to the crows.

Eloisine and Meranee, twins, were ten years old when luck forsook their mother Toussine. A school had just opened in the village, and a teacher came twice a week to teach the children their letters in exchange for a few pennyworth of foodstuff. One evening as they were learning their alphabet, Meranee said her sister had all the light and told her to move the lamp to the middle of the table. And so just one little word gave bad luck an opening. 'Have it all, then!' said Eloisine, giving the light an angry shove. It was over in an instant: the china lamp was in pieces and the burning oil was spreading all over Meranee's legs and shoulders and hair. A living torch flew out into the darkness, and the evening breeze howled around it, fanning the flames. Toussine caught up a blanket and ran after the child, shouting to her to stand still, but she rushed madly hither and thither, leaving a luminous track behind her like a falling star. In the end she collapsed, and Toussine wrapped her in the blanket, picked her up, and went back toward the house, which was still burning. Jeremiah comforted Eloisine, and they all sat in the middle of their beautiful path, on the damp grass of evening, watching their sweat, their life, their joy, go up in flames. A big crowd had gathered: the Negroes stood their fascinated, dazzled by the magnitude of the disaster. They stared at the flames lighting up the sky, shifting from foot to foot, in two minds – they felt an impulse to pity, and yet saw the catastrophe as poetic justice. It made them forget their own fate and compare the cruelty of this misfortune with the ordinariness of their own. At any rate, it's one thing that won't happen to us, they said.

Meranee's suffering was terrible. Her body was one great wound attracting more and more flies as it decayed. Toussine, her eyes empty of all expression, fanned them away, put on soothing oil, and grew hoarse calling on death, which, being no doubt occupied elsewhere, refused to come. If anyone offered to replace Toussine at the bedside for a while, she would say, smiling gently: 'Don't worry about me. However heavy a woman's breasts, her chest is always strong enough to carry them.' She spent seventeen days and seventeen nights cajoling death, and then, ill luck having gone elsewhere, Meranee expired. Life went on as before, but without one vestige of heart left, like a flea feasting on your last drop of blood, delighting in leaving you senseless and sore, cursing heaven and earth and the womb that conceived you.

Against sorrow and the vanity of things, there is and will always be human fantasy. It was thanks to the fantasy of a white man that Toussine and Jeremiah found a roof. He was a Creole called Colbert Lanony, who in the old days just after the abolition of slavery had fallen in love with a strange and fascinating young Negress. Cast out by his own people, he had sought refuge in a desolate and inaccessible wasteland far from the eyes that looked askance at his love. Nothing remained of all that now but some fine blocks of stone mouldering away in the wilderness, colonnades, worm–eaten ceilings, and tiles bearing witness still to the past and to an outlawed white man's fancy for a Negress. To those who were surprised to find a house like that in such a place, the local people got into the habit of saying, 'It's L'Abandonnée', and the name later came to be used for the hamlet itself. Only one room on the first floor was habitable, a sort of closet, where the window openings were covered with sheets of cardboard. When it rained the water trickled through a hole in the roof into a bucket, and at night the ground floor was the resort of toads, frogs, and bats. But none of this seemed to bother Toussine, who had gone to live there like a body without a soul, indifferent to such details. As was the custom, she was visited there the first nine evenings by all the people of the village, who came to pay their respects to the dead and to keep the living company. Toussine did not weep or complain, but sat upright on a bench in a corner as if every breath of air were poison. People did not want to desert a ship like Toussine, but the sight of her was so unbearable they cut the ceremony short, just coming in, greeting her, and leaving, full of pitying kindness, thinking she was lost forever.

The leaf that falls into the pond does not rot the same day, and Toussine's sorrow only grew worse with time, fulfilling all the gloomy predictions. At first Jeremiah still went to sea three times a week, but then only twice, then once, then not at all. The house looked as deserted as ever, as if there were no one living there. Toussine never left the room with the cardboard windows, and Jeremiah collected their food from the woods around – purslane, scurvy grass, pink makanga bananas. Before, the women going to market used to take a path that led by the ruined house; it was a shortcut to the main road and Basse–Terre, where they sold their wares. But now they were afraid, and they made a big detour through the forest rather than go near the pig–headed Toussine, who didn't speak, wouldn't even answer, but just sat staring into space, a bag of bones as good as dead. Every so often, when the conversation came around to her and Jeremiah and little Eloisine, a man would shin up a tree, peer towards the house, and report that it was still the same; nothing had changed, nothing had moved.

Three years went by before people began to talk about them again. As usual, a man climbed a tree and looked towards the ruins; but this time he didn't say anything, and showed no sign of coming down. When questioned he only signed for someone else to come up and look. It was the second man who announced that Toussine, the little stranded boat, the woman thought to be lost forever, had come out of her cardboard tower and was taking a little walk outside in the sun.

Glad as they were at this news, the Negroes still waited, hesitating to rejoice outright until the kid was safely caught and tethered and they were sure they hadn't sharpened their knives for nothing. And as they looked, this is what they saw: Toussine was cutting down the weeds around the ruined house. She shivered a moment, went in, then came out again almost at once and began to cut down brushwood and scrub with the furious energy of a woman with something urgent to do and not a minute to lose.

From that day on the place began to be a little less desolate and the market women went back to using the shortcut to Basse–Terre. Toussine had taken her family into prison with her, and now she brought them back to life again. First Eloisine was seen in the village again, as slight and brittle as a straw. Next poor Jeremiah came down to the beach, filled his eyes with the sea and stood staring, fascinated, then went back smiling up the hill as in the days when the song of the waves sounded in his head. It could be seen plainly written across his brow that he would go back to sea again. Toussine put curtains up at the windows, and planted Indian poppies around the ruin, Angola peas, root vegetables, and clumps of Congo cane for Eloisine. And then one day she planted the pip of a hummingbird orange. But the Negroes did not rejoice yet. They still watched and waited, from a distance. They thought of the old Toussine, in rags, and compared her with the Toussine of today – not a woman, for what is a woman? Nothing at all, they said, whereas Toussine was a bit of the world, a whole country, a plume of a Negress, the ship, sail, and wind, for she had not made a habit of sorrow. Then Toussine's belly swelled and burst and the child was called Victory. And then the Negroes did rejoice. On the day of the christening they came to Toussine and said:

'In the days of your silks and jewels we called you Queen Toussine. We were not far wrong, for you are truly a queen. But now, with your Victory, you may boast that you have put us in a quandary. We have tried and tried to think of a name for you, but in vain, for there isn't one that will do. And so from now on we shall call you "Queen Without a Name!"'

And they ate, drank, and were merry, and from that day forth my grandmother was called the Queen Without a Name.

Queen Without a Name went on living in L'Abandonnée with her two daughters, Eloisine and my mother, Victory, until my grandfather died. Then, when her daughters came to have the wombs of women, she left them to steer the course of their lives under their own sail. She wanted to go away from the house where her fisher husband had loved and cherished her and kept her safe in her affliction, when her hair was unkempt and her dress in rags. She longed for solitude, so she had a little hut built in a place called Fond–Zombi, which was said to be very wild. An old childhood friend of hers, a famous witch called Ma Cia, lived nearby, and Toussine hoped she would put her in touch with Jeremiah. So Toussine lived in the woods and came very seldom to L'Abandonnée.

◆

Mama Victory was a laundress, wearing out her wrists on the flat stones in the rivers, and her linen emerged like new from under the heavy waxed irons. Every Friday she would go down the old path of the market women to the main road, where a horse–drawn cart had left a huge bundle of washing for her to collect. She would hoist it onto her head, climb up to L'Abandonnée, and as soon as she got there start washing the clothes, singing as she worked. All the time she was washing, drying, starching, and ironing she would go on singing. For whole afternoons she would work away at a table set up under a mango tree, singing like a happy magpie. As they passed by on their way to the road her neighbours would often call: 'You're so slight you'll work your innards out, heaving those heavy irons.' Then her eyes would smile shyly and she would answer: 'A small axe cuts down a big tree, and we'll manage, please God.' My sister Regina and I, frisking about under her feet, would hear her say to herself afterwards: 'Suffering brings scorn. Better to be envied than pitied. Sing, Victory, sing!' And she would go on with her song.

We lived outside the village on a kind of plateau overhanging the first houses. Our mother was not the sort of woman to unpack her heart everywhere: she looked on human speech as a loaded gun, and, to use her own expression, talking often felt to her like an issue of blood. She would sing, say a few words about the dead, those imprinted on her eyes as a child, and that was all. Our thirst for the present remained unsatisfied. So in the afternoon, when the air grew like limpid water, my sister Regina and I would take ourselves off to the broad terrace surrounding Monsieur Tertullien's pit, where all the local cocks fought on Sundays. Monsieur Tertullien also kept a small bar, and people used to gather on his veranda with glasses of rum and absinthe, laughing and squabbling and speaking ill of those they thought could not stand up for themselves. One day as we were there picking up tittle-tattle as usual, we heard them talking about our mother. Victory had no status and no ornament in this world – not so much as a pair of earrings, only a couple of bastards. So why did she avoid them all as if they were a pack of lepers? The words seemed to bury themselves in the depths of the earth, like a lost seed with no hope of sprouting: everyone scratched idly and cracked the joints of their fingers, tired even before they had opened their mouths. Then, with visible reluctance, the oldest inhabitant opened his lips and said very slowly: 'Why won't you people ever admit it? Everyone lives at a certain height above the ground – it's in the blood. The Lougandors have always liked to fly high, grow wings, raise themselves up. And', he concluded decisively, 'Victory still hasn't even reached her true height.' And then, noticing we were there, the oldest inhabitant coughed and smiled shyly at us, and the conversation shifted to other things. Back home, when we tried to question our mother, we got the same mysterious answer we always got:

'They can say whatever they like. Some people can't sleep easy unless they've spoken ill of someone else. But I am what I am, just at my right height, and I don't go begging in the streets to fill your bellies'.

◆

Queen Without a Name had not been too pleased with the way her daughter was steering her boat on the waters of life. But when Haut–Colbi came to live in our tower she began to think Victory wasn't such a bad sailor after all. To those who criticised her daughter's conduct she would say in a soft, amused voice: 'My friends, life is not all meat soup, and for a long time yet men will know the same moon and the same sun and suffer the same pangs of love.' In fact, she was overjoyed at the mere idea of having my innocence cast a halo around her white hair, and when she came to fetch me she went away from L'Abandonnée blessing my mother.

It was the first time I'd been away from home, but I wasn't at all upset. On the contrary, I felt a kind of excitement, going along the white chalky road bordered with filaos with a grandmother whose earthly existence I'd thought was over. We walked in silence, slowly, my grandmother so as to save her breath and I so as not to break the spell. Towards the middle of the day we left the little white road to its struggle against the sun, and turned off into a beaten track all red and cracked with drought. Then we came to a floating bridge over a strange river where huge locust trees grew along the banks, plunging everything into an eternal blue semidarkness. My grandmother, bending over her small charge, breathed contentment: 'Keep it up, my little poppet, we're at the Bridge of Beyond.' And taking me by one hand and holding on with the other to the rusty cable, she led me slowly across that deathtrap of disintegrating planks with the river boiling below. And suddenly we were on the other bank. Beyond: the landscape of Fond–Zombi unfolded before my eyes, a fantastic plain with bluff after bluff, field after field stretching into the distance, up to the gash in the sky that was the mountain itself, Balata Bel Bois. Little houses could be seen scattered about, either huddled together around a common yard or closed in on their own solitude, given over to themselves, to the mystery of the forest, to spirits, and to the grace of God.

Queen Without a Name's cabin was the last in the village; it marked the end of the world of human beings and looked as if it were leaning against the mountain. Queen Without a Name opened the door and ushered me into the one little room. As soon as I crossed the threshold I felt as if I were in a fortress, safe from everything known and unknown, under the protection of my grandmother's great full skirt. We had left L'Abandonnée in the early morning and now the evening mist was about to descend. Grandmother lit a lamp that hung from the main beam of the ceiling, turned down the wick to save oil, gave me a furtive kiss as if by chance, and took me by the hand to introduce me to her pig, her three rabbits, her hens, and the path that led to the river. Then, as the mist had fallen, we went back indoors.

In the cabin there was an iron bedstead covered with the poor man's sheet – four flour bags with the print still showing despite much washing. The bed alone took up half the available space. The other half contained a table, two chairs, and a rocker of plain unvarnished wood. Grandmother opened a can and took out two manioc cookies. Then, to wash all that dryness down, we sipped water out of the earthenware jar that occupied a place of honour in the middle of the table. By the faint light of the lamp I plucked up courage to look at Grandmother, to look her in the face for the first time directly and without disguise. Queen Without a Name was dressed in 'mammy' style with a head scarf. It was drawn tight over her brow and fell down her back in three narrow, nonchalant points. She had an almost triangular face, a finely drawn mouth, a short, straight, regular nose, and black eyes that were faded like a garment too often exposed to sun and rain. She was tall and gaunt though almost unbent; her feet and hands were particularly thin. She sat up proud and straight in her rocker looking me over thoroughly as I examined her. Under that distant, calm, happy look of hers, the room seemed suddenly immense, and I sensed there were others there for whom Queen Without a Name was examining me, then kissing me with little sighs of contentment. We were not merely two living beings in a cabin in the middle of the night, but, it seemed to me, something different, something much more, though I did not know what. Finally she whispered dreamily, as much to herself as to me: 'I thought my luck was dead, but today I see I was born a lucky Negress and shall die one.'

Such was my first evening in Fond–Zombi, and the night was dreamless, for I had already dreamed in broad daylight.

Grandmother was past the age for bending over the white man's earth, binding canes, weeding and hoeing, withstanding the wind, and pickling her body in the sun as she had done all her life. It was her turn to be an elder; the level of her life had fallen; it was now a thin trickle flowing slowly among the rocks, just a little stirring every day, a little effort and a little reward. She had her garden, her pig, her rabbits, and her hens. She made manioc cookies on a tin sheet, coconut cakes and barley sugar, and crystallised sweet potatoes, sorrel, and 'forbidden fruit', which she took every morning to Old Abel, whose shop was next to our house. I helped her as best I could: I fetched water, ran after the pig and the hens, ran after the hairy–shelled land crabs, so delicious salted, ran after weeds with the 'little bands' of other children in the canefields belonging to the factory, ran with my little load of fertiliser, ran all the time with something on my head – the drum of water, the weed basket, the box of fertiliser that burned my eyes at every gust of wind or trickled down my face in the rain, while I dug my toes into the ground, especially on the slopes, so as not to drop the box and my day's pay with it.

Sometimes there would be the sound of singing somewhere; a painful music would invade my breast, and a cloud seemed to come between sky and earth, covering the green of the trees, the yellow of the roads, and the black of human skins with a thin layer of grey dust. It happened mostly by the river on Sunday morning while Queen Without a Name was doing her washing: the women around about would start to laugh, laugh in a particular way, just with their mouths and teeth, as if they were coughing. As the linen flew the women hissed with venomous words, life turned to water and mockery, and all Fond–Zombi seemed to splash and writhe and swirl in the dirty water amid spurts of diaphanous foam. One of them, a lady by the name of Vitaline Brindosier, old, round, and fat, with snow–white hair and eyes full of innocence, had a special talent for upsetting people. When souls were heavy and everything proclaimed the futility of the black man's existence, Madame Brindosier would flap her arms triumphantly, like wings, and declare that life was a torn garment, an old rag beyond all mending. Then, beside herself with delight, laughing, waving her fine round arms, she would add in a bittersweet voice: 'Yes, we Negroes of Guadeloupe really are flat on our bellies!' And then the other women would join in with that strange laugh of the mouth and teeth, a kind of little cough, and suddenly darkness would descend on me and I would wonder if I hadn't been put on earth by mistake. Then I would hear Queen Without a Name whispering into my ear: 'Come away, Telumee, as fast as you can. They're only big whales left high and dry by the sea, and if the little fish listen to them, why, they'll lose their fins!' With the washing heaped on our heads and my grandmother leaning on my shoulder, we would leave the river and go slowly back to her little cabin. Sometimes she would stop, perspiring, by the side of the road, and look at me with amusement. 'Telumee, my little crystal glass', she would say thought-fully, 'there are three paths that are bad for a man to take: to see the beauty of the world and call it ugly, to get up early to do what is impossible, and to let oneself get carried away by dreams – for whoever dreams becomes the victim of his own dream'. Then she would set off again, already murmuring a song, some beguine from the old days to which she would give a special inflection, a sort of veiled irony, the object of which was to convey to me that certain words were null and void, all very well to listen to but better forgotten. Then I'd shut my eyes and grip Grandmother's hand, and tell myself it had to exist, some way of dealing with the life Negroes bear so as not to feel it pressing down on one's shoulders day after day, hour after hour, second after second.

When we got home we would spread the linen out on the nearby bushes and that would be the end of the day. It was the moment when the breeze rose and climbed gently up the hill, filled with all the scents it had picked up on the way. Grandmother settled herself in her rocker in the doorway, drew me beside her, up against her skirts, and, sighing with pleasure at every movement of her fingers, peacefully set about doing my braids. In her hands the metal comb scratched nothing but the air. She moistened each lock with a drop of carapate oil to make it smooth and shiny, and, deft as a seamstress, separated strands, arranged them in little bunches and then in stiff plaits that she pinned up all over my head. And, only stopping to scratch her neck or shoulder blade or an ear that irritated her, she would give a delicate rendering of slow mazurkas, waltzes, and beguines, as sweet as syrup, for, with her, happiness expressed itself in melancholy. She sang 'Yaya', 'Ti–Rose Congo', 'Agoulou', 'Trouble Brought on Yourself', and many other splendid things from the old days, many of the lovely forgotten things that no longer charm the ear of the living. She knew old slave songs, too, and I used to wonder why, as she murmured those, Grandmother handled my hair even more gently than before, as if they turned her fingers liquid with pity. When she sang ordinary songs, Queen Without a Name's voice was like her face, where the cheekbones were the only two patches of light. But for the slave songs her pure voice detached itself from her old woman's face, soaring up into amplitude and depth, and reaching distant realms unknown to Fond–Zombi, so that I wondered if Queen Without a Name, too, had not come down on earth by mistake. I listened to the heartrending voice, to its mysterious appeal, and the waters of my mind began to be troubled, especially when Grandmother sang:

> Mama where is where is where is Idahe
> She is sold and sent away Idahe
> She is sold and sent away Idahe.

Then Grandmother would bend down and stroke my hair and say something kind about it, though she knew very well it was shorter and more tangled than it should be. And I always loved to hear her compliments, and as I leaned, sighing, against her stomach, she would put her hand under my chin, look into my eyes, and say, with an expression of astonishment:

'Telumee, little crystal glass, what have you got inside that body of yours to make an old Negress's heart dance like this?'

Translated by Barbara Bray
Extract from *The Bridge of Beyond.*

Myriam Warner-Vieyra

Myriam Warner–Vieyra, from Guadeloupe, has lived in Senegal for many years. Widow of the late Paulin Vieyra, the well-known film producer and critic, Myriam Warner-Vieyra has three children. She is a librarian and researcher at the University of Dakar, Senegal.

Myriam Warner–Vieyra's novels portray the predicament of the West Indian heroine whose attempts to find happiness and self-fulfilment are constantly thwarted. This is the story of the protagonist of Le Quimboiseur l'avait dit *(Paris, Présence Africaine, 1980, translation:* As the Sorcerer Said, *Longman, 1985) set in Paris, and* Juletane *(Présence Africaine, 1982, translation: Heinemann, 1987) set in West Africa. Her most recent work,* Femmes Echouées, *(Broken Women, Présence Africaine, 1988) a collection of nine Caribbean short stories, continues to reflect Warner–Vieyra's gently ironic, somewhat pessimistic vision.*

Juletane

Thursday, August 24, 1961, 1.00 p.m.

Despite a very restless night, I feel fine today. I stayed in bed till lunch time. Ndeye and Mamadou have not come back yet. The radio is broadcasting the speech made by the head of government, from the holy city. I catch words: national effort, development, first four year plan, etc. Why does Awa turn the radio up so loud? Especially to listen to a speech she cannot understand a word of, since her French never got beyond her first few scarcely intelligible efforts . . . I go and search the living–room, hoping to find something to read. Apart from Ndeye's rosewater literature, there is the national daily from the previous day. I flick through the adventures of Kouan Ndoye 'The treasure of the Mossi', by Buster Diouf. Nothing of any substance. I go back to my room and pick up the notebook which is on my bed. I open it and allow the past to surge up in a flood of memories . . .

The day I arrived in the country, nothing happened the way I had imagined it would. I was not coldly received by the family, quite the opposite. As soon as we had disembarked, a whole crowd of aunts, cousins, sisters, and even my rival, took me by the hand and kissed me. The women were all talking at once. The national language mingled with French. One of the aunts tapped me on the cheek, showering me with what were certainly words of welcome. I didn't understand a single word and contented myself with smiling. I lost Mamadou in the crowd. We were reunited half an hour later. After a twenty minute ride in an old black taxi with hard seats, we reached Thirty–third Street, Uncle Alassane's house, where we were to live. The women took charge of me.

For a moment I managed to forget my troubles. All around me there were nothing but smiling faces. I forced myself to smile with everyone too. Refreshments were served. I greeted any number of children of neighbours, of relatives, more or less distant, who had come to welcome us.

The local Imam took both my hands, palms upraised, recited a few verses of the Koran and, to my great astonishment, spat in my hands, which I passed over my face, as the other women did. About two hours after our arrival, the meal was served: a delicious dish of rice and fish, with *diwunor*, a sort of melted butter. The one that I had eaten in Paris, at friends, resembled it only very distantly. Seated around the bowl I could dissect my rival at leisure. She put the best pieces before me, smiling at me so insistently that I wondered if it were from kindness or from mockery. In any case I decided on a truce, especially since, having refused the spoon I was offered, I had to concentrate on making little balls of rice which I then put into my mouth, like the others. Although my desire to leave was very strong I had to yield to the reality that it was not going to be a simple matter. In fact, the expenses of our journey had swallowed up almost all our savings. We had just enough money to live very frugally until Mamadou found a job.

After we had eaten, I was able to see Mamadou alone, in the little room which we had been given. Once more I tried very calmly to bring up the subject of our separation, because for me that was the only real solution. I did not want half a husband, neither did I want to take a little girl's father away from her. Mamadou refused to see my point of view.

'You are making a mountain out of something insignificant . . . I was forced to marry Awa because the family had arranged it from when I was very young. The only woman that I chose, that I love, is you . . . My one concern is to find a job and a place to live as quickly as possible. Everything else is secondary.'

When this long tirade was over, far from being reassured, I wondered what love meant for Mamadou. I could not understand that he could have married someone simply to please his family . . . I did not want to

138

believe that he had the dishonesty not to tell me before our marriage and, now, the audacity to be surprised that I should refuse to accept a situation that I had not chosen.

After eight days of this ambiguity, Uncle Alassane, with whom we were living, had a talk with Mamadou and communicated to him the decisions and wishes of the family: they would accept my coming most willingly, but on no account would they agree to a separation from Awa who had waited for him faithfully for five years. Awa had gone back home to her native village, to Mamadou's parents' house, where she had been living since her marriage. From the next weekend on Mamadou would have to go to her. Mamadou told me that he had no choice, and that if we refused we would be ostracised by the whole community, that it would be impossible for us to live in the country and that he had absolutely no intention of going to live anywhere else. So, he proposed that I should agree until he got a job and a place for us to live; then he would find a reason to break with Awa. In short, I was to accept having a husband for five days, since Awa agreed to have him on weekends in the village. It seemed to me that I was on another planet, for I no longer understood what was going on around me, what was being said. As far as I was concerned, a husband was above all the most intimate of beings, another self, not an object to be lent or shared.

In a week Mamadou became a different person, a stranger I had just met. I no longer understood his reactions. I was choking with anguish and with unprecedented rage. He remained very calm, happy to be alive, to have come back home to his country and his friends. He would carry on conversations for hours in his native language, with no regard for me. We had to pay a great number of visits to friends and relatives. Whenever we went out he would introduce me, then forget me in a corner, like some discarded object, surrounded by a group of women who were smiling and kind, but who spoke no French. I saw him at a distance, chatting with the men. Neither could I understand this sort of segregation where women seemed to have no importance in a man's life, except for his pleasure or as the mother of children. They were not companions and confidantes. An aura of mystery surrounded the affairs of the husband who, as sole master, made all the decisions without ever worrying about the wishes and desires of the women. The wives, ignorant of their husband's real financial means, spent their time vying with each other as to the number of outfits and jewels they had, the messenger's wife wanting to have as many as the director's. This sometimes created tragic situations when at the end of a month a husband found himself with debts which far exceeded his total salary.

139

Constantly tense, on edge, I had no appetite. The delicious midday rice and fish, with daily repetition, no longer tasted as it had the first day. The smell of it nauseated me. I was losing weight, my skirts, which now were too big, made me look like a scarecrow. So when it was time for Mamadou's first weekend with Awa I was in a sorry state, physically and mentally. I tried to accept it, telling myself that in any case it was all over between us; that as soon as I had the chance I would go back to France. I would get a divorce. However it was too much for me to bear. I remained locked in our room without eating or drinking. Mamadou did not come back on Sunday evening as expected, he arrived on Monday at lunchtime, looking happy.

'Awa sends her regards, the family too,' he said, smiling.

'You can do without giving me a message like that,' I replied.

In spite of all my resolutions I was dying of jealousy. I could not keep myself from thinking of Mamadou with another woman as a sacrilege. Mamadou my only treasure, my most precious possession! When I married him, it was more than a husband, it was a whole family that I had found. He had become the father who had died too soon, the friend whom I had always dreamed of. I had never kept anything about myself from him; even my present pain and sorrow, I did not have the decency to hide from him.

The second weekend, my anguish was so acute that I lost all notion of time. Today, I can remember nothing, it is as if I was unconscious for two days.

The third weekend when Mamadou left for Awa's, his uncle took me to the hospital. I was deeply depressed, really raving or to use the doctor's expression I suffered 'fits of delirium'. I do not know what happened to me. I vaguely remember being overcome with a sudden, desperate rage during the night between Sunday evening and Monday morning. I began breaking everything in my room and banging my head against the walls. I did not come to my senses completely until four days later in the hospital. Aunt Khady, Uncle Alassane's wife was standing next to my bed. She explained to me as best she could, with lots of gesticulating, what I was doing there. It was a Thursday. I had been in a semi-conscious state for four days, probably because of the injections I had been given to calm me. I felt good, my mad rage had given me relief, the rest-cure had done me good. Mamadou arrived. His presence irritated me. I could not understand how the man I had loved, that I still loved, had in so short a time become this stranger. For a year we had been together and he had never mentioned his first family, nor this child who was his daughter. Why? What I blamed him for most of all was that he had hidden the truth from me. He had not shouldered his responsibilities and then he had waited for the family and Uncle Alassane to make all the decisions. What a pathetic case! Or was I the one who was being unreasonable? I was surprised at the behaviour of the people around me. The very ground seemed to be crumbling under my feet, I was struggling in a strange, irrational world.

I wonder if it was a good thing to have started this diary, to be trying to remember a past more filled with sorrows than with joys; to dwell on a present built on troubles, on solitude, despair and on a vague feeling of acceptance of a numb existence to which the regrets and resentments of the past have given way? Stirring up all that, isn't it provoking a sleeping tiger?

Ndeye's laughter and raucous, unpleasant voice bring me back to everyday reality. She is back from her visit to the Marabout; Mamadou and two colleagues who travelled with them are back as well. They are in the drawing room. I hear the clinking of glasses which Ndeye is taking from the sideboard. In spite of the household's financial difficulties there is always enough to buy beer, Ndeye's favourite drink, and Mamadou's whisky. Mamadou's two colleagues won't leave until the bottle of Scotch is empty. Ndeye, for once very astute, divides a new bottle in two or three and never gives those two a full bottle, since she knows their practices very well. Yet they have just celebrated *Maouloud* meditating and reciting the holy Koran. Apparently they are good Moslems; at home, they keep no alcohol, so as not to shock their families; besides, it is more economical to drink at someone else's house. Mamadou, who is more candid in this matter, buys his whisky and drinks it openly in his own house. At his parents' I suspect he is just as hypocritical. Yes, everything is a show, the essential is to appear rich, generous, temperate, a good Moslem, open and honest, a good husband. Meanwhile you are stone broke, selfish, alcoholic, lying, you never take care of your children and you neglect your wives. Only the latest wife counts, the empty-headed creature whom you call a modern woman, whom you shower with jewels. I hear snatches of their conversation. Mamadou says he is thinking of going to France for his next leave with Ndeye who is dying to see Paris. I can't hear what the others say. All the same I wonder where he thinks he will get the money for this trip. As for me, I never dream of Paris or anywhere else any more. I have buried once and for all everything that goes on outside this house. My life unfolds in a room five paces by four and under the mango tree in the yard where I eat my meals. Once more the radio is blaring – this time the eight o'clock news. I exchange my newspaper for my bed. No shower, no dinner either, as long as the visitors are in the house – I don't remember if Mamadou asked me to do that, I think I decided on it on my own – except when it comes to Ndeye's friends who always sit under my window in the courtyard and who disturb me with their gossip. Then I do my best to scandalise them.

The more Helene read the more she felt drawn towards this woman. She felt her suffering and the difference between them. She was sure she could never love a man to the point where she lost her reason over him. Her love affair in Paris, when she was twenty, had proved to be a real vaccination, which protected her perfectly against falling in love.

At the time she had believed a fellow countryman's declarations of love. He had formally asked for her hand in marriage. They had even exchanged letters with their respective families. Their parents had arranged a big dinner party back home in honour of their engagement. Helene was in her second year at the school of social work in Paris and Hector in his third year of medical school. They had agreed to wait two years before marrying, long enough to allow Helene to finish her studies and to work for a year in order to save something towards setting up house. The two years went by quickly and uneventfully.

Two months before the wedding day Hector had sent his best friend to announce to Helene that he had been married the previous day to a French girl who was expecting his child. He had not wanted to tell her because he wanted to save them both from a painful scene. To top it all off, he had the nerve to say that the marriage was a matter of honour and that he still loved her.

Helene had forced herself to keep her dignity, to hold her head high and not to cry in front of his friend. She looked at him with contempt. 'The hypocritical little black, full of complexes, who thinks by marrying a white woman he is acquiring a passport to success!' she thought to herself. 'And isn't it a matter of honour when you have been engaged to a childhood sweetheart for two years?'

When Hector's friend departed, Helene had locked herself in her room for two days with her grief; weeping, moaning, cursing Hector, giving full vent to her disappointment. When she managed to compose herself, her mind was made up. A woman could live by herself. She had sworn never again to suffer because of a man. She made a bonfire in her bathroom sink with Hector's letters and photos and barricaded her heart with a block of ice. She asked to be transferred overseas. Since then she had worked in several African countries. She had set out to pay Hector back through every man she met. She would use them for a while, then as soon as they seemed to be becoming involved, she would stop seeing them without any explanation. She had agreed to marry Ousmane because she wanted a child and because in accordance with her old–fashioned ideas, she preferred the child to be born in a legitimate union. One thing for sure, she thought, she would never put up with any infidelity on Ousmane's part.

Helene lit another cigarette. She had started smoking to look emancipated and liberated and had acquired a taste for it. Now she smoked two packets a day. She intended to stop one of these days, it was the only concession she would make to Ousmane, who did not smoke. She went to the kitchen to pour herself a whisky on the rocks. Her parents had been scandalised, the last time she was home on holiday, because she preferred to have whisky rather than their delicately—flavoured little punches.

She had seen Hector again for the first time since their broken engagement. He had settled in their homeland and had a successful medical practice. She had accepted an invitation to dinner at his house out of curiosity, to see the kind of woman he had preferred to her. He had introduced her as a childhood friend, without mentioning their previous relationship.

Hector's wife was a small blonde, dumpy, faded, dressed like a scarecrow, without charm; she seemed much older than her years. She did not work but looked after her home and her six children. She fussed constantly after her offspring who were particularly turbulent and indisciplined.

He told Helene, as he took her back home, how much he regretted not having married her. His life, it appeared, was a living hell. Helene had burst out laughing. No, there was no way Hector could move her, she had her block of ice firmly in place around her heart. She had told him about her life in Africa, free, pleasant and with no ties. Then to amuse herself, she had excited him. They made love in the car, on the beach. Skilfully she had managed to keep him with her until the small hours of the morning so as to infuriate his good wife, and then left him sheepish and drained. She had accepted an invitation to see him again a few days later, but had not gone. She had not seen him again during her stay on the island.

Smiling at the memory of the trick she had played on Hector, Helene went to lie down, fully dressed, her glass near at hand, and buried herself once more in her young compatriot's diary.

Translated by Betty Wilson
Extract from *Juletane*.

DOMINICA

Jean Rhys

Jean Rhys was born in Dominica in the 1890s and came to England when she was 16. After attending drama school, she drifted into a series of jobs – chorus girl, mannequin, artist's model. In 1917 she met Jean Lenglet, a half–Dutch, half–French writer, whom she married in 1919. They lived in various European capitals until 1923 when he was arrested and went to prison. Rhys began her writing career at this time, assisted by Ford Madox–Ford with whom she became 'involved'. Their affair ended in 1927, just about when her husband came out of prison. Jonathan Cape published The Left Bank *(short stories) in that year and she went to England to try to find a publisher for her first novel,* Quartet, *her marriage to Lenglet having ended. In England she met a literary agent, Leslie Tilden Smith, who was to become her second husband. (She lived with him from 1929, marrying him in 1934; he died in 1945.)*

Between 1928 and 1939 she produced most of her work: After Leaving Mr Mackenzie *(Cape, 1930),* Voyage in the Dark *(Constable, 1934), and* Good Morning, Midnight *(Constable, 1939), short stories and autobiographical reminiscences and, according to at least one of her biographers, a first draft of* Wide Sargasso Sea. *She returned with Tilden Smith to Dominica in 1936, a trip thought by some to have been important in her eventual writing – or rewriting? – of* Wide Sargasso Sea. *After the publication of* Good Morning Midnight *in 1939, Rhys slipped almost completely out of sight and was generally thought to have died. In fact she had continued to write and in 1947 had married Max Hamer, Leslie Tilden Smith's cousin. In 1966 she made a dramatic re–appearance with the publication of* Wide Sargasso Sea *by André Deutsch, who reissued all her novels between 1967 and 1973. They were also republished in paperback by* Penguin. Wide Sargasso Sea *won the Royal Society Award and the W.H. Smith Award. In 1978 she received the CBE. Two collections of her short stories,* Tigers are Better Looking *and* Sleep It Off, Lady, *were published by Deutsch in 1968 and 1976. A third,* Tales of The Wide Caribbean *(Heinemann) came out in 1985. She died in 1979 at the age of 84.*

I Used to Live Here Once

She was standing by the river looking at the stepping stones and remembering each one. There was the round unsteady stone, the pointed one, the flat one in the middle – the safe stone where you could stand and look round. The next wasn't so safe for when the river was full the water flowed over it and even when it showed dry it was slippery. But after that it was easy and soon she was standing on the other side.

The road was much wider than it used to be but the work had been done carelessly. The felled trees had not been cleared away and the bushes looked trampled. Yet it was the same road and she walked along feeling extraordinarily happy.

It was a fine day, a blue day. The only thing was that the sky had a glassy look that she didn't remember. That was the only word she could think of. Glassy. She turned the corner, saw that what had been the old pavé had been taken up, and there too the road was much wider, but it had the same unfinished look.

She came to the worn stone steps that led up to the house and her heart began to beat. The screw pine was gone, so was the mock summer house called the ajoupa, but the clove tree was still there and at the top of the steps the rough lawn stretched away, just as she remembered it. She stopped and looked towards the house that had been added to and painted white. It was strange to see a car standing in front of it.

There were two children under the big mango tree, a boy and a little girl, and she waved to them and called 'Hello' but they didn't answer her or turn their heads. Very fair children, as Europeans born in the West Indies so often are: as if the white blood is asserting itself against all odds.

The grass was yellow in the hot sunlight as she walked towards them. When she was quite close she called again, shyly: 'Hello.' Then, 'I used to live here once,' she said.

Still they didn't answer. When she said for the third time 'Hello' she was quite near them. Her arms went out instinctively with the longing to touch them.

It was the boy who turned. His grey eyes looked straight into hers. His expression didn't change. He said: 'Hasn't it gone cold all of a sudden. D'you notice? Let's go in.'

'Yes let's,' said the girl.

Her arms fell to her sides as she watched them running across the grass to the house. That was the first time she knew.

From the anthology *Tales of the Wide Caribbean*.

Let Them Call it Jazz

I don't want more wine. I want to go to bed early because I must think. I must think about money. It's true I don't care for it. Even when somebody steal my savings – this happen soon after I get to the Notting Hill house – I forget it soon. About thirty pounds they steal. I keep it roll up in a pair of stockings, but I go to the drawer one day, and no money. In the end I have to tell the police. They ask me exact sum and I say I don't count it lately, about thirty pounds. 'You don't know how much?' they say. 'When did you count it last? Do you remember? Was it before you move or after?'

I get confuse, and I keep saying, 'I don't remember,' though I remember well I see it two days before. They don't believe me and when a policeman come to the house I hear the landlady tell him, 'She certainly had no money when she came here. She wasn't able to pay a month's rent in advance for her room though it's a rule in this house.' 'These people terrible liars,' she say and I think 'It's you a terrible liar, because when I come you tell me weekly or monthly as you like.' It's from that time she don't speak to me and perhaps it's she take it. All I know is I never see one penny of my savings again, all I know is they pretend I never have any, but as it's gone, no use to cry about it. Then my mind goes to my father, for my father is a white man and I think a lot about him. If I could see him only once, for I too small to remember when he was there. My mother is fair coloured woman, fairer than I am they say, and she don't stay long with me either. She have a chance to go to Venezuela when I three–four year old and she never come back. She send money instead. It's my grandmother take care of me. She's quite dark and what we call 'country–cookie' but she's the best I know.

She save up all the money my mother send, she don't keep one penny for herself – that's how I get to England. I was a bit late in going to school regular, getting on for twelve years, but I can sew very beautiful, excellent – so I think I get a good job – in London perhaps.

146

However here they tell me all this fine handsewing take too long. Waste of time – too slow. They want somebody to work quick and to hell with the small stitches. Altogether it don't look so good for me, I must say, and I wish I could see my father. I have his name – Davis. But my grandmother tell me, 'Every word that come out of that man's mouth a damn lie. He is certainly first class liar, though no class otherwise.' So perhaps I have not even his real name.

Last thing I see before I put the light out is the postcard on the dressing table. 'Not to worry.'

Not to worry! Next day is Sunday, and it's on the Monday the people next door complain about me to the police. That evening the woman is by the hedge, and when I pass her she says in very sweet quiet voice, '*Must* you stay? *Can't* you go?' I don't answer. I walk out in the street to get rid of her. But she run inside her house to the window, she can still see me. Then I start to sing, so she can understand I'm not afraid of her. The husband call out: 'If you don't stop that noise I'll send for the police.' I answer them quite short. I say, 'You go to hell and take your wife with you.' And I sing louder.

The police come pretty quick – two of them. Maybe they just round the corner. All I can say about police, and how they behave is I think it all depend who they dealing with. Of my own free will I don't want to mix up with police. No.

One man says, you can't cause this disturbance here. But the other asks a lot of questions. What is my name? Am I tenant of a flat in No. 17? How long have I lived there? Last address and so on. I get vexed the way he speak and I tell him, 'I come here because somebody steal my savings. Why you don't look for my money instead of bawling at me? I work hard for my money. All–you don't do one single thing to find it.'

'What's she talking about?' the first one says, and the other one tells me, 'You can't make that noise here. Get along home. You've been drinking.'

I see that woman looking at me and smiling, and other people at their windows, and I'm so angry I bawl at them too. I say, 'I have absolute and perfect right to be in the street same as anybody else, and I have absolute and perfect right to ask the police why they don't even look for my money when it disappear. It's because a dam' English thief take it you don't look,' I say. The end of all this is that I have to go before a magistrate, and he fine me five pounds for drunk and disorderly, and he give me two weeks to pay.

When I get back from the court I walk up and down the kitchen, up and down, waiting for six o'clock because I have no five pounds left, and I don't know what to do. I telephone at six and a woman answers me very short and sharp, then Mr Sims comes along and he don't sound too pleased either when I tell him what happen. 'Oh Lord!' he says, and I say I'm sorry. 'Well don't panic,' he says, 'I'll pay the fine. But look, I don't think . . .' Then he breaks off and talk to some other person in the room. He goes on, 'Perhaps better not stay at No. 17. I think I can arrange something else. I'll call for you Wednesday – Saturday latest. Now behave till then.' And he hang up before I can answer that I don't want to wait till Wednesday, much less Saturday. I want to get out of that house double quick and with no delay. First I think I ring back, then I think better not as he sound so vex.

I get ready, but Wednesday he don't come, and Saturday he don't come. All the week I stay in the flat. Only once I go out and arrange for bread, milk and eggs to be left at the door, and seems to me I meet up with a lot of policemen. They don't look at me, but they see me all right. I don't want to drink – I'm all the time listening, listening and thinking, how can I leave before I know if my fine is paid? I tell myself the police let me know, that's certain. But I don't trust them. What they care? The answer is Nothing. Nobody care. One afternoon I knock at the old lady's flat upstairs, because I get the idea she give me good advice. I can hear her moving about and talking, but she don't answer and I never try again.

Nearly two weeks pass like that, then I telephone. It's the woman speaking and she say, 'Mr Sims is not in London at present.' I ask, 'When will he be back – it's urgent,' and she hang up. I'm not surprised. Not at all. I knew that would happen. All the same I feel heavy like lead. Near the phone box is a chemist's shop, so I ask him for something to make me sleep, the day is bad enough, but to lie awake all night – Ah no! He gives me a little bottle marked '*One or two tablets only*' and I take three when I go to bed because more and more I thinking that sleeping is better than no matter what else. However, I lie there, eyes wide open as usual, so I take three more. Next thing I know the room is full of sunlight, so it must be late afternoon, but the lamp is still on. My head turn around and I can't think well at all. At first I ask myself how I get to the place. Then it comes to me, but in pictures – like the landlady kicking my dress, and when I take my ticket at Victoria Station, and Mr Sims telling me to eat the sandwiches, but I can't remember everything clear, and I feel very giddy and sick. I take in the milk and eggs at the door, go in the kitchen, and try to eat but the food hard to swallow.

It's when I'm putting the things away that I see the bottles – pushed back on the lowest shelf in the cupboard.

There's a lot of drink left, and I'm glad I tell you. Because I can't bear the way I feel. Not any more. I mix a gin and vermouth and I drink it quick, then I mix another and drink it slow by the window. The garden looks different, like I never see it before. I know quite well what I must do, but it's late now – tomorrow. I have one more drink, of wine this time, and then a song come in my head, I sing it and I dance it, and more I sing, more I am sure this is the best tune that has ever come to me in all my life.

The sunset light from the window is gold colour. My shoes sound loud on the boards. So I take them off, my stockings too and go on dancing but the room feel shut in, I can't breathe, and I go outside still singing. Maybe I dance a bit too. I forget all about that woman till I hear her saying, 'Henry, look at this.' I turn around and I see her at the window. 'Oh yes, I wanted to speak with you,' I say, 'Why bring the police and get me in bad trouble? Tell me that.'

'And you tell *me* what you're doing here at all,' she says. 'This is a respectable neighbourhood.'

Then the man come along. 'Now young woman, take yourself off. You ought to be ashamed of this behaviour.'

'It's disgraceful,' he says, talking to his wife, but loud so I can hear, and she speaks loud too – for once. 'At least the other tarts that crook installed here were *white* girls,' she says.

'You a dam' fouti liar,' I say. 'Plenty of those girls in your country already. Numberless as the sands on the shore. You don't need me for that.'

'You're not a howling success at it certainly.' Her voice sweet sugar again. 'And you won't be seeing much more of your friend Mr Sims. He's in trouble too. Try somewhere else. Find somebody else. If you can, of course.' When she say that my arm moves of itself. I pick up a stone and bam! through the window. Not the one they are standing at but the next, which is of coloured glass, green and purple and yellow.

I never see a woman look so surprise. Her mouth fall open she so full of surprise. I start to laugh, louder and louder – I laugh like my grandmother, with my hands on my hips and my head back. (When she laugh like that you can hear her to the end of the street.) At last I say, 'Well, I'm sorry. An accident. I get it fixed tomorrow early.' 'That glass is irreplaceable,' the man says. 'Irreplaceable.' 'Good thing,' I say, 'those colours look like they sea-sick to me. I buy you a better windowglass.'

He shake his fist at me. 'You won't be let off with a fine this time,' he says. Then they draw the curtains. I call out at them. 'You run away. Always you run away. Ever since I come here you hunt me down because I don't answer back. It's you shameless.' I try to sing 'Don't trouble me now'.

Don't trouble me now
You without honour.
Don't walk in my footstep
You without shame.

But my voice don't sound right, so I get back indoors and drink one more glass of wine – still wanting to laugh, and still thinking of my grandmother for that is one of her songs.

It's about a man whose doudou give him the go–by when she find somebody rich and he sail away to Panama. Plenty people die there of fever when they make that Panama canal so long ago. But he don't die. He come back with dollars and the girl meet him on the jetty, all dressed up and smiling. Then he sing to her, 'You without honour, you without shame.' It sound good in Martinique patois too: 'Sans honte'.

Afterwards I ask myself, 'Why I do that? It's not like me. But if they treat you wrong over and over again the hour strike when you burst out that's what.'

Too besides, Mr Sims can't tell me now I have no spirit. I don't care, I sleep quickly and I'm glad I break the woman's ugly window. But as to my own song it go *right* away and it never come back. A pity.

Next morning the doorbell ringing wake me up. The people upstairs don't come down, and the bell keeps on like fury self. So I go look, and there is a policeman and a policewoman outside. As soon as I open the door the woman put her foot in it. She wear sandals and thick stockings and I never see a foot so big or so bad. It look like it want to mash up the whole world. Then she come in after the foot, and her face not so pretty either. The policeman tell me my fine is not paid and people make serious complaints about me, so they're taking me back to the magistrate. He show me a paper and I look at it, but I don't read it. The woman push me in the bedroom, and tell me to get dress quickly, but I just stare at her, because I think perhaps I wake up soon. Then I ask her what I must wear. She say she suppose I had some clothes on yesterday. Or not? 'What's it matter, wear anything,' she says. But I find clean underclothes and stockings and my shoes with high heels and I comb my hair. I start to file my nails, because I think they too long for magistrate's court but she get angry. 'Are you coming quietly or aren't you?' she says. So I go with them and we get in a car outside.

I wait for a long time in a room full of policemen. They come in, they go out, they telephone, they talk in low voices. Then it's my turn, and first thing I notice in the court room is a man with frowning black eyebrows. He sit below the magistrate, he dressed in black and he so

150

handsome I can't take my eyes off him. When he see that he frown worse than before.

First comes a policeman to testify I cause disturbance, and then comes the old gentleman from next door. He repeat that bit about nothing but the truth so help me God. Then he says I make dreadful noise at night and use abominable language, and dance in obscene fashion. He says when they try to shut the curtains because his wife so terrify of me, I throw stones and break a valuable stain-glass window. He say his wife get serious injury if she'd been hit, and as it is she in terrible nervous condition and the doctor is with her. I think, 'Believe me, if I aim at your wife I hit your wife – that's certain.' 'There was no provocation,' he says. 'None at all.' Then another lady from across the street says this is true. She heard no provocation whatsoever, and she swear that they shut the curtains but I go on insulting them and using filthy language and she saw all this and heard it.

The magistrate is a little gentleman with a quiet voice, but I'm very suspicious of these quiet voices now. He ask me why I don't pay my fine, and I say because I haven't the money. I get the idea they want to find out all about Mr Sims – they listen so very attentive. But they'll find out nothing from me. He ask how long I have the flat and I say I don't remember. I know they want to trip me up like they trip me up about my savings so I won't answer. At last he ask me if I have anything to say as I can't be allowed to go on being a nuisance. I think, 'I'm nuisance to you because I have no money that's all.' I want to speak up and tell him how they steal all my savings, so when my landlord asks for month's rent I haven't got it to give. I want to tell him the woman next door provoke me since long time and call me bad names but she have a soft sugar voice and nobody hear – that's why I broke her window, but I'm ready to buy another after all. I want to say all I do is sing in that old garden, and I want to say this in decent quiet voice. But I hear myself talking loud and I see my hands wave in the air. Too besides it's no use, they won't believe me, so I don't finish. I stop, and I feel the tears on my face. 'Prove it.' That's all they will say. They whisper, they whisper. They nod, they nod.

Next thing I'm in a car again with a different policewoman, dressed very smart. Not in uniform. I ask her where she's taking me and she says 'Holloway', just that, 'Holloway'.

I catch hold of her hand because I'm afraid. But she takes it away. Cold and smooth her hand slide away and her face is china face – smooth like a doll and I think, 'This is the last time I ask anything from anybody. So help me God.'

The car come up to a black castle and little mean streets are all around it. A lorry was blocking up the castle gates. When it get by we pass through and I am in jail. First I stand in a line with others who are waiting to give up handbags and all belongings to a woman behind bars like in a post office. The girl in front bring out a nice compact, look like gold to me, lipstick to match and a wallet full of notes. The woman keep the money, but she give back the powder and lipstick and she half–smile. I have two pounds seven shillings and sixpence in pennies. She take my purse, then she throw me my compact (which is cheap) my comb and my handkerchief like everything in my bag is dirty. So I think, 'Here too, here too.' But I tell myself, 'Girl, what you expect, eh? They all like that. All.'

Some of what happen afterwards I forget, or perhaps better not remember. Seems to me they start by trying to frighten you. But they don't succeed with me for I don't care for nothing now, it's as if my heart hard like a rock and I can't feel.

Then I'm standing at the top of a staircase with a lot of women and girls. As we are going down I notice the railing very low on one side, very easy to jump, and a long way below there's the grey stone passage like it's waiting for you.

As I'm thinking this a uniform woman step up alongside quick and grab my arm. She say, 'Oh no you don't.'

I was just noticing the railing very low that's all – but what's the use of saying so.

Another long line waits for the doctor. It move forward slowly and my legs terrible tired. The girl in front is very young and she cry and cry. 'I'm scared,' she keeps saying. She's lucky in a way – as for me I never will cry again. It all dry up and hard in me now. That, and a lot besides. In the end I tell her to stop, because she doing just what these people want her to do.

She stop crying and start a long story, but while she is speaking her voice get very far away, and I find I can't see her face clear at all.

Then I'm in a chair, and one of those uniform women is pushing my head down between my knees, but let her push – everything go away from me just the same.

They put me in the hospital because the doctor say I'm sick. I have cell by myself and it's all right except I don't sleep. The things they say you mind I don't mind.

When they clang the door on me I think, 'You shut me in, but you shut all those other dam' devils *out*. They can't reach me now.'

At first it bothers me when they keep on looking at me all through the night. They open a little window in the doorway to do this. But I get used to it and get used to the night chemise they give me. It very thick, and to my mind it not very clean either – but what's that matter to me? Only the food I can't swallow – especially the porridge. The woman ask me sarcastic, 'Hunger striking?' But afterwards I can leave most of it, and she don't say nothing.

One day a nice girl comes around with books and she give me two, but I don't want to read so much. Beside one is about a murder, and the other is about a ghost and I don't think it's at all like those books tell you.

There is nothing I want now. It's no use. If they leave me in peace and quiet that's all I ask. The window is barred but not small, so I can see a little thin tree through the bars, and I like watching it.

After a week they tell me I'm better and I can go out with the others for exercise. We walk round and round one of the yards in that castle – it is fine weather and the sky is a kind of pale blue, but the yard is a terrible sad place. The sunlight fall down and die there. I get tired walking in high heels and I'm glad when that's over.

We can talk, and one day an old woman come up and ask me for dog-ends. I don't understand, and she start muttering at me like she very vexed. Another woman tell me she mean cigarette ends, so I say I don't smoke. But the old woman still look angry, and when we're going in she give me one push and I nearly fall down. I'm glad to get away from these people, and hear the door clang and take my shoes off.

Sometimes I think, 'I'm here because I wanted to sing' and I have to laugh. But there's a small looking glass in my cell and I see myself and I'm like somebody else. Like some strange new person. Mr Sims tell me I too thin, but what he say now to this person in the looking glass? So I don't laugh again.

Usually I don't think at all. Everything and everybody seem small and far away, that is the only trouble.

Twice the doctor come to see me. He don't say much and I don't say anything, because a uniform woman is always there. She look like she thinking, 'Now the lies start.' So I prefer not to speak. Then I'm sure they can't trip me up. Perhaps I there still, or in a worse place. But one day this happen.

We were walking round and round in the yard and I hear a woman singing – the voice come from high up, from one of the small barred windows. At first I don't believe it. Why should anybody sing here? Nobody want to sing in jail, nobody want to do anything. There's no reason, and you have no hope. I think I must be asleep, dreaming, but I'm awake all right and I see all the others are listening too. A nurse is with us that afternoon, not a policewoman. She stop and look up at the window.

It's a smoky kind of voice, and a bit rough sometimes, as if those old dark walls themselves are complaining, because they see too much misery – too much. But it don't fall down and die in the courtyard; seems to me it could jump the gates of the jail easy and travel far, and nobody could stop it. I don't hear the words – only the music. She sing one verse and she begin another, then she break off sudden. Everybody starts walking again, and nobody says one word. But as we go in I ask the woman in front who was singing. 'That's the Holloway song,' she says. 'Don't you know it yet? She was singing from the punishment cells, and she tell the girls cheerio and never say die.' Then I have to go one way to the hospital block and she goes another so we don't speak again.

When I'm back in my cell I can't just wait for bed. I walk up and down and I think. 'One day I hear that song on trumpets and these walls will fall and rest.' I want to get out so bad I could hammer on the door, for I know now that anything can happen, and I don't want to stay lock up here and miss it.

Then I'm hungry. I eat everything they bring and in the morning I'm still so hungry I eat the porridge. Next time the doctor come he tells me I seem much better. Then I say a little of what really happen in that house. Not much. Very careful.

He look at me hard and kind of surprised. At the door he shake his finger and says, 'Now don't let me see you here again.'

That evening the woman tells me I'm going, but she's so upset about it I don't ask questions. Very early, before it's light she bangs the door open and shouts at me to hurry up. As we're going along the passages I see the girl who gave me the books. She's in a row with others doing exercises. Up Down, Up Down, Up. We pass quite close and I notice she's looking very pale and tired. It's crazy, it's all crazy. This up down business and everything else too. When they give me my money I remember I leave my compact in the cell, so I ask if I can go back for it. You should see that policewoman's face as she shoo me on.

There's no car, there's a van and you can't see through the windows. The third time it stop I get out with one other, a young girl, and it's the same magistrates' court as before.

The two of us wait in a small room, nobody else there, and after a while the girl say, 'What the hell are they doing? I don't want to spend all day here.' She go to the bell and she keep her finger press on it. When I look at her she say, 'Well, what are they *for*?' That girl's face is hard like a board – she could change faces with many and you wouldn't know the difference. But she gets results certainly. A policeman come in, all smiling, and we go in the court. The same magistrate, the same frowning man sits below, and when I hear my fine is paid I want to ask who paid it, but he yells at me. 'Silence.'

I think I will never understand the half of what happen, but they tell me I can go, and I understand that. The magistrate ask if I'm leaving the neighbourhood and I say yes, then I'm out in the streets again, and it's the same fine weather, same feeling I'm dreaming.

When I get to the house I see two men talking in the garden. The front door and the door of the flat are both open. I go in, and the bedroom is empty, nothing but the glare streaming inside because they take the Venetian blinds away. As I'm wondering where my suitcase is, and the clothes I leave in the wardrobe, there's a knock and it's the old lady from upstairs carrying my case packed, and my coat is over her arm. She says she sees me come in. 'I kept your things for you.' I start to thank her but she turn her back and walk away. They like that here, and better not expect too much. Too besides, I bet they tell her I'm terrible person.

I go in the kitchen, but when I see they are cutting down the big tree at the back I don't stay to watch.

At the station I'm waiting for the train and a woman asks if I feel well. 'You look so tired,' she says. 'Have you come a long way?' I want to answer, 'I come so far I lose myself on that journey.' But I tell her, 'Yes, I am quite well. But I can't stand the heat.' She says she can't stand it either, and we talk about the weather till the train come in.

I'm not frightened of them any more – after all what else can they do? I know what to say and everything go like a clock works.

I get a room near Victoria where the landlady accept one pound in advance, and next day I find a job in the kitchen of a private hotel close by. But I don't stay there long. I hear of another job going in a big store – altering ladies' dresses and I get that. I lie and tell them I work in very expensive New York shop. I speak bold and smooth faced, and they never check up on me. I make a friend there – Clarice – very light coloured, very smart, she have a lot to do with the customers and she laugh at some of them behind their backs. But I say it's not their fault if the dress don't fit. Special dress for one person only – that's very expensive in London. So it's take in, or let out all the time. Clarice have two rooms not far from the store. She furnish them herself gradual and she gives parties sometimes Saturday nights. It's there I start whistling the Holloway Song. A man comes up to me and says, 'Let's hear that again.' So I whistle it again (I never sing now) and he tells me 'Not bad'. Clarice have an old piano somebody give her to store and he plays the tune, jazzing it up. I say, 'No, not like that,' but everybody else say the way he do it is first class. Well I think no more of this till I get a letter from him telling me he has sold the song and as I was quite a help he encloses five pounds with thanks.

I read the letter and I could cry. For after all, that song was all I had. I

155

don't belong nowhere really, and I haven't money to buy my way to belonging. I don't want to either.

But when that girl sing, she sing to me, and she sing for me. I was there because I was *meant* to be there. It was *meant* I should hear it – this I *know*.

Now I've let them play it wrong, and it will go from me like all the other songs – like everything. Nothing left for me at all.

But then I tell myself all this is foolishness. Even if they played it on trumpets, even if they played it just right, like I wanted – no walls would fall so soon. 'So let them call it jazz,' I think, and let them play it wrong. That won't make no difference to the song I heard.

I buy myself a dusty pink dress with the money.

Abridged, from the anthology *Tales of the Wide Caribbean*.

Phyllis Shand Allfrey

Phyllis Shand Allfrey was born in Dominica in 1900. One of four sisters, she grew up there in comfortable circumstances in a family with a long tradition of service. While in England – London – during her twenties, she joined the Fabian Society, the British Labour Party and the Parliamentary Committee for West Indian Affairs. She married Robert Allfrey and returned to the Caribbean in the early 1950s, having just published The Orchid House *(Constable, 1953), her first novel. She soon became involved in Dominican politics, founding the Dominican Labour Party. In the first elections of the (now defunct) West Indies Federation, she was elected a Federal MP and became Minister of Labour and Social Affairs in the Federal Government. After the Federation folded in 1961, Allfrey returned to Dominica where she and her husband ran the* Dominica Herald *until 1965, when they began to publish their own newspaper,* The Star. *On her retirement from politics she turned to literature once more, beginning a new novel,* In the Cabinet. *However, her involvement in local politics continued to prove a distraction. Natural and personal catastrophe also seemed to conspire to keep her from resuming her literary pursuits: her daughter Phina died in Botswana, and, more recently, Hurricane David ravaged Dominica, ruining the Allfrey house and destroying their belongings. She died in 1986.*

The Orchid House *is the story of a Dominican white creole family, especially its women, told by Lally, the black nurse. It can be seen as,* inter alia, *a symbolic representation of the passing of power from coloniser to colonised. The extract here clearly contrasts the vitality and energy of black Dominicans with the pale thinness of the Master and the heavy tiredness that engulfs physical and personal environments in the family, on what Lally calls significantly 'the longest day of my life'.*

The Master Comes Home

That was the longest day of my life, I do honestly believe. The children took ages over changing into their afternoon dresses. Miss Natalie was fretful. You just had to look at her and she would cry a little, and then her face had to be washed again. I put the thermometer into her mouth as she stood there waiting for me to button up her frock behind and tie her sash. Now that I think of it, it always came natural to Miss Natalie to stand still and have things done for her. But her temperature was normal. So I tightened the elastic which kept Miss Joan's straw hat in place, and I let the puppy out and we started off, and it always seemed that we were some sort of procession, like the Corpus Christi when Olivet is a Child of Mary. Miss Stella walked first with her head in the air, and after her Miss Joan, leading the puppy on a string, and after that I came along, short of breath even in those days, and holding on to my white piqué skirt came little Miss Natalie.

On that day, as he sometimes did, young Baptiste clanged the gate behind him and followed slowly after us. He had a book in his hand. Miss Joan was forever lending him her books against my wishes, for the dirt of that kitchen was not fit for *Little Arthur's History* or the *Red Fairy Book* or *Sylvie and Bruno*. I was tired of scolding her about this, so I let it pass now and again. But I always took the books from him when I caught him at it, and breathed on them and rubbed them with my apron.

'You'll put him outside himself,' I used to tell Miss Joan. 'Encouraging a black boy to read so much.'

'He reads better than I do,' Miss Joan would answer. 'He doesn't even like all our books. He says they're silly.'

'The insolence of him, complaining about your English godmother's birthday presents,' I'd say. But Miss Joan would reply: 'I think they're silly too, sometimes.'

157

She always seemed to know when he was coming up alongside, though his bare feet made no noise, and she would wait for him and slip another book into his hand: he would pass his over to her and run off. But once he thought I was far enough away for him to linger, and I heard him say in a disrespectful manner, 'Haven't you got anything *real*?'

'No, but I'll borrow something good from Miss Rebecca and sneak it into the kitchen,' Miss Joan said. I made a big disturbance that time, and reported Baptiste to his mother, who gave him a proper flogging.

It was natural for the people in the streets to speak their mind aloud as we passed, and to say that Miss Stella's legs were like matchsticks, and how she favoured her father and the little one favoured St Agnes in the holy pictures, but the middle one, that was Miss Joan, she was Madam's own daughter except for her hair. They were all observing us hard that day because they all knew that the Master was coming home, and they had plenty to say, and there were some words I hoped the children would not understand. Well, we were heading for that library which the American millionaire had given to the islanders, and filled up with books of his own choice, but after a while Miss Rebecca who was put there to manage it, she took out a lot of the books and had them burnt or thrown in the sea, beginning with a gentleman called Tolstoy and running through all the German–sounding books during the war, and so on. But we never went there to bother about books. We went there because the library was built almost on the edge of the cliff, and from the library grounds you could see ships coming in, you could see horizon-wards almost as far as Martinique on the left. And there we met Mimi Zacariah and Master Andrew, but Miss Rosamund was sick in bed with the fever. So Mimi and I talked about temperatures for a little while, and got out our embroidery, for we made a little money on the side selling drawn-thread nightgown tops to the tourists.

Miss Stella, Miss Joan and Master Andrew swung on the lianas of the banyan tree until they felt sick and giddy and their hands were raw with gripping those long strands as they whizzed through the air. But Miss Natalie sat quietly beside Mimi and me. 'Go and play,' I said to Miss Natalie, giving her a little bit of a push. 'You are all right. You haven't got a fever today.'

'I'm aflaid,' said Miss Natalie. 'The others are too lough. I'm aflaid because Daddy is coming home. I don't want a stlange man in our house.'

'Now, look out on the horizon,' said Mimi Zacariah. 'There's a ship coming in. Did you ever hear of a ship, Miss Natalie, which didn't bring luck to someone? That may even be your father's ship, coming home to bring him back to your mother. Think how long she has been lonely.'

But Miss Natalie hid her face in my embroidery, so that she couldn't see the ship, which was only a tramp cargo boat after all. 'I'm aflaid,' said Miss Natalie.

'Well,' said Mimi Zacariah, getting sour in the voice and showing the yellows of her eyes, 'being afraid is as catching as the kaffir-pox, to my mind.' Now this put anger into me, for I would not have it said that we were afraid of receiving our Master, who had gone out to fight while some hearty gentlemen in the island had stayed at home. I looked at the other children, who were now playing hide–and–seek in the guinea–grass almost on the edge of the cliff. There was no use in telling them to keep out of the guinea–grass. Mimi and I had given them into God's hands as far as that cliff was concerned; only my God saw things in a Methodist way and Mimi's saw things in a Catholic way. But so far they had not tumbled over. 'It's a curious thing,' I said to Mimi, 'with Mr MacArthur having that Scotch name and that red complexion and the parrot on his shoulder and all, that he should have a little boy like Master Andrew who is as light and dark as those Spanish pictures of Madam's!'

'Oh, I wouldn't bring the parrot into it,' said Mimi. And though she pursed her mouth we did not argufy any more, but did a lot of good silent work on our embroidery until the sun began to drop and it was time to go home.

When I got back with the children Madam was all beautifully dressed up in her eyelet–muslin with the red and green twisted girdle, and her hair done up in those wonderful snaky top–coils. She was standing by the piano, propping a sonata on the rack and then exchanging it for another. She told me to bundle the children to bed. 'The Master's ship will drop anchor at dinner-time,' Madam said. 'I want you to be free to help Christophine.' But the children did not want to go to bed. They were angry with Madam. 'It would have been more truthful if she had stuck out my Stephen Heller's exercises, or Stella's dull minuet,' said Miss Joan crossly. But they all plunged under their mosquito nets the minute I promised to carry the puppy up to them to say goodnight. And in about ten minutes all three of them were sleeping soundly. So I didn't have to bring the puppy up after all; but I gave the poor little thing a dish of breadcrumbs and gravy.

Old Master came to see Madam before dinner, and when I brought in the cocktails he stood there with an arm over Madam's shoulders. He was saying to her that it had been a long time, yes, a very long time, and she had been pretty patient, but she mustn't worry. 'Time and war change people,' said Old Master seriously. 'But I think you are both young enough, oh yes, I think you are both young enough.' He did not stay very long. I let him out of the gate myself, and I untied the muffler on the bell–clapper so that we could all hear the bell loud and clear when the messenger from the bay reported Master's ship on the horizon. I stood there at the gate watching the thin little moon struggling through the clouds. It had grown to be a heavy night, the breeze had died. I was feeling heavy, too, and tired. I thought of the house, which had been a house only of women for six years. I thought that I must be different from the others of my dark skin, for I had small love for men. They made everything of a different quality and sound and smell. They would bring into a house deep voices and smoke and a feeling in the air. I suddenly thought of Christophine and the dinner, and looked round to see what was going on, for I could hear faint grunts and snores from the kitchen. I found her lying under the dresser, dead drunk. Someone had given her an extra chopée of black rum to celebrate with, and she had celebrated already. Her fourth child, Olivet, was sitting on a mat at her feet, fanning her in silence. When Olivet was born Madam dismissed Christophine, as she always did when a new baby came by a new father. 'I don't mind your not being married,' said Madam, 'but I do think it is rather unfair to the children to have these incessant fights over the various fathers, and Father Toussaint has asked me to co–operate with him in disciplining you.' But Madam could not keep from smiling when she made these speeches, for in all Madam disciplined Christophine six times, and always when the new baby was old enough to crawl it used to crawl in our kitchen, and the children (my little white ones) would recover from their stomach–aches and bad appetites and everything would be the same again.

I took and poured a calabash of cold water over Christophine's face to bring her together again, and I told Olivet to roll the crapaud's legs in a little flour and chop up the red pepper and beat up the special English marshmallow sauce that came from the Pharmacerie to be poured over the special fruit salad. For the island cows wouldn't squeeze out a pint of cream not to please anyone, not even the Prince of Wales when he stepped ashore in his plus fours. The milk that came from the hills, and that started out thin enough God only knows, reached Maison Rose coloured a lovely pale blue, because of all the streams the carriers passed on the way. It was never a wonder to me that my three little ones could not hide their bones decently under some fat, in spite of the Allenbury's food I had boiled up for hours and months when they were babies.

I went again to the front gate while the water took effect on

Christophine. There I saw Bill Buffon the boatman with his gold earring hanging on one ear and his silly smile. He was sitting with his feet in the open gutter, which was still sweet with the remains of Madam's bath water. 'Boat's only half–hour away,' said Buffon to me. 'I'll be the one,' he said, 'to row Madam out to meet Master.' And he grinned again, stupid. But Buffon has a good heart, for all his rags and foolishness. I never saw such a man for smelling out a hurricane, or keeping his boat right side up in rough sea. And he truly loves the family. The family is everything to a man like Buffon and to a woman like me. I suppose that in coming years poor people won't take such stock of families, royal families and ordinary high families like Madam and the Master's. But it's a comfort to have a family to tend and admire, at least I have always found it so.

'Did you smell the rum off Christophine?' I asked Buffon angrily. You must remember that by this time I was tired and sick of everything. But Buffon said that he had come to tell Madam that he had mended the leak in *Sainte Ursule* and bought a new oar from the master of a Guadeloupe schooner, all for the Master's sake. 'La pluie ka vini,' said Buffon; and indeed it was beginning to drizzle. So we went and sat in the downstairs hall, and I leaned against the wall and fell asleep. I only woke up when I heard the loud rattle of anchor dropping, and then I heard Christophine singing *O Vierge* in her feast–day voice, and I saw that Buffon had gone, and with him Madam.

Afterwards Buffon told me how it went at the meeting. The drizzle was still falling, like spun glass beads between the boat and the ship. Madam wore her Maltese shawl over the eyelet–hole muslin, and she took the rudder. I saw in my mind the picture of Madam steering that boat, with her eyes and the little moon and the light rain shining. I saw the picture, not because of what Buffon said, but because of what he did with his hands when he told me. As the boat drew alongside, the passengers crowded near the head of the gangway; but there was one who hung behind and still leaned over the rail as if in a dream, and that one was the Master. Buffon says that the Master took Madam's hand and held it as if he was seeing her for the first time. Then Buffon got bashful and looked at the sea, so he couldn't see whether they kissed or not.

I looked the Master over for wound–marks when he came into the house, and there was nothing that you could see on the outside. But he was very pale and thin, with hollow cheeks, and he looked as if he had forgotten all about us, although he was polite enough. Goodness knows what had guided him back to Maison Rose to be a husband and a father, for he had the look of a wanderer without direction. Anyhow he ate up his dinner right enough, and went into the kitchen afterwards to compliment Christophine on her cooking, and then he went upstairs with Madam to see the children again. The sight of the three children, so large in their beds compared with the little creatures he had left, seemed to amaze him, for he had little to say.

In the meantime Buffon had gone back to the bay–front and carted the Master's luggage to Maison Rose on an iron barrow. The luggage he brought back was not exactly what he took away; even the trunk had changed, and instead of his suitcases there were two chests with bands round them, weighing the devil and all. Madam asked him where his clothes were and he picked up a little leather case fit to lay by a christening–robe in. 'I don't know,' said the Master. 'It's been a long time: but I brought back some exciting trophies.' So Buffon sweated up the stairs with the boxes, and the Master opened them, and then he nailed some of the stuff up on the walls of the hall and drawing-room – outlandish Arab helmets studded with imitation jewels, daggers and great clumsy pistols you never would imagine capable of shooting anyone, a tin German hat and a grand smoking pipe with a long tube, a fine brassy shield and arm–pieces to match, and some more fancy nonsense bits with the old bloodstains long dry on them. Buffon thought these things were wonderful, and stood by twisting his cap and saying, 'Lawd, that's something!' But Madam and I could not endure the noise of hammering in the night and we were afraid that the children would wake up. After a long while, when I was rocking in the chair in my own room, everything was quiet, quiet without even the sound of voices. I went out to see if the puppy was all right and I saw a light still in the drawing–room, so I took the puppy in my arms and carried him up to show the Master.

He was sitting alone. Madam had gone to bed. He was reading a book and smoking, and the whole room was full of the sick faint smell of flowers and cigarette smoke, for after the rain the air was heavy again.

I said to myself, Lally, you must show friendliness. You must help to bring the Master out of himself and the bad war days and back to his family. I spoke to him kindly and respectfully and I laid the little dog at his feet. I told him that the children had bought it for him. '*Flanders* they called it, sir,' I said.

The Master put down his book and looked at the little dog. He looked at it queerly. I did not feel comfortable. 'An extraordinary name for a dog,' said the Master.

There was his book on the table where he had put it down. His finger, thin and white, pressed on the page to keep the place. Because he was staring at me and then at the little dog, I shifted from one foot to the other and I fixed my eyes on the book. It was French, and I cannot read French, being an English Negress, though Christophine can. I saw the title, *A La Recherche du Temps Perdu*, but it meant nothing to me. I saw the words where his finger pressed, and though I could not understand them, the whole look of the print, the whole feeling of something foreign on the page, in the air, made me very unhappy.

The little dog lay down beside the Master and shut its eyes. I turned to go, and the Master said: 'Tell me, Lally, does the mail–boat leave tonight or is there much cargo to load? I have an important letter to post.'

'I can't be sure, sir,' I said. 'But if you give me the letter I'll find Buffon and he will take it off in his boat.'

The Master gave me a letter, and I said goodnight. I left the puppy with him. I had the feeling that I could do nothing useful in that drawing–room then. There's English words, I thought, which might be said tonight, and the Master sits reading a French book like a guest in the Bellevue Hotel. I read the address on the letter as I went out to find Buffon. It was then that I saw the name for the first time: H. Lilipoulala, Port-au-Prince.

Extract from *The Orchid House*.

Paule Marshall

Paule Marshall, born in 1929, grew up in Brooklyn, New York, but both her parents were Barbadian and she has lived for long periods in the Caribbean. Many of her stories are about characters who are West Indian and who have West Indian connections. She has written three novels: Brown Girl, Brownstones, *originally published in 1959 and reissued in 1981 by the Feminist Press,* The Chosen Place, The Timeless People *(N.Y., Harcourt, Brace & World,1969) and* Praise Song for the Widow *(N.Y., Putnam's,1983). She has also produced a collection of stories* Reena and Other Stories *(N.Y., Feminist Press, 1983) and a collection of novellas,* Soul Clap Hands and Sing *(1961). Paule Marshall has taught creative writing at Yale, Columbia, and University of Massachusetts (Boston) and at the Iowa Writers' Workshop. She has one son and resides in New York.*

The novella 'Barbados', one of Marshall's earlier works, was written in 1958 during a year spent in Barbados. Paule Marshall sees the women, who are not the main characters in these novellas, as 'bringers of truth' to the male protagonists. The women, she says 'come to realise their own strength as a result of the encounter'. She intended also, she states, 'to use the relationships between the old men and the young women in the stories to suggest themes of a political nature'.* These earlier works anticipate themes and concerns still very topical in the 1980s. In 'Barbados', Mr Watford, an elderly Barbadian who has lived for many years in the United States, has finally retired and come home. There he comes into contact with a young girl and through her finally confronts himself.

Barbados

The next day, coming from the grove to prepare his noon meal, he saw her. She was standing in his driveway, her bare feet like strong dark roots amid the jagged stones, her face tilted toward the sun – and she

*Paule Marshall commenting on 'Barbados' in *Reena and Other Stories*, Feminist Press, Old Westbury, New York, 1983, p. 51.

might have been standing there always waiting for him. She seemed of the sun, of the earth. The folktale of creation might have been true with her: that along a river bank a god had scooped up the earth – rich and black and warmed by the sun – and moulded her poised head with its tufted braids and then with a whimsical touch crowned it with a sober brown felt hat which should have been worn by some stout English matron in a London suburb, had sculpted the passionless face and drawn a screen of gossamer across her eyes to hide the void behind. Beneath her bodice her small breasts were smooth at the crest. Below her waist, her hips branched wide, the place prepared for its load of life. But it was the bold and sensual strength of her legs which completely unstrung Mr Watford. He wanted to grab a hoe and drive her off.

'What it 'tis you want?' he called sharply.

'Mr Goodman send me.'

'Send you for what?' His voice was shrill in the glare.

She moved. Holding a caved-in valise and a pair of white sandals, her head weaving slightly as though she bore a pail of water there or a tray of mangoes, she glided over the stones as if they were smooth ground. Her bland expression did not change, but her eyes, meeting his, held a vague trust. Pausing a few feet away, she curtsied deeply. 'I's the new servant.'

Only Mr Watford's cold laugh saved him from anger. As always it raised him to a height where everything below appeared senseless and insignificant – especially his people, whom the girl embodied. From this height, he could even be charitable. And thinking suddenly of how she had waited in the brutal sun since morning without taking shelter under the nearby tamarind tree, he said, not unkindly, 'Well, girl, go back and tell Mr Goodman for me that I don't need no servant.'

'I can't go back.'

'How you mean can't?' His head gave its angry snap.

'I'll get lashes,' she said simply. 'My mother say I must work the day and then if you don't wish me, I can come back. But I's not to leave till night falling, if not I get lashes.'

He was shaken by her dispassion. So much so that his head dropped from its disdaining angle and his hands twitched with helplessness. Despite anything he might say or do, her fear of the whipping would keep her there until nightfall, the valise and shoes in hand. He felt his day with its order and quiet rhythms threatened by her intrusion – and suddenly waving her off as if she were an evil visitation, he hurried into the kitchen to prepare his meal.

But he paused, confused, in front of the stove, knowing that he could not cook and leave her hungry at the door, nor could he cook and serve her as though he were the servant.

165

'You know anything about cooking?' he shouted finally.

'Yes, please.'

They said nothing more. She entered the room with a firm step and an air almost of familiarity, placed her valise and shoes in a corner and went directly to the larder. For a time Mr Watford stood by, his muscles flexing with anger and his eyes bounding ahead of her every move, until feeling foolish and frighteningly useless, he went out to feed his doves.

The meal was quickly done and as he ate he heard the dry slap of her feet behind him – a pleasant sound – and then silence. When he glanced back she was squatting in the doorway, the sunlight aslant the absurd hat and her face bent to a bowl she held in one palm. She ate slowly, thoughtfully, as if fixing the taste of each spoonful in her mind.

It was then that he decided to let her work the day and at nightfall to pay her a dollar and dismiss her. His decision held when he returned later from the grove and found tea awaiting him, and then through the supper she prepared. Afterward, dressed in his white uniform, he patiently waited out the day's end on the portico, his face setting into a grim mold. Then just as dusk etched the first dark line between the sea and sky, he took out a dollar and went downstairs.

She was not in the kitchen, but the table was set for his morning tea. Muttering at her persistence, he charged down the corridor, which ran the length of the basement, flinging open the doors to the damp, empty rooms on either side, and sending the lizards and the shadows long entrenched there scuttling to safety.

He found her in the small slanted room under the stoop, asleep on an old cot he kept there, her suitcase turned down beside the bed, and the shoes, dress and the ridiculous hat piled on top. A loose night shift muted the outline of her body and hid her legs, so that she appeared suddenly defenseless, innocent, with a child's trust in her curled hand and in her deep breathing. Standing in the doorway, with his own breathing snarled and his eyes averted, Mr Watford felt like an intruder. She had claimed the room. Quivering with frustration, he slowly turned away, vowing that in the morning he would shove the dollar at her and lead her like a cow out of his house . . .

Dawn brought rain and a hot wind which set the leaves rattling and swiping at the air like distraught arms. Dressing in the dawn darkness, Mr Watford again armed himself with the dollar and, with his shoulders at an uncompromising set, plunged downstairs. He descended into the warm smell of bakes and this smell, along with the thought that she had been up before him, made his hand knot with exasperation on the banister. The knot tightened as he saw her, dust swirling at her feet as she swept the corridor, her face bent solemn to the task. Shutting her out with a lifted hand, he shouted, 'Don't bother sweeping. Here's a dollar. G'long back.'

The broom paused and although she did not raise her hand, he sensed her groping through the shadowy maze of her mind towards his voice. Behind the dollar which he waved in her face, her eyes slowly cleared. And, surprisingly, they held no fear. Only anticipation and a tenuous trust. It was as if she expected him to say something kind.

'G'long back!' His angry cry was a plea.

Like a small, starved flame, her trust and expectancy died and she said, almost with reproof, 'The rain falling.'

To confirm this, the wind set the rain stinging across the windows and he could say nothing, even though the words sputtered at his lips. It was useless. There was nothing inside her to comprehend that she was not wanted. His shoulders sagged under the weight of her ignorance, and with a futile gesture he swung away, the dollar hanging from his hand like a small sword gone limp.

She became as fixed and familiar a part of the house as the stones – and as silent. He paid her five dollars a week, gave her Mondays off and in the evenings, after a time, even allowed her to sit in the alcove off the parlor, while he read with his back to her, taking no more notice of her than he did the moths on the lamp.

But once, after many silent evenings together, he detected a sound apart from the night murmurs of the sea and village and the metallic tuning of the steel band, a low, almost inhuman cry of loneliness which chilled him. Frightened, he turned to find her leaning hesitantly toward him, her eyes dark with urgency, and her face tight with bewilderment and a growing anger. He started, not understanding, and her arm lifted to stay him. Eagerly she bent closer. But as she uttered the low cry again, as her fingers described her wish to talk, he jerked around, afraid that she would be foolish enough to speak and that once she did they would be brought close. He would be forced then to acknowledge something about her which he refused to grant; above all, he would be called upon to share a little of himself. Quickly he returned to his newspaper, rustling it to settle the air, and after a time he felt her slowly, bitterly, return to her silence . . .

Like sand poured in a careful measure from the hand, the weeks flowed down to August and on the first Monday, August Bank Holiday, Mr Watford awoke to the sound of the excursion buses leaving the village for the annual outing, their backfire pelleting the dawn calm and the ancient motors protesting the overcrowding. Lying there, listening, he saw with disturbing clarity his mother dressed for an excursion – the white head tie wound above her dark face and her head poised like a dancer's under the heavy outing basket of food. That set of her head had haunted his years, reappearing in the girl as she walked toward him the first day. Aching with the memory, yet annoyed with himself for remembering, he went downstairs.

The girl had already left for the excursion, and although it was her day off, he felt vaguely betrayed by her eagerness to leave him. Somehow it suggested ingratitude. It was as if his doves were suddenly to refuse him their song or his trees their fruit, despite the care he gave them. Some vital part which shaped the simple mosaic of his life seemed suddenly missing. An alien silence curled like coal gas throughout the house. To escape it he remained in the grove all day and, upon his return to the house, dressed with more care than usual, putting on a fresh, starched uniform, and solemnly brushing his hair until it lay in a smooth bush above his brow. Leaning close to the mirror, but avoiding his eyes, he cleaned the white rheum at their corners, and afterward pried loose the dirt under his nails.

Unable to read his papers, he went out on the portico to escape the unnatural silence in the house, and stood with his hands clenched on the balustrade and his taut body straining forward. After a long wait he heard the buses return and voices in gay shreds upon the wind. Slowly his hands relaxed, as did his shoulders under the white uniform; for the first time that day his breathing was regular. She would soon come.

But she did not come and dusk bloomed into night, with a fragrant heat and a full moon which made the leaves glint as though touched with frost. The steel band at the crossroads began the lilting songs of sadness and seduction, and suddenly – like shades roused by the night and the music – images of the girl flitted before Mr Watford's eyes. He saw her lost amid the carousings in the village, despoiled; he imagined someone like Mr Goodman clasping her lewdly or tumbling her in the canebrake. His hand rose, trembling, to rid the air of her; he tried to summon his cold laugh. But, somehow, he could not dismiss her as he had always done with everyone else. Instead, he wanted to punish and protect her, to find and lead her back to the house.

As he leaned there, trying not to give way to the desire to go and find her, his fist striking the balustrade to deny his longing, he saw them. The girl first, with the moonlight like a silver patina on her skin, then the boy whom Mr Goodman sent for the coconuts, whose easy strength and the political button – 'The Old Order Shall Pass' – had always mocked and challenged Mr Watford. They were joined in a tender battle: the boy in a sport shirt riotous with color was reaching for the girl as he leapt and spun, weightless, to the music, while she fended him off with a gesture which was lovely in its promise of surrender. Her protests were

168

little scattered bursts: 'But, man, why you don't stop, nuh? . . . But, you know, you getting on like a real-real idiot . . .'

Each time she chided him he leaped higher and landed closer, until finally he eluded her arm and caught her by the waist. Boldly he pressed a leg between her tightly closed legs until they opened under his pressure. Their bodies cleaved into one whirling form and while he sang she laughed like a wanton with her hat cocked over her ear. Dancing, the stones moiling underfoot, they claimed the night. More than the night. The steel band played for them alone. The trees were their frivolous companions, swaying as they swayed. The moon rode the sky because of them.

Mr Watford, hidden by a dense shadow, felt the tendons which strung him together suddenly go limp; above all, an obscure belief which, like rare china, he had stored on a high shelf in his mind began to tilt. He sensed the familiar specter which hovered in the night reaching out to embrace him, just as the two in the yard were embracing. Utterly unstrung, incapable of either speech or action, he stumbled into the house, only to meet there an accusing silence from the clock, which had missed its eight o'clock winding, and his newspapers lying like ruined leaves over the floor.

He lay in bed in the white uniform, waiting for sleep to rescue him, his hands seeking the comforting sound of his doves. But sleep eluded him and instead of the doves, their throats tremulous with sound, his scarred hands filled with the shape of a woman he had once kept: her skin, which had been almost bruising in its softness; the buttocks and breasts spread under his hands to inspire both cruelty and tenderness. His hands closed to softly crush those forms, and the searing thrust of passion, which he had not felt for years, stabbed his dry groin. He imagined the two outside, their passion at a pitch by now, lying together behind the tamarind tree, or perhaps – and he sat up sharply – they had been bold enough to bring their lust into the house. Did he not smell their taint on the air? Restored suddenly, he rushed downstairs. As he reached the corridor, a thread of light beckoned him from her room and he dashed furiously toward it, rehearsing the angry words which would jar their bodies apart. He neared the door, glimpsed her through the small opening, and his step faltered; the words collapsed.

She was seated alone on the cot, tenderly holding the absurd felt hat in her lap, one leg tucked under her while the other trailed down. A white sandal, its strap broken, dangled from the foot and gently knocked the floor as she absently swung her leg. Her dress was twisted around her body – and pinned to the bodice, so that it gathered the cloth between her small breasts, was the political button the boy always wore.

She was dreamily fingering it, her mouth shaped by a gentle, ironic smile and her eyes strangely acute and critical. What had transpired on the cot had not only, it seemed, twisted the dress around her, tumbled her hat and broken her sandal, but had also defined her and brought the blurred forms of life into focus for her. There was a woman's force in her aspect now, a tragic knowing and acceptance in her bent head, a hint about her of Cassandra watching the future wheel before her eyes.

Before those eyes which looked to another world, Mr Watford's anger and strength failed him and he held to the wall for support. Unreasonably, he felt that he should assume some hushed and reverent pose, to bow as she had the day she had come. If he had known their names, he would have pleaded forgiveness for the sins he had committed against her and the others all his life, against himself. If he could have borne the thought, he would have confessed that it had been love, terrible in its demand, which he had always fled. And that love had been the reason for his return. If he had been honest he would have whispered – his head bent and a hand shading his eyes – that unlike Mr Goodman (whom he suddenly envied for his full life) and the boy with his political button (to whom he had lost the girl), he had not been willing to bear the weight of his own responsibility . . . But all Mr Watford could admit, clinging there to the wall, was, simply, that he wanted to live – and that the girl held life within her as surely as she held the hat in her hands. If he could prove himself better than the boy, he could win it. Only then, he dimly knew, would he shake off the pursuer which had given him no rest since birth. Hopefully, he staggered forward, his step cautious and contrite, his hands quivering along the wall.

She did not see or hear him as he pushed the door wider. And for some time he stood there, his shoulders hunched in humility, his skin stripped away to reveal each flaw, his whole self offered in one outstretched hand. Still unaware of him, she swung her leg, and the dangling shoe struck a derisive note. Then, just as he had turned away that evening in the parlor when she had uttered her low call, she turned away now, refusing him.

Mr Watford's body went slack and then stiffened ominously. He knew that he would have to wrest from her the strength needed to sustain him. Slamming the door, he cried, his voice cracked and strangled, 'What you and him was doing in here? Tell me! I'll not have you bringing nastiness round here. Tell me!'

She did not start. Perhaps she had been aware of him all along and had expected his outburst. Or perhaps his demented eye and the desperation rising from him like a musk filled her with pity instead of fear. Whatever, her benign smile held and her eyes remained abstracted until his hand reached out to fling her back on the cot. Then, frowning, she stood up, wobbling a little on the broken shoe and holding the political button as if it was a new power which would steady and protect her. With a cruel flick of her arm she struck aside his hand and, in a voice as cruel, halted him. 'But you best move and don't come holding on to me, you nasty, pissy old man. That's all you is, despite yuh big house and fancy furnitures and yuh newspapers from America. You ain't people, Mr Watford, you ain't people!' And with a look and a lift of her head which made her condemnation final, she placed the hat atop her braids, and turning aside picked up the valise which had always lain, packed, beside the cot – as if even on the first day she had known that this night would come and had been prepared against it . . .

Mr Watford did not see her leave, for a pain squeezed his heart dry and the driven blood was a bright, blinding cataract over his eyes. But his inner eye was suddenly clear. For the first time it gazed mutely upon the waste and pretense which had spanned his years. Flung there against the door by the girl's small blow, his body slowly crumpled under the weariness he had long denied. He sensed that dark but unsubstantial figure which roamed the nights searching for him wind him in its chill embrace. He struggled against it, his hands clutching the air with the spastic eloquence of a drowning man. He moaned – and the anguished sound reached beyond the room to fill the house. It escaped to the yard, and his doves swelled their throats, moaning with him.

Extract from the collection *Soul Clap Hands and Sing*.

GRENADA

Merle Collins

*Merle Collins is from Grenada where she has worked as a teacher and researcher.
She was a member of the National Women's Organization in Grenada and is
currently completing a doctorate at The London School of Economics. A collection of
her poetry* Because the Dawn Breaks *(London, Karia Press) appeared in 1985.
She is a member of African Dawn, a group which performs poetry to African music,
and is actively concerned with creole language issues. With Rhonda Cobham she co-
edited* Watchers and Seekers: Creative Writing by Black Women in
Britain *(Women's Press, 1987), to which she also contributed.* Angel, *her first
novel, (Women's Press, 1988) is set in Grenada.*

*Collins lists Caribbean politics and society and the Grenada revolution as major
influences on her as a writer and these constitute her subject matter in* Angel. *A
considerable virtue of the work, however, is its convincing rendering of 'small
matters' as it grapples with these larger issues. Indeed the latter are allowed to
emerge in and through the ordinary everyday business of a young girl growing up and
a family making a life in a small Caribbean island. The extract which follows, in
which Angel and her family wait to hear the results of the scholarship examination,
illustrates this point.*

Angel

'Angel?'

Angel didn't answer. The only time people were allowed not to
answer one another in the house was when they were at prayer.

'. . . lead us not into temptation, but deliver us – from – evil, Amen.'

'Angel? You praying for ever dis mornin?'

Angel's eyes focused on Christ with the globe. 'Glory be to the father
and to the son and to the holy ghost, as it was in the beginning,' Christ
smiled down at her, 'is now an ever shall be, world without end, Amen!'

Angel went out to the kitchen.

'Go an tidy the rooms an sweep dem out. Sweep out the dining-room an fix the table for breakfast. Simon will sweep the yard when he wake up.'

Angel moved off, grumbling, making sure to keep well out of Doodsie's reach. She knew that a hand could reach out from nowhere and land none too gently on her. By the time Allan had come back in from feeding the cows, they were all ready with breakfast and Simon had swept the yard.

'So today is the great day!' Doodsie sat down and pulled the bowl of callaloo towards her.

'You mean the exam results?' asked Allan. 'She better pass.'

'She better had. Huh! She better had! Anyway, she do it arready an we jus have to let God do the res an hope for the best.'

'So nex year is your turn, young man.' Allan looked meaningfully at Simon, who looked at his plate. 'Pass de pear for me, Doodsie.'

Doodsie handed him the avocado.

'These pears really big, yes, an dey sweet too. Which tree dey come out in? De one at the top of the hill?'

'Hm-hm! Is a good crop.' He glanced at Simon, who looked as though he hoped he might have been forgotten. 'Look, your turn is nex year, you know! An ah lookin out for you! You better be sure you know what you doin!'

'Ye–e–s,' said Doodsie slowly. 'And Angel have another chance at it again nex year if she don pass. She young still. But if they don't pass we will have to try an see how it possible to pay for their schoolin.'

'They better pass! A whole eighty children in the country gettin free high school if they pass an we talkin about if they don't pass? They better pass!'

Two flies buzzed together across the table, settled on the avocado.

'Mu dey, fly!' Angel flapped her hands at them.

'Use de cloth, Angel!' said Doodsie. 'Cover the plate.'

'Mu dey, fly?' said Allan. 'That is any way for people going to school every day to talk? When for you to correct us, youself sayin "Mu dey, fly"?'

Simon giggled. Angel cut her eyes at him.

'If youall finish, bring you plate in de kitchen,' advised Doodsie, 'an stop sitting down dey breakin allyou neck as if somebody give you a jail sentence!'

Angel stood washing up the wares in the kitchen. She could hear her mother talking quietly with her father. He agreed that if the worst came to the worst, he would have to find money to send Simon to high school.

'And Angel?' Doodsie asked.

'Huh! Look, that's a different thing, you know. We might have to choose. We mightn be able to send both of them, and Angel is a girl. They grow up and before you know it is confusion, they don even finish school or they finish, get married, their name not even yours again and somebody else get the praise.'

Is true, thought Doodsie, but she goin still! She threw some scraps through the window. The clean–neck hen rushed to the spot, picked up the piece of bread quickly. From across the yard, the big deep–brown cock saw her and came rushing forward, his wings kicking out. The fowl squawked and ran off. The cock gave chase.

Throughout that morning, out in the field, measuring the task, cracking the cocoa, Allan kept stopping to rest on the handle of his cutlass stuck in the ground, thinking of what he wanted for his children. Simon should be a doctor, not to catch hell in this land like he was doing, killing out his soul case for little or no money. Simon should be a doctor. He would be so proud. Angel should be a nurse or something. If I ever see her with any little man, he thought, I break she tail. He thought of his sister, of how suddenly one day she had stopped being his playmate and was carrying her first child at the age of twelve. He had felt strangely betrayed. And the same had happened with his other sisters, one after the other. And Cristalene, he thought, look at Cristalene today! His mother always said that girl children were too difficult. He spat between his teeth and shouted to the workers to hurry. I would break her blasted neck, he thought angrily.

Throughout that morning, Doodsie was very quiet. Every time Angel tried to say something to her, she would suck her teeth in irritation and brush her away. Angel stood in the kitchen helping her to peel the provision for lunch and watching Simon through the window as he stood in the yard heaving up limes and hitting them with the coconut bat as they fell back down. Doodsie was silent for a while.

◆

Angel said nothing. Doodsie stood at the back door of the kitchen looking up into the damp gloom under the cocoa trees. The air was quite still. She go get de bes if even ah have to scrub floor to give er. She won be like me. By the time I was her age, ah go to six different school arready. Every time Mammie move to another work, so meself behin er. Never could have time to learn nutting. Always like a big chupid-i in de class. As if it were yesterday, Doodsie could see the ring of children around her, small waists jerking this way and that, hands beating to the musical tempo of the taunt. Duncie Duncie Mama Palavi, Duncie, Duncie.

'Look, you big for ten years. You body develop arready an you look more than you age. I tell you arready be careful. Any day now you could expect that ting I tell you about.'

Angel frowned. She hated it when these conversations started. She remembered the day she had pulled up her bodice to show a little boy in the yard her chest. Doodsie had seen her. She had almost half–killed her with licks. She didn't like it when her mother started talking about things like this.

'Anybody interfere with you on the street come an tell me. An study you head. Nobody does expec good out of little girl an all those you tink is you frien just waitin to see you fall for them to laugh. They not interested in you. Any time you see man smilin for you, is because they want to drag you down with them. So study you head. Learn you lesson an don grin grin wid nobody, because the moment you turn you back is laugh they laughing to see how they fool you. You see me in de kitchen here is bluggoe I peeling day in day out an is all for somebody else pocket. I could never have a cent because ah workin without thanks, without pay. You big enough now to know that you father have other children, other people to mind, that he never have enough for us, that the more I work inside is the more he have to give outside.'

The rain had started to drizzle.

'Bon Jé, an ah did mean to wash today, yes! Simon, if ah doh tell you to come in out of the rain, you doh know!'

Simon dashed to the kitchen door. 'De rain only drizzlin, Mammie. Watch de mountain! It won come!'

'Go an siddown inside an if it stop you could go back out!' She pushed open the kitchen door for him to enter. 'Go an see what you brother doin! He wake up an eat, but ah think he musbe sleepin' again!'

'Ah never see a boy could sleep so!'

Simon rushed off inside. Doodsie looked at Angel. 'So study you head. Nobody could be more interested in you than you is in youself. You see for youself dat if ah doh have drawers to put on an ah ask for a dollar for one is confusion.' She looked at Angel. 'Put a little bit o salt in de pot!' Angel stretched behind the coalpot to get the pan of salt off the shelf. 'Study youself. Ah don't want that for you. If you get you own education, nobody is you boss. Ah want the best for Simon too, but he is man, so he start off . . .'

'Mammie,' Simon shouted from the drawing–room, 'ah could go back outside?'

Doodsie looked outside. Glanced up at the mountain. 'Yes. It look like

175

it was just a passing cloud. Simon, now, because he is man, he start off as boss arready. You have to work for it. Study youself!'

Angel said nothing. For some reason she felt like crying. From outside, Simon shouted.

'Mammie! Mammie! Watch!'

He had perfected the skill of hitting the lime the moment it reached eye level. The bat flashed out. Lime centred. Simon looked eagerly up at his mother.

'Good. Bravo! Do it again!'

'Eh!' Angel sucked her teeth. 'I could do that too. That not hard. Dat is someting den?'

'Hush you mout an peel de bluggoe, girl.'

They worked in silence. Doodsie looked thoughtful. Angel was irritable, moving her head to keep off the sandflies, stamping her feet, sucking her teeth. The flies buzzed and worried. The sandflies looked for bare skin and stung.

'Ay! Mammie! Look Rupert!'

'Ay, papa! You wake up? How Mammie baby? You wet! Come lemme change you!' She picked up Rupert and went out of the kitchen.

Angel swept the kitchen. She thought about the scholarship exam. It hadn't been really hard, except that stupid general knowledge paper. Doodsie came back out to the kitchen. Rupert toddled quietly behind her, looking sleepy. She peeled a banana, handed it to him.

'Sit down dey, papa. Look! Pass the callaloo for me, Angel!'

Angel picked up the bunch of leafy green callaloo, handed it to her mother.

'Come, les siddown in de dining–room here and get dat ready!'

Angel sat down. 'Simon now, things different for him. He is man. He growin up to be in charge. You father say Simon education sure if even he don pass scholarship. I say that even if I have to go back on me knees and scrub floor in white people house an leave dis job here dat not payin, yours go be sure, too. But notice what ah tellin you. You not stupid. You could understand. Tings easier for a man. Don shame youself an me. Show dem dat nobody could pull you down. You hear me?'

Angel didn't answer.

'You hear me, Angel?'

'Yes, Mammie,' quietly, with tears sounding at the back of her throat.

'The results go announce on radio tonight. You tink you pass?'

'Yes, Mammie.'

'You sure?'

'Is only the general knowledge ah didn do too good an ah don know

176

how much marks dat carry, but ah tink ah do de arithmetic good an ah know the English was good, so ah tink ah pass.'

'I hope so, chile. Ah really hope so. All you teachers say you very young an you have another chance still but ah would be glad if we could pass de hurdle. You wastin de callaloo, Angel. Just peel off the threads, don throw away dese big junk!' Doodsie took the big junk out of the pan, peeled off the thin thread, put the callaloo into the bowl. 'Ah warning you to study you head. Don take on no little boy that tryin to pull you down, because dat is where confusion start an you life mash up an ah don want dat for you. You hearin me?'

'Yes, Mammie.'

That night, they were all grouped around the radio, waiting for the seven o'clock news. Doodsie's knitting was on her lap. Allan was in a good mood, talking about his cricket days. He used to be the best batsman in the team, he said, had scored a century more than once.

'Is true, Mammie?'

'So he say!'

'Eh! Youself, Doodsie, you know is true.'

Doodsie laughed.

'Dey say he good in truth, although not as good as he sayin.'

'You could still bat good, Daddy?'

Angel and Simon leaned against him. Rupert looked up from the corner where he sat absorbed, using shoes for building. Whatever he found, he used for building. He was always building something, putting shoe upon shoe upon shoe, book upon book upon book, standing back and looking with joy at the result.

'Eh, what do you? None of these fellahs caan touch me, you know. Ask you mudder how dey use to call me.'

Doodsie laughed. 'Bradman!'

'Who is Bradman?' asked Simon and Angel in unison.

'One hell of a cricketer!' Allan leaned back in his seat, ready for the story.

'Uh! Papa Boast.'

'This is the Windward Islands Broadcasting Service. Here is the news read by . . .'

Angel settled down on the floor.

'The British government today announced . . .'

Doodsie said, 'Lemme put dis chile to bed,' picked up Rupert and went towards the room door. Angel started whispering to Simon.

'Hush youall mout an let people listen to the news,' said Allan. 'Youall children jus don listen to news!'

Angel and Simon fidgeted. Tried to look as if they were listening.

Heard nothing until: 'The results of this year's scholarships examination were announced today. The following are the names of those who passed the examination. First: Mark Antoine, St George's RC Boys.'

'Uh–huh! RC get first again! Dat school good, you know!'

'Uh–huh!'

'Ay–ay! Second, third, fourth – and fifth too! wo–o–o–y!' Allan laughed excitedly. 'Nobody caan touch dem, non!'

'Is de belt dat talking dey, you know! Ole Man Henson makin dem understand. Is his pass more dan dose chilren own, yes!'

'Ay! Mammie! Andrea! Andrea come eighth, Mammie!'

'What! Miss Barnes mus be laughin!'

'Woy!'

They fell silent, listening. Angel started to think of the general knowledge paper. Twenty–second. Still no Angel. Simon looked at his sister. He saw the tears start to gather in her eyes. He started tearing the bits of paper in his hand into small pieces, biting his lips and bending over to stare at his feet. He glanced at his father's face. Allan cleared his throat. Doodsie sighed.

'Twenty–fifth: Angel McAllister, St Paul's Government.'

The room exploded. Doodsie was laughing and shouting, Allan looking quietly pleased, Angel crying, Simon on the floor somersaulting.

'Well, we make it, we make it, eh, girl.' Doodsie hugged her, an unusual treat.

'Yes,' said Allan 'you make the McAllister name call. Dat good.'

'Meself,' said Doodsie, 'I don have name, but we make it.'

The announcer was now saying that those who had passed should visit the school of their choice with their parents during the coming week.

It had been decided long before that the convent would be the best for her, since the children and Allan were Catholics; and, anyway, Doodsie felt that the convent gave girls just the sheltered, good type of education that was best. Allan agreed. He trusted Doodsie's judgement in things like this.

Extract from *Angel*.

178

Dionne Brand

Dionne Brand was born in Trinidad and has lived in Toronto for the past 19 years. Brand is already well known for her work as a poet. She has published five books of poetry: 'Fore day Morning *(Toronto, 1978),* Earth Magic *(children's poetry, Toronto, 1980)* Primitive Offensive *(1983),* Chronicles of the Hostile Sun *(1984) and* Winter Epigrams and Epigrams to Ernesto Cardenal in Defence of Claudia *(1983). Her short stories have appeared in several publications. Her first prose collection,* Sans Souci and Other Stories *(1988), was published by Williams-Wallace International, Toronto, as were her three preceding publications. The extract from* 'Photograph' *is from this collection.*

Despite her long absence from the land of her birth, Brand's Caribbean voice remains uncompromised and her evocation of Caribbean places and situations is sharp and moving. 'Photograph' *deals with a situation which is a very frequent feature of Caribbean life: being brought up by a grandmother. Ms Brand sensitively explores the effects of the mother's absence on the mother/daughter relationship as well as the very special bond created between the grandmother and her young granddaughters for whom she is responsible.*

Photograph

We had debated what to call my mother over and over again and came to no conclusions. Some of the words sounded insincere and disloyal, since they really belonged to my grandmother, although we never called her by those names. But when we tried them out for my mother, they hung so cold in the throat that we were discouraged immediately. Calling my mother by her given name was too presumptuous, even though we had always called all our aunts and uncles by theirs. Unable to come to a decision we abandoned each other to individual choices. In the end, after our vain attempts to form some word, we never called my mother by any name. If we needed to address her we stood about until she noticed that we were there and then we spoke. Finally, we never called my mother.

All of the words which we knew belonged to my grandmother. All of them, a voluptuous body of endearment, dependence, comfort and infinite knowing. We were all full of my grandmother, she had left us full and empty of her. We dreamed in my grandmother and we woke up in her, bleary–eyed and gesturing for her arm, her elbows, her smell. We jockeyed with each other, lied to each other, quarrelled with each other and with her for the boon of lying close to her, sculpting ourselves around the roundness of her back. Braiding her hair and oiling her feet. We dreamed in my grandmother and we woke up in her, bleary-eyed and gesturing for her lap, her arms, her elbows, her smell, the fat flesh of her arms. We fought, tricked each other for the crook between her thighs and calves. We anticipated where she would sit and got there before her. We bought her achar and paradise plums.

My mother had walked the streets of London, as the legend went, with one dress on her back for years, in order to send those brown envelopes, the stamps from which I saved in an old album. But her years of estrangement had left her angry and us cold to her sacrifice. She settled into fits of fury. Rage which raised welts on our backs, faces and thin legs. When my grandmother had turned away, laughing from us, saying there was no place to beat, my mother found room.

Our silences which once warded off hunger now warded off her blows. She took this to mean impudence and her rages whipped around our silences more furiously than before. I, the most ascetic of us all, sustained the most terrible moments of her rage. The more enraged she grew, the more silent I became, the harder she hit, the more wooden, I. I refined this silence into a jewel of the most sacred sandalwood, finely–grained, perfumed, mournful yet stoic. I became the only inhabitant of a cloistered place carrying my jewel of fullness and emptiness, voluptuousness and scarcity. But she altered the silences profoundly.

Before, with my grandmother, the silences had company, were peopled by our hope. Now, they were desolate.

She had left us full and empty of her. When someone took the time to check, there was no photograph of my grandmother, no figure of my grandmother in layers of clothing and odd–sided socks, no finger stroking the air in reprimand, no arm under her chin at the front window or crossed over her breasts waiting for us.

My grandmother had never been away from home for more than a couple of hours and only three times that I could remember. So her absence was lonely. We visited her in the hospital every evening. They had put her in a room with eleven other people. The room was bare. You could see underneath all the beds from the doorway and the floors were always scrubbed with that hospital smelling antiseptic which reeked its own sickliness and which I detested for years after. My grandmother lay in one of the beds nearest the door and I remember my big sister remarking to my grandmother that she should have a better room, but my grandmother hushed her saying that it was alright and anyway she wouldn't be there for long and the nurses were nice to her. From the chair beside my grandmother's bed in the hospital you could see the parking lot on Chancery Lane. I would sit with my grandmother, looking out the window and describing the scene to her. You could also see part of the wharf and the gulf of Paria which was murky where it held to the wharf. And St Paul's Church, where I was confirmed, even though I did not know the catechism and only mumbled when Canon Farquar drilled us in it.

Through our talks at the window my grandmother made me swear that I would behave for my mother. We planned, when I grew up and went away, that I would send for my grandmother and that I would grow up to be something good, that she and I and Eula and Ava and Kat and Genevieve would go to Guayaguayare and live there forever. I made her promise that she would not leave me with my mother.

It was a Sunday afternoon, the last time that I spoke with my grandmother. I was describing a bicycle rider in the parking lot and my grandmother promised to buy one for me when she got out of hospital.

My big sister cried and curled herself up beneath the radio when my grandmother died. Genevieve's face was wet with tears, her front braid pulled over her nose, she, sucking her thumb.

When they brought my grandmother home, it was after weeks in the white twelve–storey hospital. We took the curtains down, leaving all the windows and doors bare, in respect for the dead. The ornaments, doilies and plastic flowers were removed and the mirrors and furniture covered with white sheets. We stayed inside the house and did not go out to play. We kept the house clean and we fell into our routine of silence when faced with hunger. We felt alone. We did not believe. We thought that it was untrue. In disbelief, we said of my grandmother, 'Mama can't be serious!'

The night of the wake, the house was full of strangers. My grandmother would never allow this. Strangers, sitting and talking everywhere, even in my grandmother's room. Someone, a great aunt, a sister of my grandmother, whom we had never seen before, turned to me sitting on the sewing machine and ordered me in a stern voice to get down. I left the room, slinking away, feeling abandoned by my grandmother to strangers.

I never cried in public for my grandmother. I locked myself in the bathroom or hid deep in the backyard and wept. I had learned as my grandmother had taught me, never to show people your private business.

When they brought my grandmother home the next day, we all made a line to kiss her goodbye. My littlest sister was afraid; the others smiled for my grandmother. I kissed my grandmother's face hoping that it was warm.

Extract from the collection *Sans Souci and Other Stories*.

Rosa Guy

Rosa Guy was born in Trinidad in 1928 and came to the United States in 1932 with her family. She grew up in Harlem, the setting for many of her novels. Her family name was Cuthbert; she married Warner Guy, now deceased, and has one son. Rosa Guy's first novel, Bird at my Window, *was published in 1966 (Lippincott) and since that time she has written several novels, especially for and about young people, as well as short stories and a play. Her novels include* The Friends *(Holt, 1973);* Ruby: a Novel *(Viking, 1976);* The Disappearance *(Delacorte, 1979) which was named on the 'Best Books for Young Adults 1979' list by the Young Adult Services Division of the American Library Association;* A Measure of Time *(Holt, 1983) and* I Heard a Bird Sing *(Delacorte, 1986).*

Rosa Guy draws upon her West Indian heritage and her experiences in a black immigrant family from the Caribbean, forced to adapt and survive in Harlem, and addresses the problems of ghetto life and the difficulties facing talented and gifted young people in such circumstances. She has been especially appreciated for creating characters who deal with contemporary pressures and serve as role models for her young readers and has thus made a significant contribution in the often neglected area of literature for young adults. The extract 'Désirée Dieu-Donné' is from My Love, My Love *or* The Peasant Girl *(London, Virago, 1987). The story is a retelling of Hans Christian Anderson's 'The Little Mermaid', set in a Caribbean island. Folk tale though it is, it concerns issues of poverty, race, class and the vicissitudes of life in a small tropical island ravaged by storms and in danger of losing its forests.*

182

Rosa Guy's abilities as a raconteur convert a fable for young people into a story with universal application.

Désirée Dieu-Donné

The work of Désirée Dieu-Donné – her heart's work, her life's work – began. And Madame Mathilde worked along with her. When she wanted herbs, Madame Mathilde sent servants to fetch them from the Madame Bonsanté of the closest peasant village. When she needed teas brewed and poultices made, Madame Mathilde instructed the servants in the kitchen to prepare them. And it was she who brought them up to young Daniel's room, and helped prepare him for his daily bath. She stood by while the peasant girl massaged him.

What care! Désirée massaged his legs and feet to the tips of his toes, his arms and hands to the fingertips. She rubbed his back and shoulders with oils. She applied poultices to his crippled leg, which still held the earlier rot, and to his head. She forced him to drink teas to cleanse his blood, teas to calm him, teas to make him sleep. And she asked Madame Mathilde to prepare the potion of soup made up of blood, marrow, and bones, to give him strength.

And nights, when Madame Mathilde left them alone, Désirée curled up beside Daniel on the bed, listening to him breathe, ready to comfort him. When he cried out from his nightmares, she held his head against her breasts and sang:

> *Dor, dor petit popée*
> *You are not alone*
> *I am here to guard you in your sleep*
> *Over the mountains, and over the deep*
> *Through floods, famine, hunger and strife*
> *I shall be here until you make me your wife.*

And so her song had changed. Of course. This had been the wish of the gods. It had been her wish. To be with Daniel Beauxhomme, to make him well. To bring life back to him and to Asaka. To bring comfort and peace to Mama Euralie and Tonton Julian, and to peasants everywhere.

183

Ahh, the papillons grew restive. They beat against the cage. Had she not achieved her wishes? They wanted to be gone now. But Désirée Dieu-Donné held them captive still.

And in the days and weeks that followed, Daniel Beauxhomme grew strong, stronger. The peasant girl sensed it from his lessening weight on her shoulders when they strolled around the grounds in the evenings. In his room during the day, she saw it in his clearing gray eyes, and in the bronze returning to his pale skin. But more, she knew it through her own growing weakness.

She had poured her strength into him. She refused sleep, waiting for his moans. Relentlessly she fought the forces of night that threatened him, disturbing his sleep. Then one night, weakened from the battle, she moaned. He awakened. Finding himself in her arms, he drew her into his. She moaned again. He drew her closer still. Suddenly they were awake – alert. In each other's arms, tied there by an unexplained magic, giving to each other new delights.

Now their nights grew restless with the heat of a new need. Their days, cushioned by calm, held a new tenderness. They looked into each other's eyes and thrilled at the depth of their own beauty, a new knowledge of their most secret selves. Indeed, they had fallen deeply in love.

They talked, and Désirée told Daniel of finding him on the road, crushed and near dead on that darkest of nights. She told him of the care she had taken, forcing him to live. She spoke of singing to him, and of how, in the calm after the storm, he had looked at her, and she at him, and how they had pledged themselves one to the other with their eyes.

Twilights, guarding their aloneness, they plunged into the deep woods. There, before the setting of the sun, they discovered their love anew – in the unfolding of buds into flowers, in the shrilling of birds to their mates, in the movements of brilliantly coloured caterpillars, soon to become butterflies.

Désirée climbed trees and threw down fruits for the crippled Daniel to catch. They ate them while peering through crisscrossing branches at the sky, seeing one star appear, then another and still another until the world was but stars. They let waterfalls beat on their bodies and swam in pools lit by moonlight. They stretched out enfolded in each other's arms, while in the dark, owls hooted overhead and chirping insects questioned their wisdom in a low, throaty chu – urp? Chu – urp? Chu – urp?

And the captive papillons, their mission fulfilled, shook the cage, demanding to be free. But Désirée Dieu-Donné held them captive still . . .

Madame Mathilde read the tale of love in the bright eyes of the young couple. Troubled, she called Désirée aside one day. 'Ti Moune,' she said. 'The crisis for young Daniel has passed. There's no longer need for you to stay.'

'But where shall I go?' Désirée demanded.

'I have no answer to give you. Monsieur Gabriel has gone off to France. Whenever he returns, you can be sure he will reward you well for his son's good health.'

The woman's answer troubled Désirée, and confused her. She went to Daniel Beauxhomme. 'Daniel,' she said. 'Madame Mathilde says you no longer need me. She wants me to leave. She said that your father will reward me for your good health. But how can he repay me for your health, when your life was mine to save?'

'There's no need for you to worry, my love,' Daniel said to her. 'You shall be with me always.' When Madame Mathilde next came, he said, 'Chère Mathilde, you have told Désirée she must leave. I say she cannot. I shall lose my health and strength if she ever leaves. And the next time I shall die. Désirée Dieu-Donné has earned my heart with her care. It now belongs to her.'

'A curse,' the good woman cried. 'The gods have entrapped me! Monsieur Gabriel will punish me. You are my responsibility. As he left, he warned me to keep my eyes sharp and my senses alert. Oh, how I fear his anger.'

'Madame Mathilde,' the young man answered. 'In this room Mistress Désirée Dieu-Donné is responsible for me. To you I give a new responsibility. Make my mistress into a grande demoiselle whom even my father will be unable to resist.'

And so, the following weeks, the hotel was filled with excitement: dressmakers were hired, and hairdressers, and shoemakers. Beauticians and manicurists came and went. A buzzing, a gossip spread through the hotel and even into the grande ville. Everyone had heard about and was talking about the handsome Daniel Beauxhomme having chosen for himself a peasant as mistress.

Accomplished designers fashioned clothes and shoes of extraordinary beauty; their reputations in high circles demanded this. Lovely women, they made themselves ugly with jealousy; how did a black, a peasant, win the heart of Daniel Beauxhomme, a grand homme, whom they all desired? How did a peasant, a black, come to live in the Hotel Beauxhomme among the rich, whereas they, with their copper-coloured or light tan or brown skin, and with all their accomplishments, had never been accepted but as highly paid courtesans?

As they fitted clothes on Désirée, or dressed her hair, these women kept up a stream of graceless remarks to each other, loud enough for Désirée's ears: 'What do you think will happen when Andrea Galimar comes back home from school in France?' Or, 'I thought the Galimars and the Beauxhommes were to become one big family.' Or, 'I hear Andrea Galimar is more beautiful than ever. She always had the fairest skin – almost white.' Or, 'I hear that now Andrea is so–o–o polished.' Or, 'I wonder why Monsieur Gabriel Beauxhomme decided so suddenly to dash off to France?'

When Désirée had gone from the room the remarks were more direct: 'My God, did you ever see anyone so black?' Or, 'Does she really think she can hold on to that grand homme?' Or, 'One thing Désirée Dieu-Donné will never have to face – a priest. Who ever heard of a rich mulatto marrying a black – rich or poor?' Or, 'What a name, Dieu-Donné. God–given indeed! What God gave, God surely can take away.'

Désirée and Daniel, insulated by their love, saw and heard only each other. After their evening walks and baths, they went into their rooms, where they looked out from the balconies. From one they admired the city sprawling beneath them; from another they looked out at the distant sea, calm in the moonlight as if waiting to display turbulence or gaiety or, as everyone knew, its overpowering savagery.

'I'm almost as strong as ever,' Daniel Beauxhomme exclaimed one night as they looked out at the mountains surrounding the hill. 'I have almost recovered my health and, except for my lame leg, my beauty. I thought I had lost both forever, and perhaps my life, in the wildness of my youth. How lucky I am that you exist, Désirée. How blessed to have you with me, child of the storm. Tell me, in this entire world, what can I give you?'

Désirée smiled. Happiness, she wanted to say. But she was already happier than ever. To be your wife, she wanted to say. But did that need to be said? Then she thought of Mama Euralie, of Tonton Julian. Looking up at the bare tops of the Black Mountains, she said, 'There is an old man in my village, Monsieur Bienconnu. He says that once upon a time the mountains of this Jewel of the Antilles were green. He said they were thick with forests of hardwood trees reaching up to the sun. He said that a variety of bush and herbs grew among the trees, guarding their roots and supporting the goddess Asaka, who caused fertility and all growing things to live. Agwe respected Asaka then. He worked with her. Together they brought forth an abundance that protected the land and the people.

'I want those mountains green again. I want hardwood trees reaching for the sun again. I want Agwe to be kind and never to punish the good

Asaka again. I want them to work together to end misery on this Jewel of the Antilles.'

As Daniel's arms tightened around her, Désirée looked down. In the shadows of the trees she saw a figure lurking. A man – a part of the darkness. He wore a top hat, and the cigar he smoked glowed in the dark. Désirée cried out.

'What is it?' Daniel Beauxhomme asked.

'There's someone in the garden. I'm afraid. It's someone who means us harm.'

Daniel Beauxhomme rushed from the room. She saw him as he strode through the garden, searching. He came back a short time later. 'No one is out in the gardens,' he said, 'except that fellow Lucifus doing his rounds.'

◆

'The men are handsome. They are all kind. But I cannot leave Daniel,' Désirée answered.

'Young Daniel is well. Your work here is done. Seek happiness elsewhere, while there is still time.'

'Daniel is my happiness,' Désirée said. 'I am his. Madame Mathilde, I thought you loved him.'

'I do.'

'Then why don't you wish him well?'

'I love him. And I love you,' the good woman said. 'And it's your happiness for which I am concerned. Your one chance for happiness is for you to leave now. Go as far away from this island as air and space will allow.'

'I cannot leave this island, Madame Mathilde. I belong to this island, as Daniel belongs to it. The gods willed it so.'

'Then the gods did curse you,' the woman cried. 'They know how deep the love of peasant and patron runs. How strong the bonds that bind them. But hatred runs deeper.

'We peasants hate them because they reject our blackness. They hate us because we remind them of theirs. My child, that is the curse of the Antilles, created by the enslavement of our fathers.

'Désirée Dieu-Donné, you are the best of us: woven from the fragments of orphans; imbued with the swollen hopes, the courage of dreamers; sensitised with the hearts of lovers; made compassionate through the tears of the poor, mourning those lives wasted for having lived. All have washed over you, deceiving you into believing that all things are possible. You are the best in us – our humanity.

187

'Oh, the gods did choose well. But how dared they choose so tender a flower to bear the burden of our shared guilt!

'Go, dearest Désirée Dieu-Donné. Go, before this love destroys you – destroys us. Go now, my child. Go while this chance has been given to you – or, my dear, the ocean will not be big enough to hold our tears . . .'

Terrified by the woman's intensity, Désirée ran. She ran into the garden and stood looking around at the flowers, smelling their fragrance, seeing in the cultivation of the garden and the surrounding woods the accumulated rewards for her devotion. Then she cried out, 'Daniel Beauxhomme and Désirée Dieu-Donné are one. All this belongs to us.'

Then, in a frenzy, she went looking for still another papillon. She searched the gardens and the orchard. She had given up in despair when one alit next to her at the side of the pool. Patiently, Désirée reached out her arm. She was about to close her hand around it when a snarl from the other side of the pool forced her to turn.

Lucifus stood there. He kept staring at her, his ugly face twisted. Squat, massive of shoulders, he clenched and unclenched his hands. His red eyes reflected anger and hatred of this peasant–turned–lady.

He had heard about her, and resentment had kept him looking for her. Curiosity at never seeing her had fanned his resentment. Now he recognised her as the peasant girl who had sat with the artisans at the hotel entrance – elusive, untouchable.

And as he stood there, angry now that he recognised her, a change came over him. Désirée saw it. Papa Gé had taken possession of him. He became part of the darkness. His tongue darted from his hissing, blood–red mouth. He grinned around a cigar. Becoming agile, he jumped across the pool and reached for Désirée. But even though possessed, the groundskeeper found his arms shackled by Désirée's elegance. He dared not touch her. Instead he leered, spat, and was gone.

Désirée, her hand still outstretched, turned quickly to seize the papillon. But the butterfly sensed her terror and flew beyond reach. Overwhelmed by fear Désirée stood staring at the empty space where the papillon had been as though she had turned to stone.

Extract from *My Love, My Love or The Peasant Girl*.

Marion Patrick-Jones

Marion Patrick–Jones was born in Trinidad in the 1930s. She attended the prestigious (all–girls) St Joseph's Convent in Port–of–Spain and was the first woman admitted to the Imperial College of Tropical Agriculture (now the St Augustine campus of the University of the West Indies). She worked for a year after that in a ceramics factory in Brooklyn, New York, then returned to Trinidad to a job at the Carnegie Free Library, and a diploma in library science. In 1959 she enrolled for graduate studies in social anthropology at London University, becoming during her time in London one of the founders of CARD (Campaign Against Racial Discrimination). She currently lives in Paris where she works with UNESCO and is active in race relations.

Her two novels, Pan Beat *(1973) and* J'Ouvert Morning *(1976) were published by Columbus Publishers, Trinidad.* J'Ouvert Morning *looks at the life of a Trinidadian middle class family held together, ironically, by their isolation, variously seeking refuge from a sense of failure in the umpromising harbours of drink, philandering, money and position, religion and radical politics. Marion Patrick–Jones's drunken Elizabeth – 'Stinking Fur Liz', as she is nicknamed – is feisty, robust and self-affirming even in her dissoluteness. The bonding (across social class) of Elizabeth and Rosie who share womanness, Trinidadianness, and a personally defined and highly prized independence, is a contribution to gender discourse that is well ahead of its time.*

Elizabeth

For Elizabeth Grant one thing made this day different: she had met her nephew, Junior, and he had spoken to her. She had been standing near to Rosie's tray on Frederick Street ole talkin' about the price of khus khus grass and wooden hangers when Junior hopped out of a pick up taxi, held her by the elbow and said, 'Aunt Liz, how you doing?' Until Junior had come she had been dividing her time between Rosie and commenting on the big shots who had passed her by. She knew them all, she assured Rosie, personally. It was early in the day and she was not yet drunk. She had already done her morning's quota of duties. She had been to mass, paid her periodic visit to some 'boys' who were starting a tailoring co–operative, cussed out a policeman who had moved her on

189

the day before, collected a loaf of hops bread and cheese from a parlour in Duncan Street. The last stop before she wandered to a rum shop was always Rosie's tray. She and Rosie had become friendly over Ray Burnett and over politics. Rosie had spent most of her life – since she was fifteen – selling cigarettes, matches, sweets, khus khus grass, and of late coconut–shell shac shacs especially put on for American tourists. She sat, legs apart, straw hat on, before a store front on Frederick Street. From there she viewed the scene around, registering each minute change in this person or that. Snippets of passing conversation were saved, sorted out, added to. The size of each person's shopping paper bag was noticed as well as which store had issued it. From all of this Rosie worked out the news of the day. Rosie had known them all when they were what Elizabeth called 'snotty–nosed kids', but which Rosie primly called 'runny–nosed children'! She had watched their parents shopping down town, or lingering at the street corners. There were some people in whom Rosie was particularly interested; those who had made it. They fascinated her. She had, she swore, picked them out when they were still young, noted their return to Frederick Street after being abroad, or the way they walked after having made a good marriage. Rosie's other preoccupation was with 'independence'. She counted the number of girls who had been discharged from the big bright stores, or the salesmen who were in a job today and out tomorrow and came to the conclusion that the only safety was in 'independence'. She was independent behind her tray sitting on the turned–over empty box which served her as a stool. She was not, she stressed, dependent on Ray Burnett for a job, or Bullseye Charlie for police protection, nor on any madam for a week's pay. She could, she added, dispose of her sugar cakes as she damn well felt like. She always kept one for Elizabeth. She had been doing that ever since Elizabeth was a girl at Convent school breaking Sister Marie's instructions never to eat in the street. Rosie always discussed the news with Elizabeth. They had a high regard for each other's intelligence. It was Rosie who had first warned Elizabeth that Ray Burnett was a son–of–a–bitch. She knew it from the precise skimping way he walked and she had heard he and Bullseye Charlie threatening to clean up the town and drive her off the streets. Elizabeth had bust the warning when the boys were marching in 1970 and Rosie had had time to hide her tray, wrap a red cloth around her head and join their parade. She hadn't lost a thing and now Rosie's sugar cakes were bought by all the Black Power people. Rosie's tray was Elizabeth's main vantage point for Frederick Street, and it was through Rosie that Elizabeth had made friends in the barrack yards Behind the Bridge. Everyone was related to Rosie. Rosie had just whispered that John's wife

Elaine was looking more and more like a soucouyant, up bright and early 'foreday mornin' haunting down town, and that Ray Burnett and Bulleseye Charlie looked as if the devil was catching up with them they were suddenly so mild, when Junior caught Elizabeth by the elbow. Rosie was particularly fond of Junior, she liked the way he wore his collar braked back like a man and he was always asking for his Aunt Elizabeth. The people Rosie liked were never those she prophesied would go far. It was a point on which she and Elizabeth disagreed. Junior had stood around for a while, shutting Rosie up with his presence and forcing her to push two shac shacs before a goggled, camera swinging, shirt—outside tourist. 'Aunt Liz,' he told Elizabeth, 'where you been hidin', man, I haven't seen you for weeks.'

'I have,' Elizabeth assured him, pulling herself up, straightening an old fur around her shoulders, and pulling down her dress skirt, 'been busy. Getting the country along proper lines is a hell of a job. You aren't finished with one thing when another starts up.'

Junior agreed with her. Only the night before he and the boys had said the same thing. They had begun by wondering what they would do for Christmas. They would lime parangs at Arima now that the old custom had been revived. They had moved in imagination from one parang to the other, from one house to the other, dancing and singing and feteing. After that they had discussed a J'Ouvert morning band. They would play all the crazy people on the island. The little problem was who was crazy. They argued and argued over that. Each mad person had a backer among the boys who would produce cogent reasons for the person being perfectly sane. Everyone agreed that Elizabeth Grant was not mad at all, she had simply done what they all wished they could do. She had ditched the lot, 'told them', Junior had said, 'where to go and what to do when they got there', and she served as a reminder of the hypocrisy of their parents. She had been their friend, one of them – until she began shaking up the place. At first Junior had been ashamed of Aunt Elizabeth. Whenever she came to their house in Ellerslie Park a scandal would break out bringing the street to their verandahs. He had feared meeting her, dirty half drunk on the corner of some street. He had had to live down the taunt of having an aunt who was known as 'Stinking Fur Liz'. As time went on shame turned to pride. He had moved into a group of boys who called themselves 'The Gettysburg Patriots'. Gettysburg had been chosen because someone had read Abraham Lincoln's address the day before they had to choose a name. Their main job was to bring Trinidad Culture to the schoolroom. They had emerged after the cultural anguish which followed the attempted revolution of 1970. They wrote poetry, painted, beat pan, went in force to parangs and calypso tents – and idolized Elizabeth. Last night he had been delegated to draw Elizabeth in as an honorary member of their group. They wanted her experience for the planning of their carnival J'Ouvert band.

The band this J'Ouvert was to be the culmination of their defiance, the manifesto of a new generation for a new society. The idea had arisen that night when his mother had stood on the veranda, her ragged hysterical voice one with her nervous face. There was something bordering on insanity in the way that she had come out, yelled, retreated, slamming doors and windows as if to escape something which was more than the harmless music that they were beating. Her housecoat was tied tightly around her waist, a pair of long hanging earrings jumped backwards and forwards. She seemed a wild haunted apparition which, in some inverted way, made what they were doing a revolution. After she had left they had named each other: Fidelista, Che Chica, Karlie Marx, Mao Meow, Malcom etcetera, and they had hit on the idea of a J'Ouvert band as their advertisement that the end had come. Elizabeth would lead it, carrying high the banner of the destruction from which would spring some unplanned future. The Pure One, they called her. Elizabeth the pure. For wasn't she untouched by the corruption, the disease that hollowed out his mother's eyes into dark mascara and ringed pencil? He had come upon Elizabeth once, carefully chalking a poem on a pavement to be erased by the passing feet hours later. He had seen her with a bundle of stolen faded flowers aimlessly talking to them and to herself. It was this Elizabeth to which he returned.

◆

This evening Elizabeth was less drunk than she had been for months. The houses seemed starker, the streets straight, people distinguishable. She began her thinking where the calendar had interrupted her. It was impossible to analyse the 'whys' in silence. Each attempt brought with it a desire to take another drink from the nip bottle she carried along with her. 'I cannot let Junior meet me looking like an old hag,' she told herself, 'I used to be beautiful. When I walked into a room the whole room stopped, man. I'm not going to drink tonight. I'm going to talk over the past with Junior and plan for the future. Know your own past and the future will fend for itself. So we begin with the past.' She kicked a tin can across the pavement, 'sounds like church bells, it's time for the "Angelus". Proof and the stars come out, one by one, one bright in the blue sky and then it's dark and on they come. Where shall I start. The wise men wandered over the desert until they came to a child in a

192

manger. They followed stars. Wild dreams in the sky and proof one comes up, look yonder, Junior, proof one then two then a dozen and the Milky Way. Dreams that's where you begin and then madness. I'm not mad. But if I'm not, then what am I?' She stopped to consider it. 'Dusk they call it. Twilight. Lasts a second and down the darkness and on the stars, flip on switch and on the stars. Can't count them. Shining above us. So on they walked across the desert to a hope that is a star. High in the sky, snap my fingers at them. Snap, snap thumb and finger. Last night I counted five hundred sitting on the pavement in one small space. Now if I had walked I could have found five hundred more, collected into an apron, gathered into a skirt, stars and they'd jump around sparkle around, spill over a Christmas tree. Eyes up, head up totter totter, I can almost walk straight heel first, toe next and in a line. Who says I'm drunk? The rum shops close at night for then they're the stars to give hope. But in the day oh they're cosy and we drink and klup klurp drink and kloop swallow and arrgh belcch, all drinking, waiting, equal. Looking alike and smelling alike and descending into hell. Finished. Not not that. Alike and ended and drunk and oh there's dreams in each eye. You can dream awake when you're drunk. The world merges into a cloud and there's nothing left that isn't fancy. All furry and slouched praying and all full of hope, drunk. Straight from the bottle, that's courage for you. Straight in a line toe after heel and a little bit, sway, like dem first–class women shaking their hips. Sway Liz. Whew I used to be one of those and sometimes when I'm not drunk I remember and I feel myself pulled back in and going mad. When I'm not drunk something says: "Liz that's the way it is and it's no use fighting it." It has always been like that, anything else is an illusion. But when I'm drunk then I see the truth that lives, faces, counters, buildings all are only part of a masquerade unreal world of pretence or hope. It's a choice. Sober and pretend, drunk or hope. Can't have both. Told that to Rosie this morning and she didn't believe me. I could see her thinking there goes crazy stinking Liz. But tell me who's sane if they don't go mad? Rosie is mad, give me a sugar cake that she could have sold to a bigtime tourist trying to escape into a holiday. Afraid, alone. I am so afraid of going back and afraid of staying out. There's a contradiction and I'm alone both ways. I can feel the pull back, back before the stars and back into it all and the past forgiven. What was the past? Let's see! It drops like darkness, swish down and I can't remember. If I drink I'll remember a little bit. But what? I feel as if, as if, Junior, I can't tell. It makes me laugh the encounter with the future that is Junior or the future that hangs around waiting, waiting to be conceived. Carnival and we re–

create the past in the present, I can tell him that. I'm afraid of that past and the future will exclude those like me, who like me, as if we weren't of one robe seamless and woven together without a stitch. Yourself is the best person to talk to. Once upon a time, so fairy stories begin because the past is only a tale, I used to address the people. Now I address myself and talk to myself a world within ours and body and head and feet and I can feel the aloneness as when, as now I hold out my finger–tips to trip them along the bars of a fence. Fast and it pains and you know that you exist and that hurt exists outside of you. Like people. So I talk to myself. I can mutter like water dripping down a wet hillside plip plop and a wet frond of a fern trembles. Plip and it glistens. Thoughts remain unstolen, and mad they are unsold unused, drunk they can be rustled apart to be stuck back into a puzzle. Carnival is the re–creation of the past. I said that before, didn't I?'

'Confessions. I have wanted to be great. Forgiveness for presumption. Forgive me father for I have sinned, I have wanted to be a saint. I confess that I hate it all and fear it all and love it all and that I would go back if the road was not blocked by the past and pot–holed by the future. Confession. I drink. Not too much, that's the problem, only enough to unload guilt on to a bottle. Junior is wrong. My mother suffered and my father suffered sacrificing today for what? For nothing any of us can repay them with. We sell them if we succeed and we sell them if we fail. Confession. I am the other side of Ray Burnett and of Elaine Grant. I hate them and I hate myself. HATE that's the way you spell hate. Creep up like a ghost and shoosh onto them out of the dark. Mother of the opt outs and the cop outs and those who refuse to build a future at all have mercy on us. We live roofless not even "Zandolie find your hole" applies to us. Escaping torment in the illusion of drink and sanity in the illusion of madness. It's a fraud, it's not Stinking Fur Liz. I want to cry. To cry for myself. I used to be beautiful, do you know that? And clean, do you know that? I used to be and I want to be and I dare not be.'

'Lord and our Lady, mercy. Power to the powerless, mercy. And we are the most powerless of all, threatening like my vomit yesterday – no, I wasn't drunk – to be spewed up, hiccuped up. Power, darlings, power. That's Junior, a power band, I'll lead it as I did that day when we sang to the end of the war and the beginning of peace. And I'll shoot my fist into the air, high out of despair. It will be enough to keep me sober for two damn days, drunkenness in itself.'

'And middle class. From Woodbrook. A squared sterile place that used to be a plantation and that bred us in O'Connor Street, Gallus Street, Luis Street, Carlos Street, Alfredo Street, Cornelio Street. And I love it beyond talking or drinking or vomiting. It holds on to my heart and squeeze, squeeze and I hate myself, HATE, *Hate*. And hate it. HATE, *Hate*. It was pregnant with Ray Burnett, and Elaine Grant and with me too. Only a Behind the Bridge whored with St Clair. Aunt Dora and Douglah Mouse. That is history fer yer. Come on fur, you're mink. God will awaken Woodbrook and Belmont and Cascade and Maraval and the statue will see. You're a fool Stinking Fur Liz. You love it because it sleeps. Don't touch Woodbrook, leave it as it is. *Leave it*. A monument to dreams turned into nightmares. The skimping and the saving a blasted penny a day. Junior comes, *Aunt Liz*, and I wish to return to Woodbrook out of the gutter. That's what they say. I'm in the gutter. But I made my vows. Mother Bridget was innocent. And the vows are poverty, chastity and obedience. To be innocent of money, love of power. That's Our Lady fer yer. Confession. We wanted all three. God, for a drink. Junior, I'll move a toast.

> Here's to Ash Wednesday morning.
> Hail Holy Queen, Mother of Mercy.
> Hail our life, our sweetness and our hope . . .

I haven't forgotten it, we used to say it after the rosary at lunchtime. St Joseph's Convent. Poor banished children of Eve. Ashes on your forehead in a cross. St Patrick's stands grey, sombre, shrugging aside its garden, unimpressed by the ghosts which walk and St Theresa's opens down its steps and on to the street. Pray for us Holy Mother of God. "Hallelujah. Hallelujah" said the Baptist woman, heads tied, hands clapping, shoulders swaying. "Hallelujah" she said with eyes closed and the Spirit descended groaning, shivering. "Sing it out, sing it out. Eh, but leave something for we, na. Is every t'ing so dem spirits must t'ief?" Ray Burnett's mother, high priestess of the Children of Christ reformed, forehead knotted in purple cotton, a yellow embroidered black satin stole around her neck grabbed my elbow after Junior had left. "Prayer, penance and mourning," she continued whispering to me, "for Ethopia shall arise saith the Lord. And then there shall be time for Hallelujahs and rejoicing. Scruntin' done".'

Extracts from *J'Ouvert Morning*.

Merle Hodge

Merle Hodge was born in Trinidad in 1944 and has spent most of her life living and working in the Caribbean. Author of Crick Crack, Monkey *(Deutsch, 1970; Heinemann Caribbean Writers Series, 1981) as well as short stories for children, numerous articles and reviews and a translation of a collection of poems by Leon Damas. Merle Hodge received her high school education in Trinidad and Tobago then read French at University College, London, where she obtained BA and MA degrees. She has also studied and worked in France and Denmark and travelled extensively in Europe, West Africa and the Caribbean. She has lectured in French at the University of the West Indies and taught in high schools in Trinidad and Grenada, where she worked during the Bishop regime, being there when the Americans arrived. She presently lives at Hodge Trace in St Augustine, Trinidad, with her teenage son, and lectures part–time at UWI, St Augustine. 'Attracted to and probably inspired by modern French writers such as André Gide, Albert Camus and Jean Paul Sartre', she says she also admires the style if not the vision of V. S. Naipaul. She is currently working on her second novel.*

In Crick Crack, Monkey *Merle Hodge considers – often humorously – the growing up of Tee, her young heroine, as she moves between the robust, earthy, near-idyllic life of the country where her grandmother (Ma) lives, the boisterous home of Tantie, and the pretentious middle-class household of Aunt Beatrice. Tee is caught between the radically different values of Ma and Tantie, and Aunt Beatrice, a conflict still unresolved at the end of the book. In this extract, from which the title of our anthology is taken, Ma tells Tee the story of her grandmother's insistence on being called by 'her true–true name'. The fact that the incident occurs at Ma's country place perhaps suggests something about the context in which self–knowing and self–affirming are best achieved.*

Her True-True Name

The very next day we were being hustled off to Ma, away away up in Pointe d'Espoir, with Toddan falling asleep on Mikey's lap as usual and Mikey having to climb the track with him over one shoulder and the suitcase in the other hand. When we came back it would be time for me to go to school, and Toddan they could simply lose among Neighb' Ramlaal–Wife's own when there was no one at home.

The August holidays had already begun, so that all the multitude was there. Our grandmother was a strong, bony woman who did not smile unnecessarily, her lower jaw set forward at an angle that did not brook opposition or argument. She did not use up too many words at a time either, except when she sat on the step with us teeming around her, when there was a moon, and told us 'nancy–stories. If the night was too dark or if it was raining there was no story–telling – it was inconceivable to her that one should sit inside a house and tell 'nancy–stories. At full moon there was a bonus and then we would light a black–sage fire for the mosquitoes and sand–flies and the smoke smelt like contented drowsiness. And when at the end of the story she said 'Crick crack?' our voices clambered over one another in the gleeful haste to chorus back in what ended on an untidy shrieking crescendo:

> *Monkey break 'e back*
> *On a rotten pommerac!*

And there was no murmur of protest when she ordered with finality: 'That is enough. Find allyu bed.'

On most afternoons we descended to the beach in a great band. Ma saluting houses on the way:

'Oo–oo Ma–Henrietta!'

'Oo–oo!' a voice would answer from the depths of the house or from somewhere in the backyard.

'Is me an' mih gran's passin'.'

'Right, Ma–Josephine!'

Ma brought with her a wooden box and a stick. While we splashed about in the water she sat immobile and straight–backed on her box, her hands resting together on the stick which she held upright in front of her. When someone started to venture too far out she rapped sharply on the box with the stick. And when it was time to go she rapped again: 'Awright. Come–out that water now!'

Then we walked along the sand, straggled and zig–zagged and played along the sand, to where they drew the nets in, and we 'helped' in this latter operation, fastening ourselves like a swarm of bees to the end of the rope and adding as much to the total effort as would a swarm of bees bunched at the end of the thick hauling–rope. Afterwards we swooped down and collected the tiny fishes that they left on the beach, and Ma let us roast these in the fire at home.

Ma's land was to us an enchanted country, dipping into valley after valley, hills thickly covered with every conceivable kind of foliage, cool green darknesses, sudden little streams that must surely have been

197

squabbling past in the days when Brar Anancy and Brar Leopard and all the others roamed the earth outsmarting each other. And every now and then we would lose sight of the sea and then it would come into sight again down between trees when you least expected to see it, and always, it seemed, in a different direction; that was frightening too. We went out with Ma to pick fruit, she armed with a cutlass with which she hacked away thick vines and annihilated whole bushes in one swing. We returned with our baskets full of oranges, mangoes, chennettes, Ma bent under a bunch of plantains that was more than half her size.

Ma had a spot in the market on Sunday mornings, and she spent a great part of the week stewing cashews, pommes–cythères, cerises, making guava–cheese and guava jelly, sugar–cake, nut–cake, bennay–balls, toolum, shaddock–peel candy, chilibibi . . . On these days we hung slyly about the kitchen, if only to feed on the smells; we were never afforded the opportunity of gorging ourselves – we partook of these delicacies when Ma saw fit, and not when we desired. She was full of maxims for our edification, of which the most baffling and maddening was:

> *Who ask*
> *don't get*
> *Who don't ask*
> *don't want*
> *Who don't want*
> *don't get*
> *Who don't get*
> *don't care*

For her one of the cardinal sins of childhood was gluttony: 'Stuff yu guts today an' eat the stones of the wilderness tomorrow.' (Ma's sayings often began on a note of familiarity only to rise into an impressive incomprehensibility, or vice versa, as in 'Them that walketh in the paths of corruption will live to ketch dey arse'.)

She was equal to all the vagaries of childhood. Nothing took her by surprise – she never rampaged, her initial reaction was always a knowing 'Hm'. Not that one permitted oneself the maximum of vagaries in Ma's house – her eye was too sharp and her hand too quick. But there were the odd times that somebody thought she wasn't looking. Sometimes there would be a chase, exciting but brief, when the culprit was hauled back panting to face the music in front of us all. Sometimes he was merely set free again, since he was already frightened to death and would certainly never try that one again.

Just as there were enough of us to play Hoop and Rescue and every conceivable game, so there were enough of us for the occasional outbreak of miniature gang–warfare. We sat for hours under the house in two camps proffering hearty insults. The division usually fell between those who were kept by Ma and those of us who didn't really live there. Ma's children were the 'bush–monkeys' and 'country–bookies' and they in turn made it known to us how deep was their longing for the day when we would all depart so they could have their house and their yard and their land to themselves again. This stung deep for though we knew beyond doubt that it was equally our house and yard and land yet it was those fiends who lived in the house all year round and played in the yard and went on expeditions into the land with Ma when we were not there. If hostilities lasted till a mealtime, then we placed ourselves on opposite sides of the table and eyed each other with contempt. And if they lasted until night–time, then going to bed was an uncomfortable affair, for it took rather longer to fall asleep when every muscle of your body and every inch of your concentration was taut with the effort of not touching your neighbour. But we the vacation batch always had our revenge when it was time to go home and our big–people had come to fetch us and we were all dressed up for the trip home and being fussed over – Ma's children looked a little envious then.

Ma awoke every morning with a groan quickly routed by a brief loud cheups. She rose at a nameless hour and in my half–sleep I saw a mountain shaking off mist in one mighty shudder and the mist falling away in little drops of cloud. The cheups with which Ma greeted the day expressed her essential attitude before the whole of existence – what yu mus' beat–up yuself for? In the face of the distasteful and unavoidable, the unexpected and irreversible, all that Ma could not crush or confound with a barked word or surmount with her lioness strength, she reacted to with a cheups, more or less loud, more or less long. Thus she sucked her teeth loudly and without further comment when the iron pot full of rice spitefully tipped itself over into the fire; when the sun took to playing monkey–wedding with the rain the moment she had put the final clothes–peg to her miles of washing strung from the breadfruit tree to the zaboca tree, from the zaboca tree to the house–post and from the house–post to the chicken–run post, Ma sucked her teeth and turned her back.

And there were the days of real rain. We could see it coming, down across the water, a dark ceiling letting down slow grey streamers into the horizon (that was God pee–peeing into his posie) and then it would be pounding the earth like a thousand horses coming at us through the trees. It was frightening and exciting. A sudden greyness had descended upon everything and we had seconds in which to race about the yard like mad—ants helping Ma to place her assortment of barrels and buckets in places where they would catch the water. And all the time the rain pounding nearer, racing to catch us. When the first messenger spray hit us there was pandemonium – we stampeded into the house, some squealing with a contagious excitement. We ran round shutting the windows, pulling out buckets and basins to place under the leaks, still squealing and colliding with each other. As the windows were closed one by one a cosy darkness crept in, and we felt as if our numbers were growing. We all collected into one room. Sometimes we piled onto the big—bed and made a tent of the coverlets, tying them to the four posts of the bed. Under the tent the commotion was sustained, rising to squealing pitch at every flash of lightning and crack of thunder, or every time the tent collapsed about us, or when a lath fell so that a part of the bed caved in under some of us; or when someone chose this situation of inescapable intimacy to emit an anonymous but very self—assertive poops. It was impossible to detect the owner, and chaos ensued while every man accused his immediate neighbour. In the end we had to count the culprit out by means of Ink—Pink—Mamma—Stink, and the man thus denounced was emitted bodily amidst a new burst of commotion.

Meanwhile Ma bustled about the house – we knew that she was just as excited as we were, barricaded into the darkened house with the rain drumming on the galvanise and surrounding us with heavy purring like a huge mother—cat. Ma seemed to be finding things to do so as not to yield to the temptation to come and crawl under the sheets and play tent with us. Then she came in with a big plate of sugar—cake and guava—cheese, and pretended to be scandalised at the way we were treating the bedclothes.

And when the rain had stopped we dressed up in Grampa's old jackets and went out with Ma to look at the river. This was like a ritual following upon the rain – she had to go and see the river. We walked behind her squelching joyously in the new puddles and mud. The air smelt brown and green, like when the earth was being made. From a long way off the river was calling to us through the trees, in one continuous groan, so that when we finally came to it, wet and splashed from the puddles and from the bushes we had brushed against, it was as though we had been straining along in it the whole time. Ma stopped abruptly and spread out both her arms to stop us, as though it were likely that we would keep on walking right into the fast ochre water. We counted how many trees it had risen past on the bank. If the river came down every week Ma's rapture would be quite as new.

'Eh!' she exclaimed, and then fell back into her trance. Then a little later on 'Eh!' shaking her head from side to side, 'Well yes, well yes!' We stood around her in an unlikely silence like spattered acolytes in our jumble–sale clothes, in the bright air hanging out crisp and taut to dry, and the river ploughing off with the dirt and everything drenched and bowing and satisfied and resting before the world started up again from the beginning.

We roamed the yard and swarmed down to the water and played hoop around the breadfruit tree as if we would always be wiry–limbed children whose darting about the sun would capture like amber and fix into eternity. Although Ma exclaimed upon our arrival each year at how big we'd got, yet all the holidays at Pointe d'Espoir were one August month, especially in the middle part of the day when everything seemed to set in the still, hanging brightness – our games and squabbling; the hens with their heads down scratching about the yard; the agreeable-ness of sitting clamped between Ma's knees having one's hair plaited. The cream air in the middle part of the day was like Time staring at itself in a mirror, the two faces locked dreamily in an eternal gaze.

I was Ma's own–own bold–face Tee, harden' as the Devil's shit but that is yu great great grandmother, that is she, t'ank Gord. Sometimes when the others were not about she would accost me suddenly: 'An who is Ma sugar–cake?'

'Tee!'

'An who is Ma dumplin'?'

'Tee!'

And all at once she put on an expression of mock–displeasure and snapped at me gruffly: 'Who tell yu that?'

'Ma tell mih!'

'Well Ma is a liard ol'–fool,' and she thrust a hunk of guava–cheese at me.

Ma said that I was her grandmother come back again. She said her grandmother was a tall straight proud woman who lived to an old old age and her eyes were still bright like water and her back straight like bamboo, for all the heavy–load she had carried on her head all her life. The People gave her the name Euphemia or Euph–something, but when they called her that she used to toss her head like a horse and refuse to answer so they'd had to give up in the end and call her by her true–true name.

Then Ma creased her forehead and closed her eyes and rubbed her temples and if anyone spoke she waved her hand with irritation. She sat like this for a long time. Then she would shake her head sorrowfully. She couldn't remember her grandmother's true–true name. But Tee was growing into her grandmother again, her spirit was in me. They'd never bent down her spirit and she would come back and come back and come back; if only she could live to see Tee grow into her tall proud straight grandmother.

Extract from _Crick Crack, Monkey_.

THE CARIBBEAN WRITERS SERIES

The book you have been reading is part of Heinemann's long- established series of African fiction. Details of some of the other titles available in this series are given below, but for a catalogue giving information on all the titles available in this series and in the African Writers Series write to:
Heinemann Educational Publishers
Halley Court, Jordan Hill, Oxford OX2 8EJ;
United States customers should write to:
Heinemann, 361 Hanover Street,
Portsmouth, NH 03801-3912, USA

ZEE EDGELL
Beka Lamb

Joint winner of the Fawcett Society Book Prize, Beka Lamb is the story of ordinary life in Belize. It focuses on a girl's victory over her habit of lying and her relationship with a friend. The novel records a few months of this girl's life and portrays the politics of the small colony, the influence of the matriarchal society and the dominating presence of the Catholic Church.

BERYL GILROY
Boy Sandwich

A novel conveying the ways in which three generations of a West Indian family have been affected by life in Britain and how, after time, the third generation desires to take the family back to their homeland and regain a sense of belonging.

Frangipani House

Set in Guyana, this is a beautifully written protest at institutions which isolate, and a way of life which denies respect and responsibility for the weak.

EARL McKENZIE
A Boy Named Ossie

Ossie, a young Jamaican boy, is the tool through which Earl McKenzie expertly portrays the reality of life in rural Jamaica; its humour, warmth and ambitions, as well as its terrors and tribulations.

MARLENE NOURBESE PHILIP
Harriet's Daughter

Set in Toronto, two girls, Margaret – a second generation West Indian immigrant – and Zulma – fresh up from a joyous life with her grandmother in Tobago to a tense and unhappy relationship with her mother and step-father – become friends and comrades in various adventures.

EARL LOVELACE
The Wine of Astonishment

Earl Lovelace writes about the survival of a small community with a lyricism and understanding which has established an international reputation.

A Brief Conversion and Other Stories

A collection of short stories telling of ordinary people and everyday subjects, but through a rare combination of literary excellence and accessibility each is invested with a unique magic

NAMBA ROY
No Black Sparrows

The "Sparrows" – four impoverished orphaned children – eke out a living as petty traders whilst under constant threat from the police.